Cambridge Opera Handbooks

Claude Debussy
Pelléas et Mélisande

This is a series of studies of individual operas written for the opera-
goer or record-collector as well as the student or scholar. Each
volume has three main concerns: historical, analytical and interpretative. There is a detailed description of the genesis of each work,
the collaboration between librettist and composer, and the first
performance and subsequent stage history. A full synopsis considers
the opera as a structure of musical and dramatic effects, and there is
also a musical analysis of a section of the score. The analysis, like the
history, shades naturally into interpretation: by a careful combina-
tion of new essays and excerpts from classic statements the editors of
the handbooks show how critical writing about the opera, like the
production and performance, can direct or distort appreciation of its
structural elements. A final section of documents gives a select
bibliography, a discography, and guides to other sources. Each book
is published in both hard covers and as a paperback.

Books published

Richard Wagner: *Parsifal* by Lucy Beckett
W. A. Mozart: *Don Giovanni* by Julian Rushton
C. W. von Gluck: *Orfeo* by Patricia Howard
Igor Stravinsky: *The Rake's Progress* by Paul Griffiths
Leoš Janáček: *Kát'a Kabanová* by John Tyrrell
Giuseppe Verdi: *Falstaff* by James A. Hepokoski
Benjamin Britten: *Peter Grimes* by Philip Brett
Giacomo Puccini: *Tosca* by Mosco Carner
Benjamin Britten: *The Turn of the Screw* by Patricia Howard
Richard Strauss: *Der Rosenkavalier* by Alan Jefferson
Claudio Monteverdi: *Orfeo* by John Whenham
Giacomo Puccini: *La bohème* by Arthur Groos and Roger Parker
Giuseppe Verdi: *Otello* by James A. Hepokoski
Benjamin Britten: *Death in Venice* by Donald Mitchell
W. A. Mozart: *Die Entführung aus dem Serail* by Thomas Bauman
W. A. Mozart: *Le nozze di Figaro* by Tim Carter
Hector Berlioz: *Les Troyens* by Ian Kemp
Alban Berg: *Wozzeck* by Douglas Jarman

Maeterlinck in his study in Ghent *c.* 1890

Claude Debussy
Pelléas et Mélisande

ROGER NICHOLS AND
RICHARD LANGHAM SMITH

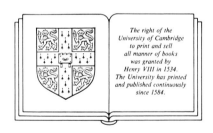

The right of the
University of Cambridge
to print and sell
all manner of books
was granted by
Henry VIII in 1534.
The University has printed
and published continuously
since 1584.

CAMBRIDGE UNIVERSITY PRESS

Cambridge
New York   New Rochelle
Melbourne   Sydney

Published by the Press Syndicate of the University of Cambridge
The Pitt Building, Trumpington Street, Cambridge CB2 1RP
32 East 57th Street, New York, NY 10022, USA
10 Stamford Road, Oakleigh, Melbourne 3166, Australia

First published 1989

Printed in Great Britain at the University Press, Cambridge

British Library cataloguing in publication data
Nichols, Roger
Claude Debussy: Pelleas et Melisande. –
(Cambridge opera handbooks).
1. Opera in French. Debussy, Claude, 1862–
1918. Pelléas et Mélisande. Critical studies
I. Title   II. Smith, Richard Langham
782.1'092'4

Library of Congress cataloguing in publication data
Nichols, Roger.
Claude Debussy, Pelléas et Mélisande / Roger Nichols and Richard
Langham Smith.
    p.   cm. – (Cambridge opera handbooks)
Bibliography.
Discography.
Includes index.
ISBN 0 521 30714 7. ISBN 0 521 31446 1 (pbk)
1. Debussy, Claude, 1862–1918. Pelléas et Mélisande. I. Smith,
Richard Langham.   II. Title.   III. Series.
ML410.D28N48 1988
782.1 – dc 19   88–16172

ISBN 0 521 30714 7 hard covers
ISBN 0 521 31446 1 paperback

Contents

Illustrations

The illustrations are reproduced by permission of the following institutions: Fondation Maeterlinck, Ghent, frontispiece; The British Library, plates 1, 3, 4, 6; Hôtel Drouot, plate 5; Bibliothèque Nationale, Paris, plates 7, 8, 9; Bibliothèque et Musée de l'Opéra, Paris, plate 10; Royal College of Music, plate 11; Agence de Presse Photographique Bernand, plate 12, Opéra de Lyon, plate 13; Clive Barda Photography, plate 14. For the quotation from the autograph manuscript of Maurice Maeterlinck, permission is granted by the Pierpont Morgan Library, New York.

Acknowledgements

Helpful remarks and clarifications have come from many sources. Among those who have assisted in this way are Robin Holloway, Roy Howat, Robert Orledge, Susan Parsons, Sue Taylor-Horrex, Helen Phillips, Marie Rolf and also David Grayson, whose contribution to the book has extended far beyond the boundaries of his own chapter. A particular debt of gratitude is owed to Mme Irène Joachim for her invaluable insights into the opera and into the role of Mélisande.

1   The play and its playwright

BY RICHARD LANGHAM SMITH

People with strange names, living in impossible places, where there are only woods and fountains, and towers by the sea-shore, and ancient castles, where there are no towns, and where the common crowd of the world is shut out of sight and hearing, move like quiet ghosts across the stage, mysterious to us and not less mysterious to one another. They are all lamenting because they do not know, because they cannot understand, because their own souls are so strange to them and each other's souls like pitiful enemies, giving deadly wounds unwillingly. They are always in dread, because they know that nothing is certain in the world or in their own hearts, and they know that love more often does the work of hate and that hate is sometimes tenderer than love.

Arthur Symons, *Annotations by the Way*

It is a minor coincidence that the births of Debussy and Maeterlinck in 1862 were separated by exactly one week. One hundred years later, their centenaries encouraged not only a spate of studies and exhibitions but also, appropriately, a revival of Debussy's setting of *Pelléas et Mélisande* at the Opéra-Comique in Paris. Among those invited to the opening night was Maeterlinck's widow, his second wife the Comtesse Renée Maeterlinck. While remembering Debussy's centenary, the directors of the Opéra-Comique had evidently ignored that of the playwright. Mme Maeterlinck was moved to retort to their invitation in a letter to *Le Figaro*:

According to the wording of your card, you wish to invite me to be present, on the 14th December, at the revival of *Pelléas et Mélisande*, drame lyrique in five acts and thirteen *tableaux*, 'the libretto by Maurice Maeterlinck', with music by Claude Debussy. I am obliged to bring to your notice that Maurice Maeterlinck was never a librettist for operas. Claude Debussy wrote his music for the entire text of Maurice Maeterlinck's play. Do not forget that it was Claude Debussy who, bowled over and inspired by a reading of *Pelléas et Mélisande*. . . came especially to Belgium to ask for the author's permission to set the work to music.[1]

Although Mme Maeterlinck was not quite correct in her assertion that Debussy had set the entire text, she was entirely justified in her claim that Maeterlinck had never stooped to the level of being a mere librettist. Although his reputation may have declined sharply in the twentieth century (and even his most ardent champions have conceded that Debussy's opera played a considerable part in keeping him in the public eye), he had enjoyed a considerable reputation during the 1890s when he was seen not only as an innovator in Symbolist drama, but also as a widely read philosophical essayist of considerable influence.

Pelléas et Mélisande is, in fact, the fifth of Maeterlinck's first series of plays written during the 1890s. The other dramas of this period are also largely concerned with the plight of couples – *Aglavaine et Sélysette*, *Alladine et Palomides* are others – or with magic groups of three or seven – *Les Aveugles* and *Les Sept Princesses*. They are loosely legendary and mediaeval in setting, and they share common themes and preoccupations, frequently illuminating each other. Though both Wagner's *Tristan* and several plays of Shakespeare may spring to mind as forebears of *Pelléas*, Maeterlinck's pairs of lovers follow neither myth nor history, though they more than occasionally touch upon the trappings of Arthurian legend or Celtic symbolism.

The individuality and power of these plays were quickly recognised in France. In 1890, a eulogistic appraisal by the respected Octave Mirbeau of the first of the plays, *La Princesse Maleine* (also considered as a possible project by Debussy), appeared in *Le Figaro*. Overnight, it caused the breakthrough Maeterlinck needed:

M. Maurice Maeterlinck has given us the work of this age most full of genius, and the most extraordinary and most simple as well, comparable and – shall I dare say it? – superior in beauty to what is most beautiful in Shakespeare.[2]

Further plays followed, reworking the intertwining themes of love and destiny: *Pelléas* was one, *Alladine et Palomides* another, and it was this latter play that Maeterlinck called a 'decoction of *Pelléas*'. In what is often considered the final play of the first period of his work, *Ariane et Barbe-bleue* (*Ariane and Bluebeard*), published in 1902 and set to music by Paul Dukas, Mélisande appears as one of the seven wives of Bluebeard.

During the 1890s critical response from the literary world multiplied and deepened. Mallarmé himself wrote a lengthy piece on the playwright, and many other notable figures paid him some attention.

Complementary to the plays were essays by Maeterlinck in various *revues*, later published as a collection under the title *Le Trésor des Humbles*, translated as *The Treasure of the Humble*. These, together with the preface to his collected early plays (*Théâtre*, 1901) distil the themes of the dramas of this period, and are a better starting point for an understanding of *Pelléas* than the prolific interpretative views of Maeterlinck's work which have been put forward to explain the symbols of the play.

After *Ariane et Barbe-bleue* Maeterlinck changed course, admitting, in the preface to *Théâtre*, that for him, Symbolism was finished. Apart from several interesting revivals of *Pelléas* at the playwright's home at the abbey of Sainte-Wandrille in Normandy, his career in the twentieth century is of little relevance to the student of Debussy, save to remark that he, like Debussy, retained a special affection for this play. Just as Debussy had an ornamental toad known as 'Arkël', in a position of honour on his desk and sometimes taken *en voyage*, so Maeterlinck had a Bulldog called Golaud, (always kept muzzled), and both his wife and his Afghan hound were affectionately known as 'Mélisande'.

Despite the enthusiastic adoption of Maeterlinck by French literary circles, *Pelléas* suffers less than one might think from an English language approach. Being Belgian and not French, Maeterlinck leaned more towards the anglophile and teutonic than his French Symbolist counterparts, since he was deeply influenced by English literature, especially Shakespeare, the Pre-Raphaelites and Poe, all of whom he read in the original language. Indeed, in the year before he wrote *Pelléas*, Maeterlinck confessed to 'having read only four French books'.[3] In the *Cahier bleu*, an important notebook from the early 1890s which contains many important ideas in embryo and gestation, he had written in a section concerned with the poet Rossetti:

Aux allemands la musique, aux anglais la poésie, car la poésie française depuis qu'elle existe en ce siècle est née en Angleterre.

(In music, the Germans [are best]; in poetry, the English; for French poetry, from the moment of its inception in this century, was born in England.)[4]

The simplicity of Maeterlinck's style made his work eminently translatable and both plays and essays ran into several editions in translation. Of *Pelléas*, for example, there were no fewer than five translations by the early 1900s (see Bibliography), and only slightly in the wake of French critical comment on his work came a surge of critical attention in English.

Mallarmé's review of the first performance of Maeterlinck's *Pelléas* appeared in London. Writing in the *National Observer* of July 1893 he describes his reactions to the solitary matinée that took place on 17 May of that year at the Théâtre des Bouffes-Parisiens. Curiously, he already finds musical qualities in the work:

Pelléas et Mélisande sur une scène exhale, de feuillets, le délice. Préciser? Ces tableaux, brefs, suprêmes: quoi que ce soit a été rejeté de préparatoire et machinal, en vue que paraisse, extrait, ce qui chez un spectateur se dégage de la représentation, l'essentiel. Il semble que soit jouée une variation supérieure sur l'admirable vieux mélodrame. Silencieusement presque et abstraitement au point que dans cet art, où tout devient musique dans le sens propre, la partie d'un instrument même pensif, violon, nuirait par inutilité.

Pelléas et Mélisande on the stage breathes, page by page, delight. To be precise? *Tableaux*, brief and perfect: whatever there might be that was preliminary or structural has been rejected, so that there appears, extracted, its essential message that the spectator receives from the performance. It seemed that a superior variation on the admirable old melodrama was enacted. Almost silently and abstractly to the point that in this art, where everything becomes music in the real sense, even the addition of a single, pensive violin part would be unnecessary.[5]

Mallarmé's introduction of *Pelléas* in the English press was by no means the first part of the chain which connected Maeterlinck to England. Apart from the literary influences already hinted at, the visual art of the second generation Pre-Raphaelites Burne-Jones and Walter Crane was formative in Maeterlinck's conception of what his plays should look like and also of the all-pervading atmosphere of sadness with which they are infused. The haunting figures of Burne-Jones's pallid damsels, their dilated eyes on the verge of tears, distilling the world's sorrow, were clearly implicated in the genesis of Mélisande, and in *Pelléas*, as in many images of Burne-Jones, these frail figures exist in an atmosphere where violence is never far away. In the late 1880s Maeterlinck had announced a forthcoming book on the Pre-Raphaelite poets, and we know from several sources that his study in Ghent was hung with the recently available platinotypes of Burne-Jones. Maeterlinck's contemporary Iwan Gilkin, who also left us valuable accounts of the playwright's taste for Odilon Redon, wrote most perceptively of his relationship with the English artists:

[Maeterlinck's] characters are the brothers and sisters of the heroes of those tales resurrected in the 19th Century through the genius of Tennyson, Burne-

Jones and Richard Wagner. For Celtic legend has had the good fortune to be awakened from sleep by these great artists. . . This sympathy must have awakened in Maeterlinck's soul in his youth, no doubt after having seen the beautiful photographs which popularised the work of Burne-Jones.

His art does not in any way imitate the art of Burne-Jones, but responds to it and completes it. Or rather, there is a kind of exchange between these two artists. If Burne-Jones furnished Maeterlinck with the outward appearance of his characters and the visible atmosphere which envelopes them, Maeterlinck has interrogated these wonderful figures, unveiled their souls, fathomed their mystery. He has formulated their magic and musical language, expressed in words all the poetic passions which trouble their hearts, and the lofty and melancholy thoughts which are reflected in their beautiful faces.[6]

With Debussy, Maeterlinck shared a taste for the illustrated 'toy books' so prevalent during the 1890s. But while Debussy seems to have been inspired more by Arthur Rackham (the piano *Préludes* 'Ondine', 'Les fées sont d'exquises danseuses' and 'La danse de Puck' were based on Rackham illustrations), Maeterlinck preferred Walter Crane, who was particularly admired in Belgium. For the Paris première of Maeterlinck's *Pelléas* it was Walter Crane's illustrations which provided the basis for the set. Maeterlinck's schoolfriend Charles van Lerberghe had already jotted down his reactions to a reading of *Pelléas*, well before the play was staged: 'On découvre Mélisande au bord d'une fontaine' he noted. 'C'est un Walter Crane'.[7]

Further English connections developed as *Pelléas* was translated and performed, and it was in the 1898 London performance that Maeterlinck found the ideal exponents of his drama. Mrs Patrick Campbell played the part of Mélisande and Martin Harvey was Pelléas. Mrs Campbell's gold tunic was conceived by her friend Burne-Jones and was revived in 1904 in a curious performance where she repeated her Mélisande, but in French, to Sarah Bernhardt playing Pelléas *en travesti*. It was, however, the 1898 performance, with incidental music by Fauré, that most impressed Maeterlinck. Of Mrs Campbell he wrote eulogistically, admiring her capacity 'to make visible and real his too beautiful dreams'. 'Little Jack' Harvey, as Pelléas the 'boy-lover', he thought unsurpassed:

It was in the middle of the first act, when Harvey as Pelléas advanced slowly upon the scene, pale and marked by fate with mortal beauty, like a sort of pre-Renaissance Hamlet, that I heard in the very depths of my heart the secret but all-powerful cry of that mysterious voice which only sounds at great moments of existence. . . There could be no doubt – although at first my eyes did not believe it – that the Pelléas of Harvey was incomparably more Pelléas than the Pelléas of my drama.[8]

So vivid were his memories of Harvey's interpretation of the role that when he revived *Pelléas* at Sainte-Wandrille, Maeterlinck sent to England for the costume which the actor himself had designed. Lugné-Poë, the producer of the original Paris performance, had given up after several attempts to fulfil Maeterlinck's own dream of 'costumes of the eleventh [and] twelfth centuries, or else like Memling'.[9] Harvey amusingly recalled his painstaking efforts with every detail of the costume:

I knew how I ought to look, and my wife, with her quick sympathy for my own thought, was able to express it perfectly in my costume. My wig gave me endless trouble. I could not get hair which would radiate, as it were, round my head, with that kind of living force which I felt would suggest the ecstatic soul of Pelléas, until I got the effect I wanted by using the hair which grows on the chest of the Tibetan Yak. His appearance, as I saw him in my mind's eye, was mingled in my imagination with the conceptions of the Pre-Raphaelites.[10]

Harvey's costume (see plate 1) was remarkable for the wings on Pelléas's head, and it seems to have been this which so impressed Maeterlinck, despite Mrs Campbell's backstage jibe that he looked like a 'moth'. Harvey and Maeterlinck became friends and the playwright wrote subsequent parts for him. At their meeting at the rehearsals for the London performance, Harvey had asked Maeterlinck whether the character of Pelléas was in any way autobiographical. Maeterlinck's reply was that it was indeed himself, at the age of eighteen.

In the later memoirs of his youth, the *Bulles bleues*, Maeterlinck confirms this. In a piece entitled 'La première maîtresse', Maeterlinck recalls having discovered his first mistress in the arms of another man:

I surveyed the scene with a painful stupefaction, but there was nothing I could do. Already Golaud, who was not yet born, was whispering inside me:

Je n'attache aucune importance à ces choses, voyez-vous, vous ferez comme il vous plaira.

In silence, I wandered off into the lonely night believing myself the most miserable of men.[11]

It was not merely this above isolated confession which Maeterlinck connected with his early plays. His upbringing in a repressively

Photo, Caswall-Smith.

Mr. Martin Harvey
as
PÉLLÉAS
in " Pélléas and Mélisande."

Translated by Professor Mackail from the play of that name by Maurice Maeterlincke.
Produced at the Prince of Wales's Theatre, June 21st, 1898.

1   Martin Harvey as Pelléas, showing the wings on the headpiece. Maeterlinck considered Harvey his ideal Pelléas and requested the costume for
subsequent performances.

Catholic atmosphere in the misty flatlands around Ghent also contributed much to the atmosphere of these dramas, *Pelléas* being no exception.

His parents were bourgeois French-speaking *Gantois* who had been landowners for some 600 years. The critic Franz Hellens later evoked the milieu of the *bourgeoisie Gantoise*: 'there is no city where the bourgeoisie are more manifestly proud of their culture, closer to the noble aristocracy'.[12] His father's passions were bee-keeping and horticulture, both of which exerted a lasting influence on Maeterlinck himself, emerging in 'La vie des abeilles' and 'L'intelligence des fleurs'. The early poems, the *Serres Chaudes*, also recall the vast greenhouses that surrounded Maeterlinck at the family summer house at Oostacke, outside Ghent.

Installed in his bedroom in the slated tower at Oostacke, Maeterlinck spent several months of each year in the eerie tranquillity of estuary-lands and salt-marshes, frequently hung with a gauze curtain of mist, but where an unchecked wind could suddenly rise to rattle the foundations of the castle-like domain. It was an isolated world of interminable flatness whose *ennui* was broken only by the vast canals. One such canal was so close that, Maeterlinck remarked, the vast and mysterious boats (often from England) seemed to be 'sliding through the garden', just as in *Pelléas* the mysterious galleon which brought Mélisande glides past in Act I scene 3, with the *Hisse-hoé*s reinforcing the sense of unexplained and disquieting forces.[13]

The feeling of stagnation and isolation of these flatlands, which Maeterlinck later identified with Edgar Allan Poe, was by no means alleviated by his years at school. After early years in a convent, he was enrolled at the Jesuit college of Sainte-Barbe, on the outskirts of Ghent. Before Maeterlinck, it had educated Georges Rodenbach and Emile Verhaeren, important figures in turn-of-the-century Belgian literature. Contemporary with the playwright were two other figures who were to follow similar paths: Charles van Lerberghe and Grégoire Le Roy. With these two Maeterlinck developed close friendships in his late teens, and found some refuge from the narrow-minded dogma of the Jesuits who ran the somewhat squalid school. No music was taught, and modern French literature was forbidden. Moral training was of the 'fire and brimstone' kind: van Lerberghe recounted how 'each year. . . a special sermon on death would be delivered, putting the fear of God into us all. We would be told of cases of sudden death, of young men struck down without warning while in a state of mortal sin, falling into the flames of hell.'[14] Rodenbach spoke of the school in similar terms: 'Death was always present in our youth. Oh, those years when we should have been taught to love life, and when they busied themselves only with making us familiar with death. . . Changeless and bleak existence in that courtyard that blotted out the sun.'[15] With these recollections in mind, it is by no means far-fetched to suggest that the contrasts of the sunless school in Ghent with the plains of Oostacke, where all was mist and sky, may well have precipitated the setting of *Pelléas*, with its forests 'where the sun is never seen' and the sea-mists of Act I scene 3.

Added to this were the obligatory visits to nuns and madonnas. Not far from Oostacke a healing-virgin had become something of a place of pilgrimage and at the age of seventeen Maeterlinck wrote an *eclogue* to her with a fellow pupil. Visits to the nunnery (*béguinage*) were also required, and the atmosphere of silent procession has an echo in several of the early plays, including *Pelléas*, where the 'knowing' servants silently bear witness to the death of Mélisande. Maeterlinck's catholicism at this time he describes as 'provisional' and he became the writer prescribed for 'those who had lost their religion but not the religious spirit'.[16] With his friends van Lerberghe and Le Roy, Maeterlinck began to stand aloof; they considered themselves 'distinguished amateurs' with regard to their religious education.

Together they began to turn towards other things. Van Lerberghe's predilection was for virgins and fairy-princesses, fantasies discussed *à cœur ouvert* with Maeterlinck. Le Roy was more down-to-earth, conquering a pair of sister school teachers. Maeterlinck, at eighteen, took the first of many mistresses, a milliner's daughter. It seemed that his father's more sybaritic nature had got the better of any of the Jesuits' moralistic homilies. The Maeterlinck household was by no means a cosy *ménage à deux*: in common with many Ghent landowners, his father openly kept mistresses, and on one occasion Maeterlinck found himself sharing the favours of a younger woman with his father. Familial dramas of rivalry and jealousy were as much a part of his own life as misty flatlands. Verhaeren summed up Maeterlinck (who insisted on the Flemish pronunciation of his surname, with a long 'a' and a hard 'k' at the end) as 'the most eminent of those modern authors who feel in Flemish and write in French'.

The 'Flemish feeling' of *Pelléas* thus derives from Maeterlinck's transformation of the landscapes of his own experience into the settings of his early plays. In *Pelléas* this *paysage* is of prime importance. Indeed, when the characters are at their most passive, there are scenes where the only changes are in the weather and the effects of light. *Pelléas* is scarcely different from the other early plays in the elements comprising this landscape: an old castle surrounded by dark forests save for the sea on one side. There is also a vertical arrangement of higher and lower levels on stage clearly related to Maeterlinck's play of symbols. Stairs lead downwards into the castle vaults and to sombre caverns with bottomless lakes (associated with death), or aspire upward to the tower, and to Mélisande's bedroom where she both loves and dies, but where her daughter symbolises a promise of renewal, as Arkël observes. Most notable, however, is the use of different types of water mirroring different stages in the psychological development of the drama. This aspect of the symbolism of the play may well derive from the tales of Edgar Allan Poe where various types of water are used in a similar way. Whatever its origins, it is an aspect of *Pelléas* to which Debussy's reaction was strong. In the changing moods of the sea in Act I; in the love scenes by the well; in the stagnant tarns and the bright sea-air with which they contrast; even in the clouds passing over the entrance to the sea-cave – here are the sources of the water-imagery which was to preoccupy Debussy throughout his life.

Maeterlinck leaves us in no doubt about the connections between the landscape and the meaning of the play, whether it is Golaud and Mélisande lost in the dark forest, Golaud and Pelléas smelling the 'stench of death' in the castle vaults, or the lovers in the flower-garden. The landscape is always symbolic rather than decorative. Baudelaire had presaged the Symbolist attitude to landscape some years earlier:

If some assembly of trees, mountains, water and houses that we call landscape is beautiful, it is not so in itself, but only through my bestowal of beauty upon it, by the idea or feeling I attach to it. Landscape is born of the imagination.[17]

It is this view of landscape which Maeterlinck develops and which he shares not only with the English Pre-Raphaelites but also with Debussy. For it is the composer's Symbolist attitude to landscape as a reflection of a human state which allies him to the poets of his day, and invalidates any connection with pure Impressionism.

In *Pelléas*, several techniques are used to underline these links. Most obvious is the total lack of descriptive stage directions. It is not that Maeterlinck has thus abandoned any interest in the scenic parameter – on the contrary. Instead, the characters themselves continually comment on the changing weather (in a rather English way, it has been suggested) or on the details of the landscape. This clearly and effectively moves the scenic setting into the foreground when it is important to do so. The opening dialogue of Act I scene 3, drawing attention to the elemental symbolism of darkness and light, is returned to several times in the scene, which contains virtually no other action:

MELISANDE   Il fait sombre dans les jardins.
               Et quelles forêts, quelles forêts tout autour des palais.
GENEVIEVE   Oui; cela m'étonnait aussi quand je suis arrivée ici, et cela étonne tout le monde. Il y a des endroits où l'on ne voit jamais le soleil. . . Regardez de l'autre côté, vous aurez la clarté de la mer.

MELISANDE   It is dark in the gardens. And what forests, what forests there are all around the palaces.
GENEVIEVE   Yes, it used to astonish me when I arrived here, and everyone is astonished at it. There are places where one never sees the sun. . . Look on the other side, there, you will have the light of the sea.

Following Poe, the landscape elements in Maeterlinck become presagers of destiny, and characters encounter physical objects – stones or tree-trunks – if they struggle against the forces of fate. Water is particularly important. The sea is presented as mysterious and infinite, but it is an agent of destiny in that it has brought Mélisande to Allemonde – a fact stressed by the several references to the ship. The space and light of the sea attract the characters – 'nous cherchions la clarté' says Geneviève. 'Ici, il fait un peu plus clair qu'ailleurs' – (We were seeking the light. Here it is a little lighter than elsewhere.) Yet there are reminders of terrible shipwrecks: not only of the sea's sudden moods of darkness on a bright day, but of the wreckage it has thrown into the sea-cavern.

In the castle vaults the Poeian aspect is still more explicit, as stagnant water (so frequently found in both Poe's tales and his poetry) is imbued with the stench of death:

GOLAUD   Sentez-vous l'odeur mortelle qui règne ici? Selon moi, elle provient du petit lac souterrain que je vais vous faire voir. . .

> Pour Dieu! Mais ne voyez-vous pas? – Un pas de plus, vous étiez
> dans le gouffre. . . Eh bien, voici l'eau stagnante dont je vous
> parlais. Sentez-vous l'odeur de mort qui monte?
>
> (Can you smell the stench of death which hangs here? In my
> view, it comes from the underground pool that I am going to
> show you. Heavens! Can't you see? One step more and you'd
> have been in the chasm. Ah yes, there's the stagnant water about
> which I was telling you. Can you smell the stench of death which
> rises from it?)

In this scene, as in much of the play, there is no real conversation between the characters, in this case Golaud and Pelléas. Instead, Golaud's words serve to draw attention to the details of the vaults – expanding on the symbolism and exaggerating the feeling of doom: the poison of the atmosphere, the lizards on the wall.

The third element of water imagery is the fountain in the park. Owing nothing to Poe (who dealt little in matters of love) this is a pseudo-mediaeval addition, perhaps again from one of the 'toy books' where princesses and sleeping-beauties languish beside 'wells at the world's end'. Beside such wells magic spells are cast and the seeds of love are sown. To the first English translators it was no doubt obvious that 'une fontaine' should be translated as a 'well', not a fountain. Golaud finds Mélisande beside such a well, and Pelléas and Mélisande return there to nurture their love. But again, Maeterlinck does not allow the symbol to go undeveloped. Like the sea, the well brings mixed fortunes. The blind used to be cured there, Mélisande's crown and ring are lost there and it is by the same well that Pelléas falls to Golaud's sword.

Symbols often contrast with an opposite with which they may, none the less, share certain characteristics. The air, water and light from the sea contrast with the dark and oppressive forest. Where the sea hints at past and future journeys away from the destiny of Allemonde, the forest represents the inescapable present, an impenetrable barrier which surrounds the castle on all sides, hermetically sealing the kingdom from the real (but unreal) world outside. Like the sea, the forest can contain unexpected and terrible perils: Golaud's accident hints at this. The forest serves also as a massive and omnipresent reminder of the force of destiny: Golaud and Mélisande are lost in the forest and Pelléas and Mélisande cannot escape Golaud's vengeance because (or partly because) there is nowhere else but forest to escape to. The briar-rose of the scene where Mélisande lets her hair tumble from the tower, as well as the

Pre-Raphaelite well, suggest that the woods of Arthurian times may have been in Maeterlinck's mind. Burne-Jones had immortalised the adventures of the knights in the briar-wood in his series of 'Briar-Rose' paintings where knights in armour sleep among fierce but flower-adorned briars. In another canvas with much of the atmosphere of *Pelléas, Love among the ruins*, an armoured knight and a sad-eyed maiden precariously clasp each other amidst the overgrown ruins of an ancient building (see plate 2).

It is against this dualism of forest and water-places that the 'action' of the play takes place. But as with Wagner's *Tristan*, the 'action' is relatively unimportant, and the spectator must discover how and where to look in order to derive the deepest level of meaning from the play. In his hostile review of the first performance in *Le Temps*, the influential critic F. Sarcey summed up the story of *Pelléas* in one sentence, moralistically censuring its theme: 'It is the incestuous love of a married woman for her brother-in-law; the outraged husband surprises the guilty ones, kills the one and wounds the other, who dies afterwards.'[18] Apart from its inaccuracy, this summary entirely misses the point. Arthur Symons is far more penetrating: 'In *Pelléas and Mélisande* we have two innocent lovers, to whom love is guilt; we have blind vengeance, aged and helpless wisdom; we have the conflict of passions fighting in the dark, destroying what they most desire in the world.'[19]

Contemporary critics of the play found all sorts of precursors for the love-triangle. Dante's *Paolo e Francesca*, fresh in the mind from Rossetti's celebrated painting, was one. Others included *Othello*, as well as *Tristan und Isolde*, and Poe's poem 'Annabel Lee'. Given to contrivance as regards proper names, Maeterlinck seems to have taken some of his names directly from Arthurian literature, but invented others by combining prefixes and suffixes. The outline plot was conceived before settling on the names Pelléas and Mélisande, for Pelléas was at first Yniold, and Mélisande at first Claire then Geneviève. Yniold and Geneviève were then transferred to minor characters. Maeterlinck may have decided on the name Pelléas after reading (or re-reading) Malory's *Morte d'Arthur*, where there is a Sir Pelleas similarly involved in a love-triangle.[20] Sir Pelleas is in love with the lady Ettard but is betrayed by Sir Gawaine with whom he finds her sleeping. Pelleas curses Ettard and is comforted by the damozel of the lake who 'rejoiced Sir Pelleas and they loved together during their life-days'.

Tennyson, in his *Idylls of the King* tells a similar tale in the poem 'Pelleas and Ettarre'. Several features of the poem suggest that it may have influenced Maeterlinck's own *Pelléas*. It was included in his reading for the proposed book on the English poets which was in a sketched-out stage before the playwright began work on the early plays.[21] In Tennyson's poem, Sir Pelleas of the Isles is one of the 'new knights', made 'to fill the gap left by the Holy Quest':

> In hall at old Caerleon, the high doors
> Were softly sunder'd, and thro' these a youth,
> Pelleas, and the sweet smell of the fields
> Past, and the sunshine came along with him.

Tennyson plays on the recurrent image, also borrowed by Maeterlinck, of the characters lost in the dark forest. In the poem it is at first a 'sea of damsels' who are lost, later Pelleas himself:

> And one was pointing this way, and one that,
> Because the way was lost.

The damsels (reminding us of Burne-Jones's 'Golden Staircase') are led by Guinevere: Pelleas is stunned by her beauty, Parsifal-like in his 'broken utterances and bashfulness'. Guinevere mutters that she has 'lighted on a fool'. Still more reminiscent of Maeterlinck is a song within the poem, ballad-like in its harkening back to the idea of the rose:

> A rose, but one, none other rose had I,
> A rose, one rose, and this was wondrous fair,
> One rose, a rose that gladden'd earth and sky,
> One rose, my rose, that sweeten'd all mine air –
> I cared not for the thorns; the thorns were there.

Its central image of blossom and thorn is echoed by Maeterlinck, where Mélisande's hair falls from the tower and becomes entwined in a blossoming rose. As in Malory, the climax of the poem occurs when Ettarre's 'ever-veering fancy' leads her to duplicity with Gawain, which brings about Pelleas's realisation:

> I loathe her, as I loved her to my shame.
> I never loved her, I but lusted for her –
> Away!

Though both Malory and Tennyson tell a different tale, it may have been in Maeterlinck's mind to create a new episode in the life of Pelleas, for he shares character-traits with his Arthurian forebear, and the atmosphere of idealised love and violent retribution clearly carries over into Maeterlinck's *Pelléas*.

The origins of Mélisande's name are more puzzling, and perhaps deliberately so. Like much of Maeterlinck's symbolism, her name has a range of resonances. Several names in the *Morte d'Arthur* begin with Mel-, and several end in -sande. She may also have something to do with the siren Melusine whose enchanting voice arouses a passion she cannot satisfy and who leads men to self-destruction. One of her metamorphoses is that of a bird-woman. Mélisande's references to birds as well as Pelléas's frequent allusions to Mélisande's voice both give weight to this suggested influence.

A further credible source is found in Walter Crane's illustrated *Valentine and Orson*. Here the name is Bellisant (see plate 3).

> Once upon a time an Emperor, a man of might and fame
> Married a wife, and fair was she, and Bellisant her name
> And fair and happy were their lives, until an evil man
> (He was the high priest of the court) an evil tale began,
> Of how the lady was not true unto her husband dear.[22]

Maeterlinck's library contained a well-annotated copy of another book illustrated by Walter Crane: his widely circulated volume of Grimm's *Household Stories*, translated by Lucy Crane, the artist's sister. The playwright surely could not have forgotten the striking illustration of Rapunzel in this volume, where she leans out of her tower, letting her hair down for the gallant knight to climb up and save her (see plate 4).

Whatever these connections, we learn from one of the lines Debussy cut that she was a princess in torn clothes in the true children's book tradition: 'Elle était d'ailleurs vêtue comme une princesse, bien que ses vêtements fussent déchirés par les ronces)' (She was dressed, moreover, as a princess, even though her clothes were torn by briars; Act I scene 1). She again tears her clothes as she escapes from Golaud to meet Pelléas for their final tryst. There is also perhaps a musical significance in Mélisande's name, from the *Melos* prefix, and suited to her Ophelian singing as she combs her hair. The 'Y' of Yniold's name, and the *tréma* on Arkël's, add Celtic colour, as does the name Golaud, who – in slightly different spellings – was a 'seigneur de Tintagel'.[23] Golo was also the third character in another love-triangle: the mediaeval story of *Geneviève de Brabant*. 'Siegefroid, one of the noblest Palatines from the court of Tièves, was espoused to Geneviève, Duchess of Brabant, whom he con-

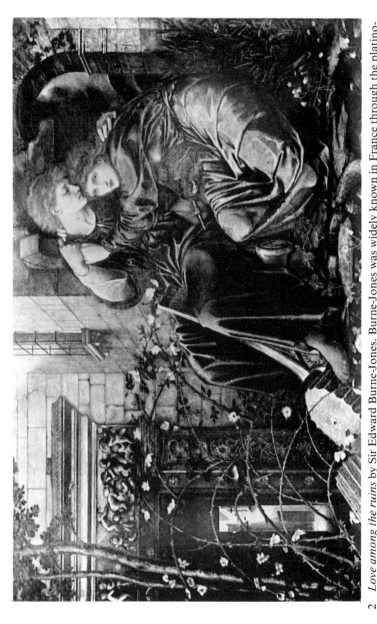

2   *Love among the ruins* by Sir Edward Burne-Jones. Burne-Jones was widely known in France through the platino-types of Frederick Hollyer. Maeterlinck's study was hung with Burne-Jones's whose themes are often strikingly reminiscent of the playwright's early dramas.

ONCE on a time an Emperor, a man of might
and fame,
Married a wife, and fair was she, and Bellisant her
name ;
And fair and happy were their lives, until an evil man
(He was the High Priest of the Court) an evil tale
began,
Of how the lady was not true unto her husband dear:
The Emperor believed the tale, and rose up in great
fear,
And drove poor Bellisant away; in haste and dire
mischance
She took her way to Pepin's Court (her brother, King
of France).

3 *The Princess Bellisant*, a possible source of Mélisande, from *Valentine and Orson*, a toy-book illustrated by Walter Crane. Both Debussy and Maeterlinck shared a passion for English 'toy-books'. Crane was particularly popular in Belgium.

demned to death because of false accusations of infidelity with a knight named Golo. Exposed with her son in a vast forest. . . Geneviève was found safe and sound after some considerable time.' As we have seen, the Christian name of this heroine was incorporated into the play at an early stage, and the parallels of the 'vast forest' and the son whose paternity is in question hardly need underlining.[24] Golaud's own name, like those of the other characters, had originally been quite different, one version being the Arthurian name 'Uther'.

Also at the back of Maeterlinck's mind may well have been the story of Bluebeard and his seven wives. The passive *princesses lointaines* of the early plays reappear as the wives of Bluebeard in *Ariane et Barbe-bleue*, Ariane representing the first of Maeterlinck's new heroines who were to have more will of their own. But it is likely that the Bluebeard tale had been in Maeterlinck's mind far earlier. He is first known through a tale by the seventeenth-century writer Perrault, but reappears in many subsequent fairy-tale anthologies, including a story illustrated by Walter Crane. A few years before Maeterlinck began *Pelléas*, an important book had been published giving the full details of the real Bluebeard who had given rise to the tales, one Gilles de Rais. This figure, who lived in Brittany in the fifteenth century, was a companion of Joan of Arc, and committed acts of charity as well as the seven terrible crimes.[25] It is clearly the same Mélisande who appears in *Ariane et Barbe-bleue*:

| MELISANDE | Mais ce sont les oiseaux. . . Les vois-tu? Ils sont là des milliers dans les grands peupliers, le long de la rivière. |
| SELYSETTE | Oh! Tu es pâle Mélisande!. . . |

| (MELISANDE | But they are the birds: can you see them? There are thousands of them in the large poplars along by the river. |
| SELYSETTE | Oh! You are pale, Mélisande.) |

This may throw some light not only on the unspecified horrors which have befallen Mélisande before Golaud finds her in the forest, but also on the character of Golaud, who has more than a little of the cruel character and physical features of his more infamous predecessor, Bluebeard. It may have been in the back of Maeterlinck's mind that Mélisande has somehow escaped with her crown from Bluebeard's clutches, and that her wish to lose the crown is a symbolic attempt to forget her terrible past.

These connections with Bluebeard, though not explicitly mentioned by Maeterlinck himself, seem to have been well-known among the early casts of the opera. Mentioned by Irène Joachim (a celebrated interpreter of Mélisande's role, see plate 10) they were also known to the first Golaud, Hector Dufranne. Maggie Teyte, another Mélisande, recounted the story as told to her by Dufranne, in an interview given in 1954 alluding to Mélisande's role in *Ariane et Barbe-bleue.*

Now you know why Mélisande is petrified by men – she was assaulted by Bluebeard so viciously that when we first see her in *Pelléas* she has lost her memory. And men cannot touch her. Throughout most of the opera she devises excuse after excuse to prevent men from touching her – even Pelléas. It is only after Golaud has pulled her violently by the hair that she returns to her senses and is wholeheartedly able to accept affection. Through brutality she has lost her mind and through brutality it has been restored. It's a kind of archaic shock treatment.[26]

Just to what extent Maeterlinck's wordplay on proper names was intended is a matter for conjecture. The assonance of the names Pelléas and Mélisande binds the two together, and it is perhaps also significant that Arkël has their '-el', while Golaud and Yniold are isolated by their '-ol's. If we are to believe some critics, this too is a part of the elaborate symbolism of the play, with the chosen names allied to predominant themes in the play: Golaud = gold; *l'eau* = *sanglot*; Pelléas = *pleurs*; Mélisande = Ophelia–*mélodie*–'prototype de la mort aquatique et amoureuse'.[27]

In thus reading between the lines, an approach has been made, willy-nilly, to the developing methods of Symbolist theatre, and of Maeterlinck's techniques in particular. Symbolism had begun as a reaction against positivist thought and its resultant theory of Art as put forward by Taine and as exemplified in the works of the Naturalists in literature and visual art. Taine, widely read in the nineteenth century, claimed that Art was based on natural scientific laws:

The modern method which I attempt to follow, and which has begun to be introduced into philosophy, consists of considering human works, and in particular works of Art, as facts and products, of which one must define the characters and find the causes: nothing more.[28]

Artists, he claims, must follow the tide of their age:

Soak your heart and mind, as ample as they are, in the ideas and feelings of your own century, and the work of Art will come of its own accord.[29]

Such views were totally antipathetic to the evolving school of Symbolism, which took Baudelaire rather than Taine as its guiding light.

4   *Rapunzel*, illustration by Walter Crane, another possible inspiration for Mélisande.

In one of the rare passages from *Le Trésor des Humbles* which pertains to his own art, from an essay 'Le tragique quotidien' (The Tragical in Daily Life), Maeterlinck shows his own awareness of these opposing aesthetics:

Indeed, when I go to a theatre, I feel as though I were spending a few hours with my ancestors, who conceived life as something that was primitive, arid and brutal; but this conception of theirs scarcely even lingers in my memory, and surely it is not one that I can share. I am shown a deceived husband killing his wife, a woman poisoning her lover, a son avenging his father, a father slaughtering his children, children putting their father to death, murdered kings, ravished virgins, imprisoned citizens – in a word, all the sublimity of tradition, but alas, how superficial and material! Blood, surface tears and death. What can I learn from creatures who have but one fixed idea, and who have no time to live, for that there is a rival, or a mistress, whom it behoves them to put to death?[30]

The clash of these diametrically opposed views of art was probably responsible for the slow acceptance of Maeterlinck's *Pelléas* for theatrical representation. Maeterlinck submitted the work to André Antoine at the Théâtre-Libre, but this impresario was too preoccupied with theatrical parallels to the techniques of Zola (where every lifelike detail possible was incorporated into the *mise-en-scène*) to have any understanding of Maeterlinck's quite opposite theatrical ideals.

Nurtured by parallel crazes for Wagner and Schopenhauer, the Symbolists evolved an opposing philosophy of art: mystical in that it sought to highlight phenomena which could not be explained by natural science; idealistic in that it sought to create other worlds – like that of Wagner's *Tristan* – where art could provide an ideal better than the natural world. At the centre of the dispute with Taine had been Taine's failure to recognise that, in the view of the Symbolists, the world had existence only in as much as it was perceived by the mysterious sensory apparatus of man himself. Rémy de Gourmont, writing in 1896, summed this up:

A new sincerity has recently come into literature and art, it is a metaphysical sincerity, on the surface *a priori*, quite young since it is only a century old, and in reality new, since it is not yet a part of our aesthetic order. This sincerity, evangelical and marvellous, liberating and refreshing, is the principle of the idealism of the world. With regard to the thinking man, the world – all that is exterior to myself – exists only according to the idea he has bestowed upon it.[31]

The precise consistency of this idealism differed between writers, and amongst writers it varied between works. Henri de Régnier claimed that 'idealism is the metaphysical key to the majority of figures of the generation which makes up the Symbolist school'.[32] It certainly played a large part in the plays of its father-figure Villiers de l'Isle Adam whose play *Axël* is the first landmark of French Symbolist drama. Mallarmé's obituary speech for Villiers ('Un homme au rêve habitué, vient ici parler d'un autre qui est mort') cites a speech of Axël to Sara, showing how he – before Maeterlinck's own aesthetic had been nourished by the damozels of Burne-Jones – could distil this idealism in the madonna-figure of a young and unattainable woman:

AXEL   Sara! I thank you that I have seen you. (*Drawing her into his arms*) I am happy, O my lily-like bride! my mistress! my virgin! my life! I am happy that we are here together, full of youth and hope, filled with a truly immortal feeling, alone, governed by unknown rulers, and all shining with mysterious gold, lost in the depths of this manor, during this dreadful night.[33]

It was from Villiers, Maeterlinck later confessed, that he learnt 'all that he knew', and we should not forget that Debussy himself had at one time considered a setting of *Axël*.

As a succinct description of Symbolism's method of probing the mysteries which scientific positivism had ignored, Mallarmé's oft-repeated dictum is hard to better:

Nommer un objet c'est supprimer les trois quarts de la jouissance du poëme qui est faite de deviner peu à peu.

(To name an object is to suppress three-quarters of the pleasure of a poem, which comes from discovering little by little.)[34]

Mallarmé's own style was complex, obtuse and untranslatable compared with that of Maeterlinck, but Maeterlinck's aesthetic was also based on the premiss that what is left unsaid may reveal more than what is said. He explains this at some length in his essay 'Le silence', first published in June 1895:

Speech is of time, silence is of eternity. Bees will not work except in darkness; thought will not work except in silence; neither will virtue work except in secrecy.
    It is idle to think that, by means of words, any real communication can ever pass from one man to another. The lips or the tongue may represent the soul. . .but from the moment that we have *something to say to each other*, we are *compelled* to hold our peace: and if at such times we do not listen to the urgent commands of silence, invisible though they be, we shall have suffered

an eternal loss that all the treasures of human wisdom cannot make good; for we shall have let slip the opportunity of listening to another soul, and of giving existence, be it only for an instant, to our own; and many lives there are in which such opportunities do not present themselves twice. . . It is only when life is sluggish within us that we speak. . .

Maeterlinck, himself known as *le grand taiseur*, goes on to remark upon the different qualities of these silences:

Though all words may be akin, every silence differs from its fellow; and, with rare exceptions, it is an entire destiny that will be governed by the *quality* of this first silence which is descending upon two souls.

The idea of silence as an essential component to love, Maeterlinck may well have taken from Rossetti, in whose work the theme of silence between lovers is frequent. ''Tis visible silence, still as the hour-glass', we read in his 'Silent Noon', and in 'Willow-wood' (announced for publication as a cantata by Debussy, but left unfinished) there is a striking image of silence:

> I sat with Love upon a woodside well
> Leaning across the water, I and he;
> Nor ever did he speak nor looked at me,
> But touched his lute wherein was audible
> The secret thing he had to tell:
> Only our mirrored eyes met silently
> In the low wave; and that sound came to be
> The passionate voice I knew; and my tears fell.

Two other qualities of silence are mentioned by Maeterlinck – a passive silence, which he considers 'the shadow of sleep, of death or non-existence', and what he calls 'les autres *grands* silences, those of death, grief or destiny' which 'do not belong to us. They come towards us at their own hour!' With his use of the word *grand* – used with resonance in the last act of *Pelléas* when Mélisande asks for the 'great' window to be opened – Maeterlinck invokes the final silence of destiny.

This exploration of silence is put into practice in *Pelléas*; and seen in this context Debussy's remark that he had used 'silence as a means of expression'[35] in the opera gains considerably in significance. Maeterlinck's ways of doing this are several. One such is the frequent introduction of unanswered questions, particularly in the case of Mélisande whose character is as much defined by what we do not know about her as by what we do. In Act I scene 2, Golaud writes to Pelléas: 'Je ne sais ni son âge, ni qui elle est, ni d'où elle vient et je

n'ose pas l'interroger, car elle doit avoir eu une grande épouvante. . .'
(I know neither her age nor who she is, nor where she comes from,
and I dare not ask her, for she must have suffered some terrible
misfortune). Her character is defined by the half-explained. The
crown is a further example – why is she so adamant about not want-
ing it back? Her silence is more expressive than explanation. By the
end of the opera, a myriad of unanswered questions has piled up.

The silence of the well is evoked in Act II. 'On n'entend rien',
remarks Mélisande. 'Il y a toujours un silence extraordinaire',
confirms Pelléas. 'On entendrait dormir l'eau' (One hears nothing.
There is always an unusual silence. You can almost hear the water
sleeping. . .). More unusual and striking, however, is the entry of the
serving women, signalling the death of Mélisande: 'La chambre est
envahie, peu à peu, par les servantes du château, qui se rangent en
silence le long des murs et attendent.' Golaud insistently asks the
serving women why they have come. 'Répondez!', he cries desper-
ately, but is answered only by the stage direction: *Les servantes ne*
répondent pas. Twice more in the act, hinting at the 'great silences of
death' referred to in *Le Trésor des Humbles*, Maeterlinck introduces
silence into the stage directions. After the doctor has confirmed that
the serving women are correct in having divined Mélisande's
moment of death, Maeterlinck indicates *un long silence*. The final
postlude to the opera also accompanies an all-important stage direction: *ils sortent en silence.*

Related to the idea that mystery is indicative of profundity are
several other ideas in *Le Trésor des Humbles*. One such is clearly
expressed in the essay 'Le tragique quotidien' (The Tragical in Daily
Life), where the character of Arkël is suggested: the silent sage, para-
doxically blind yet more visionary than anyone:

I have come to believe that an old man, seated in his armchair, waiting
patiently with his lamp beside him, giving unconscious ear to all the eternal
laws that reign about his house, interpreting without comprehending the
silence of doors and windows and the quivering voice of the light. . .does yet
live in reality, a deeper, more human and more universal life than the lover
who strangles his mistress.[36]

With his first words in the play 'Je n'en dis rien' and his resignation in
the face of destiny, Arkël sees and understands more than anyone.
Maeterlinck's reference to the 'comprehension of windows and
doors' hints at this technique whereby simple, everyday objects
become symbolic of ideas far greater than themselves.

A further technique is that of the oblique answer, a device at which Mélisande is particularly adept. Her replies to Golaud's questions are all the more meaningful because they do not answer his question. However *quotidien* they seem, they are weighted with meaning. In Act I the following exchange occurs:

GOLAUD   Quel âge avez vous?
MELISANDE   Je commence à avoir froid.

(GOLAUD   How old are you?
MELISANDE   I am beginning to feel cold.)

Similarly, in Act V:

ARKEL   Que veux-tu que je fasse?
MELISANDE   Est-il vrai que l'hiver commence?

(ARKEL   What do you want me to do?
MELISANDE   Is it true that winter is beginning?)

In both cases the oblique answer emphasises Mélisande's fear of the cold. Later she concludes the symbol, but it remains only half-explained, with the emphatic *'grand'* already mentioned:

MELISANDE   J'ai peur du froid. Ah! j'ai peur des *grands* froids.
            (I am afraid of the cold, I am afraid of the great cold.)

If Arkël is, in the words of another essay, 'Les avertis', a 'warned-one' because of his age, so too is Mélisande who, in Act II scene 2, senses that she will not live long. 'Les avertis' is full of the paradoxes of mystical writing, of the 'seeing yet not understanding' which pervades *Pelléas* and which accumulates towards the end of the play. The essay ends with the words:

They came towards us and our eyes met; we drew asunder, silently, and all was clear to us, though we knew nothing.[37]

Mélisande's non-comprehending knowledge in the final act of the play is very much in a similar vein:

Il me semble cependant que je sais quelque chose. . . Je ne comprends pas non plus tout ce que je dis, voyez-vous. . .Je ne sais pas ce que je sais. . . Je ne dis plus ce que je veux.

(Yet it seems to me that I know something. . . I don't understand, though, everything that I say, you see. . . I don't know what I know. . . I no longer say what I want to.)

Princesses lointaines such as Mélisande were common figures in the idealistic literature of Symbolism. Mélisande, sister to Rossetti's

'Blessed Damozel', was by no means the prototype of her genre, whose youth, beauty and femininity brings rejuvenation to a stagnant world. In an article published in 1891 Maeterlinck's idea that women were 'closer to God' than men had already been put forward and in *Le Trésor des Humbles* the necessity of a woman's spiritual leadership is expounded in an essay simply entitled 'On Women':

Therefore it is, perhaps, that, besides their primitive instincts, all women have communications with the unknown that are denied to us. With reverence we must draw near them, be they lowly or arrogant, inattentive or lost in dreams, be they smiling still, or plunged in tears; for they know the things that we do not know, and have a lamp that we have lost.

For women are indeed the veiled sisters of all the great things we do not see. They are indeed nearest of kin to the infinite that is about us, and they alone can still smile at it with the intimate grace of the child, to whom its father inspires no fear. It is they who preserve here below the pure fragrance of the soul, like some jewel from heaven which none know how to use; and were they to depart, the spirit would reign in solitude in a desert. Theirs are still the divine emotions of the first days; and the sources of their being lie deeper far than ours, in all that was illimitable.[38]

In the light of these idealised views, it is no wonder that Golaud is distraught at the loss of the ring symbolising his union with Mélisande: 'I would rather have lost everything I own', he remarks, 'than to have lost that ring.'

We should remember that the Pre-Raphaelite woman herself was imbued with similar qualities: most importantly, she became a personification of the poet's own idealistic aspirations. Mélisande seems to personify this view – seeing 'what we do not see', possessing the 'grace of a child', yet sexually attractive. In the play itself the idealised aspects of Mélisande are most strikingly represented in her song, so aptly set by Debussy as a monody, hinting at the Lydian mode. She was, we learn, 'born on a Sunday at noon'. Later, Arkël refers to the renewal she has brought to the world-weary kingdom of Allemonde. But these idealised qualities exist, for Maeterlinck, 'besides their primitive instincts'. The scenes where Pelléas is so overcome by Mélisande's instinctual attraction, symbolised by her hair, and the final scene, where neither can resist the pull of passion, are the crucial antitheses, and ultimately pessimistic counterpart, to the theme of spiritual development personified in Mélisande's character and in Pelléas's and Mélisande's love.

It is not fortuitous that the two actual characters most imbued with spiritual qualities in *Le Trésor des humbles* are the wise old man and the idealised woman, for it is Arkël and Mélisande who are most developed in the play. Several early criticisms of *Pelléas*, while generally sympathetic, found Golaud too much of a stock-in-trade stage villain. Common both to essays and play are references to certain symbols of the metaphysical, of a 'greater knowledge': doors, windows, keys, rings, circles of light. More fundamentally though, it is the exploration of the theme of destiny in *Le Trésor des Humbles* which most illuminates our reading of *Pelléas*.

Maeterlinck's preoccupation with the inescapable hand of destiny, implicit in his early plays, is again explicit in *Le Trésor des Humbles*. It is the old man's understandable awareness of death and experience, and Mélisande's passive acceptance of fate, because of her womanhood, that make Arkël and Mélisande the main protagonists of this deeper level of meaning of the play. In the 1890s, Maeterlinck associated resignation to fate particularly with women:

> It would seem that women are more largely swayed by destiny than ourselves. They submit to its decrees with far more simplicity; nor is there sincerity in the resistance they offer.[39]

If Mélisande is the incarnation of this view of women, it is Arkël who from his first words propounds and underlines his belief in the uselessness of any attempt to tamper with the hand of fate. That Debussy recognised his pronouncements as of overriding importance is evident from his *lent et grave* setting of Arkël's most resonant pronouncements, often underlined by particularly striking music.

Those intent on transcribing the relationships of the characters of the play into modern psychological terms are fed many key lines by Maeterlinck. The failure of the relationship between Golaud and Mélisande, for example, has been ascribed to its father–daughter basis. Golaud reminds us of Mélisande's extreme youth in Act I, and both Yniold and Mélisande remind us of Golaud's prickly grey beard. Pelléas and Mélisande, however, are referred to as 'brother and sister'. In time, we may wonder, such a relationship might have been equally doomed, for they meet 'for the last time' as if mysteriously forewarned that their love will be to no avail. Also explored with considerable delicacy is the peculiar empathy between the very old Arkël and the young Mélisande, united in their 'knowing'.

Apart from *Le Trésor des Humbles*, Maeterlinck's preface to the 1901 edition of his collected works illuminates the ideas of the early plays:

Refined poetry, if one looks at it closely, is composed of three principal elements. First, verbal beauty; next the contemplation and passionate portrayal of what exists in reality around us and in ourselves, that is to say nature, and our feelings; and finally, enveloping the whole work and its individual atmosphere, the way in which the poet depicts the *unknown* in which the characters move and have their being, from the mystery which dominates them and judges them, and which presides over their destinies.[40]

The 'verbal beauty' of *Pelléas* at once struck many supporters of the play. Maeterlinck's friend van Lerberghe noted the simple beauty of many of the images and symbols when Maeterlinck first read a draft to him in 1892. 'The words which convey the most' he noted, 'are the simplest, profoundly human, discreet in their imagery.'[41] Some phrases he saw as of particular beauty – Arkël's first 'Je n'en dis rien'; Pelléas's image of water in a muslin bag. He also suggested a few changes to Maeterlinck, foreseeing some of the lines that were to fuel the invective of the play's opponents. 'Je suis affreuse ainsi', was one such line.

Maeterlinck's second component – 'the passionate portrayal of what exists in reality around us and in ourselves, that is to say nature, and our feelings' – does not necessarily involve extension into a framework of symbolism. Simple details about characters in the play, or in the objects around them, may reflect changes or developments in their psychological state: Mélisande's 'unwell hands', the blue depths of the sea-cavern which have never been explored, Golaud's wound or Arkël's blindness. If such reflections are on the borders of symbolism, there are still larger, more recurrent and less tangible symbols which unify the whole play. The light–dark symbolism has been singled out for a separate chapter, but there are also the several references to circles: the ring, the lost crown, the circle of water, Yniold's golden ball. The circular shapes extend to scenes within the play which often consist of a circular journey – there and back – whether it is the gardens, the sea-cavern, or the vaults under the castle. Moreover, this circular motion is reflected in the overall shape of the play which never ends, for in Arkël's final line we learn that it is now the turn of the little child.

Above all Debussy shared with Maeterlinck a belief that art should explore mystery, a quality he admired in the painter Turner. In his celebrated interview with his teacher Ernest Guiraud, reported by Maurice Emmanuel, Debussy described his ideal text. At the time, it seemed to relate to his cantata *Diane au bois* but this, like many other projects was ultimately abandoned. His response to the question 'Quel poète pourra vous fournir un "poème"? would seem more precisely to apply to *Pelléas*:

Celui qui, disant les choses à demi, me permettra de greffer mon rêve sur le sien, qui concevra des personnages dont l'histoire et la demeure ne seront d'aucun temps, d'aucun lieu; qui ne m'imposera pas, despotiquement, la "scène à faire" et me laissera libre, ici ou là, d'avoir plus art que lui, et de parachever son ouvrage.

(One who states only half of what is to be said, and allows me to graft my dream on to his. One who conceives his characters as out of place and out of time, and who does not force on me a 'big scene'. One who, here and there, will allow me the freedom to have a little more art than he – to finish off his work.)[42]

2 The opera: genesis and sources

BY DAVID A. GRAYSON

Although Debussy attended the stage première of Maeterlinck's *Pelléas et Mélisande* at the Théâtre des Bouffes-Parisiens in Paris, it was evidently his prior reading of the play which captured his imagination. In 1902 he told an interviewer how the idea to set the play to music first came to him: 'One fine day, having bought the slim volume, he set about reading it and saw in it a fine subject for an opera.'[1] Louis Laloy's 1909 'authorised' biography of the composer placed this discovery in the summer of 1892,[2] shortly after the play's May publication, but the composer himself assigned it to the following year: he wrote on a slip of paper, 'Purchased and read *Pelléas* in 1893',[3] and indicated this same date in an essay published posthumously under the title 'Pourquoi j'ai écrit *Pelléas*' (Why I Wrote *Pelléas*).[4] Perhaps he came upon the play by chance, as Laloy suggested, or perhaps he learned about it from one of the articles or announcements which appeared in the press as early as January 1893 to publicise the play's forthcoming production. In either case, he must have read the play with more than casual interest.

Two years earlier, in 1891, he had hoped to write an opera based on another Maeterlinck drama, *La Princesse Maleine*, published in 1889 and as yet unperformed, but he was forced to abandon these plans when he was informed that Maeterlinck had already promised the play to Vincent d'Indy, who had expressed the 'vague intention' of setting it some day. (He never did.) This incident shows, nevertheless, that Debussy was already drawn to the work of the Belgian playwright, and it is thus quite possible that, when he came to read *Pelléas*, it was with the express intention of assessing its operatic potential. According to Laloy, Debussy was immediately taken with the play and needed only a day to decide that he wanted to set it. If he did not immediately seek Maeterlinck's authorisation, it was because (as he told the 1902 interviewer) he wanted first to allow his plans to develop. In Laloy's account, he also sought the counsel of various friends, who tried unsuccessfully to dissuade him from undertaking such a 'disastrous' project.[5] Any lingering doubts about the play's theatrical viability were probably put to rest by the performance at the Bouffes-Parisiens.

Another reason why Debussy may have waited before starting to set *Pelléas* was that in the spring and summer of 1893 he was already working on several other pieces: the orchestration of his 1891 *Marche écossaise*, the String Quartet, and the *Proses lyriques*. Also remaining to be completed were the *Prélude à l'après-midi d'un faune*, begun in 1892, and the three-act opera *Rodrigue et Chimène*, with a libretto by Catulle Mendès based on the legend of El Cid, which Debussy began in April 1890 and worked on until 1892. During the summer of 1893, he was still treating the nearly completed opera as a work in progress; he played it to Paul Dukas, who found the music praiseworthy ('the episodes are exquisite and have a harmonic finesse which brings to mind the early songs'), but thought the libretto 'uninteresting. . . a mixture of Parnassian bric-à-brac and Spanish barbarism'.[6] Debussy probably agreed with this assessment. He never finished *Rodrigue*, complaining to Gustave Charpentier that it was 'contrary to everything I wished to express. The traditional aspects of the subject call for music which is not my own.'[7]

Actually, *Rodrigue* was only the most recent in a series of theatre works which Debussy began and abandoned before he discovered *Pelléas*. The most significant of his prior efforts were partial settings of Théodore de Banville's *Diane au bois* (1881–6) and *Hymnis* (c. 1882) and Villiers de L'Isle-Adam's *Axël* (c. 1887–9).[8] He alluded to these aborted projects in 'Why I Wrote Pelléas': 'For a long time I had been striving to write music for the theatre, but the form in which I wanted it to be was so unusual that after several attempts I had almost given up the idea.' As early as October 1889, in the course of his famous conversation with his former composition teacher Ernest Guiraud, he prophetically anticipated *Pelléas* when he defined certain aspects of the 'unusual' form he sought. When asked what poet would suit his needs, Debussy replied:

Celui des choses *dites à demi*. Deux rêves associés: voilà l'idéal. Pas de pays, ni de date. Pas de scène à faire. Aucune pression sur le musicien qui parachève. . . Je rêve poèmes courts: scènes mobiles. Me f. . . des 3 unités! Scènes diverses par lieux et caractère; personnages ne discutant pas; subissant vie, sort, etc.

(One who only hints at what is to be said. The ideal would be two associated dreams. No place, nor time. No big scene. No compulsion on the musician, who must complete and give body to the work of the poet. . . My idea is of a short libretto with mobile scenes. I have no use at all for the three unities. A variety of scenes in regard to place and character. No discussion or arguments between the characters whom I see at the mercy of life or destiny.)[9]

In 'Why I Wrote *Pelléas*' he explained his attraction to Maeterlinck's Symbolist play, specifically juxtaposing it with the ideals of naturalism, with which he had little sympathy:

Le drame de *Pelléas* qui malgré son atmosphère de rêves contient beaucoup plus d'humanité que les soi-disant 'documents sur la vie' me parut convenir admirablement à ce que je voulais faire. Il y a là une langue évocatrice dont la sensibilité pouvait trouver son prolongement dans la musique et dans le décor orchestral.

(The drama of *Pelléas* – which, despite its atmosphere of dreams, contains much more humanity than so-called real-life documents – seemed to suit my intention admirably. It has an evocative language whose sensitivity could find its extension in music and in orchestral setting.)

In early August 1893 Debussy formally approached Maeterlinck through an intermediary, the poet Henri de Régnier, who wrote the following letter to the playwright:

My friend, Achille Debussy, who is a musician of the most clever and delicate talent, has begun some charming music for *Pelléas et Mélisande*, which deliciously garlands the text while scrupulously respecting it. Before going further with this work, which is not inconsiderable, he would like authorisation to continue.[10]

In his reply of 8 August, Maeterlinck thanked the poet for his 'friendly intervention' and granted the requested authorisation 'since you approve of what he has done so far'.[11] Despite Régnier's claim, there is no firm evidence that Debussy had as yet written *any* music for *Pelléas*. The composer's lifelong friend Robert Godet recalled that Debussy had jotted down a few musical ideas immediately upon reading the play (and before attending its performance) – the rhythm representing Golaud's ponderous walk, Mélisande's five-note 'arabesque', and the theme which accompanies Pelléas's line 'On dirait que ta voix a passé sur la mer au printemps' in Act IV scene 4 – but this testimony is suspect since the first two motifs named are conspicuously absent from the earliest extant sketches.[12] Even so, such jottings could hardly have justified Régnier's praise, which was probably just a conceit concocted to bolster Debussy's case. After all, considering his prior disappointment at being denied

La Princesse Maleine, it is hard to imagine that Debussy would have begun composing *Pelléas* before securing Maeterlinck's permission. According to the composer's recollections, he might have had 'a few secret thoughts about possible music' after reading the play, but he did not actually begin the work until September 1893,[13] which is also the earliest date found in a surviving manuscript.

Debussy began writing the opera, not at the beginning, but with the climactic 'love-duet' scene, Act IV scene 4. It appears that this was drafted very quickly. In a letter to Ernest Chausson of 3 September he wrote that he was 'working furiously', then, in the postscript to this letter, written perhaps a few days later, he announced that he had completed the fourth of the *Proses lyriques* and was finishing the scene from *Pelléas*.[14] Raymond Bonheur, who was among the first to hear the newly composed scene, believed that Debussy set it purely for his own pleasure and not with the intention of producing a theatre work.[15] On the other hand, Debussy may well have regarded the scene as a trial to test the play's suitability as an opera libretto, a procedure he appears to have used a few years before when he set a single scene from *Axël*.[16]

If committed to the project, Debussy was soon dissatisfied with his setting, and in a letter of 2 October, confided to Chausson his reasons for discarding the draft: he found the music too derivative ('like a duo by Mr So-and-so'), and was disturbed above all by evidence of a Wagnerian influence. The latter would have been particularly troubling and potentially embarrassing, since he had just announced his forthcoming article 'De l'inutilité du wagnérisme' (On the uselessness of Wagnerism) in the September issue of *L'Idée libre*. (The article, however, never appeared.) He told Chausson that he tore up the original draft (though part of it may still exist in the 'Meyer' MS; see Bibliography, a catalogue of the manuscript and printed sources), and reported that he was working on a new version which was 'more personal' and used 'silence . . . as a means of expression'. This second version, still quite different from the scene's ultimate form, was apparently completed by 19 October. It survives in the 'Legouix' MS, dated 'September–October 1893'. As was his habit, Debussy tried out the scene by playing it for his friends; Raymond Bonheur and the painter Henry Lerolle heard it on separate occasions in mid-October, and both responded enthusiastically.

In early November Debussy travelled to Ghent to meet Maeterlinck. According to a report in *L'Art moderne* of 12 November, the composer's purpose was to play his setting for the playwright. Debussy's detailed account of the meeting, contained in another letter to Chausson written at the beginning of December, mentions no such audition. Rather, Maeterlinck is quoted as confessing that he understands 'nothing about [music], and, faced with a Beethoven symphony', is 'like a blind man in a museum', which, while apparently true, sounds like Maeterlinck's way of avoiding having to comment – or even of having to listen to – Debussy's scene. Nevertheless, the composer was altogether pleased with the outcome of the meeting because he was able to secure Maeterlinck's authorisation to make any cuts he deemed necessary. In actual fact, this was probably his main mission in making the trip to Ghent. The playwright even suggested some cuts, which Debussy described as 'very important, *even very useful*', though unfortunately he did not identify them. Maeterlinck's agreement was necessary, not so much for what Debussy had already composed (his early draft of Act IV scene 4 made no cuts at all and included only two tiny – and perhaps inadvertent – word changes), but for what he planned to compose, now that he was apparently (even if only temporarily) satisfied with his setting of the scene which obviously attracted him most in the play. Evidently Maeterlinck did not insist that Debussy adopt the changes which had been made for the stage première (and which formed the basis for the first comprehensive revision of the play, published in 1898), most conspicuously, the substitution of 'Les trois soeurs aveugles' for 'Mes longs cheveux', Mélisande's original song from the tower in Act III. While it is not known what specific cuts Maeterlinck recommended to the composer, they may well have included the four scenes which Debussy never set: Act I scene 1, Act II scene 4, Act III scene 1, and Act V scene 1. (See chapter 3 for a discussion of these and other cuts.) The decision to omit these scenes was probably made before any music was written for them: no sketches survive and they are never discussed in the composer's correspondence.

Thus, in December 1893, when Debussy resumed work on *Pelléas* and turned to Act I, he passed over the first scene and composed the remaining three in sequence, at the approximate rate of one scene per month, completing the act in February 1894. He wrote to Chausson of his compositional struggles: 'J'ai passé des journées à la poursuite de ce "rien" dont elle est faite (Mélisande)' (I have spent days trying to capture the 'nothing' that Mélisande is made of [Act I scene 1]).

Maintenant c'est Arkël qui me tourmente: celui-là, il est *d'outre-tombe*, et il a cette tendresse désintéressée et prophétique de ceux qui vont bientôt disparaître, et il faut dire tout cela avec, do, ré, mi, fa, sol, la, si, do!!! Quel métier!

(At the moment it is Arkël who's tormenting me [Act I scene 2]. He comes from *beyond the grave*, and he has that objective, prophetic gentleness of those who are soon to die – all of which must be expressed with doh, ray, me, fah, soh, lah, te, doh!!! What a profession!)[17]

After completing Act I, Debussy appears to have suspended work on *Pelléas* until May, when he turned to the third act, bypassing the second, which was in fact the last to be composed. Act III scene 1 was perhaps still unfinished by 31 May, when Pierre Louÿs invited some friends to his home to hear the composer play scenes from the opera, but it was probably completed by 20 July, when Debussy informed Louÿs of his decision to proceed with Act III scene 2, the scene in the underground vaults. The weeks which followed were extremely productive, and Debussy detailed his accomplishments in a lengthy letter to Lerolle dated 28 August: he had completed Act III scene 2, 'pleine de terreur sournoise, et mystérieuse à donner le vertige aux âmes les mieux trempées' (full of impalpable terror and mysterious enough to make the most well-balanced listener giddy), as well as Act III scene 3, 'la scène au sortir des mêmes souterrains, pleine de soleil, mais du soleil baigné par notre bonne mère la mer' (The climb up from the vaults is done too, full of sunshine, but a sunshine reflecting our mother the sea). He expressed anxiety over the final scene of the act, in which Golaud forces his son Yniold to spy on Pelléas and Mélisande, which may explain why he briefly interrupted the composition of the act to complete Yniold's 'other' scene, Act IV scene 3, 'où j'ai essayé de mettre un peu de la compassion d'un enfant à qui un mouton donne d'abord une idée du jouet auquel il ne peut toucher, et aussi une pitié que n'ont plus les gens inquiets de confortable' (in which I've tried to get across something at least of the compassion of a child who sees a sheep mainly as a sort of toy he can't touch, and also as the object of a pity no longer felt by those who are only anxious for a comfortable life). This done, he returned to Act III to work on its final scene: 'j'ai peur, il me faut des choses si profondes et si sûres! Il y a là un "petit père" qui me donne le cauchemar' (It's terrifying, the music's got to be profound and absolutely accurate! There's a 'petit père' that gives me nightmares); this scene was probably finished in September. He was also thinking ahead to Act V and described an idea (ultimately rejected) for its scoring: to put a group of instruments on stage.

He then set *Pelléas* aside to work on other projects – the orchestration of the *Prélude à l'après-midi d'un faune*, the three *Nocturnes* for violin and orchestra (never completed, though perhaps reworked as the three *Nocturnes* for orchestra of 1897–9), and a set of three *Images* for piano (published in 1978 as 'Images (oubliées)'). *Pelléas* was resumed in January–February 1895, but we do not know which scenes were being composed at this time – quite possibly Act IV scenes 1–2, the only scenes which cannot otherwise be dated on the basis of manuscript annotations or references in the correspondence. In April, while collaborating with Pierre Louÿs on the scenario of a lyric fairy-tale called *Cendrelune*, Debussy had a sudden impulse to work on Act V of *Pelléas*, and the following month he undertook another extensive revision of Act IV scene 4. He next turned in earnest to Act V and was able to announce its completion on 20 June. Now only Act II remained. In a letter to Bonheur of 9 August he expressed surprise that, contrary to his expectations, he was finding this act so difficult to compose. More likely, it was some anticipated difficulty which had motivated the postponement of its composition in the first place. When he finally completed the act on 17 August, he explained to Lerolle why he had found its second scene especially problematic:

car c'est là où l'on commence à remuer des catastrophes, là où Mélisande commence à mentir à Golaud et à s'éclairer sur elle-même, aidée en cela par ce même Golaud, brave homme tout de même, et qui démontre qu'il ne faut pas être tout à fait franc, même avec les petites filles.

([because] that's the point where things begin to move towards the catastrophe, and where Mélisande begins to tell Golaud lies and to realize her own motives, assisted in this by the said Golaud, a solid fellow for all that; it also shows you shouldn't be completely frank, even with young girls.)

But he was quite pleased with the way scene 3 turned out:

ça essaye d'être tout le mystérieux de la nuit où parmi tant de silence, un brin d'herbe dérangé de son sommeil fait un bruit tout à fait inquiétant; puis, c'est la mer prochaine qui raconte ses doléances à la lune, et c'est Pelléas et Mélisande qui ont un peu peur de parler dans tant de mystère.

(I tried to capture all the mystery of the night and the silence in which a blade of grass roused from its sleep makes an alarming noise; then there's the sea nearby, telling its sorrows to the moon and Pelléas and Mélisande a little scared of talking, surrounded by so much mystery.)

Thus, on the basis of the composer's correspondence and the dates inscribed in manuscripts, it is possible to assemble the following compositional schedule for *Pelléas*:

Act IV scene 4	(?late August–) September–October 1893, May 1895
Act I scenes 1–3	December 1893 – February 1894
Act III scene 1	May–June (–July?) 1894
Act III scene 2	July–August 1894
Act III scene 3	August 1894
Act IV scene 3	August 1894
Act III scene 4	August–September 1894
Act IV scenes 1–2	(January–February 1895?)
Act V	April–June 1895
Act II scenes 1–3	June – 17 August 1895

There is some logic to this out-of-order sequence, for, despite some gaps and irregularities, Debussy's inclination was to conceive and compose each act as an integral unit. He started with Act IV scene 4, the 'trial' scene, which was probably central to his attraction to the play, and after several attempts was finally satisfied with it. He then turned to the beginning of the play, composing the scenes of Act I in sequence. He deferred Act II, perhaps because he anticipated difficulties with it, and started to compose the scenes of Act III in order; but he became anxious over scene 4, possibly to some extent because it involved writing a child's part, so he delayed its composition until he had completed Act IV scene 3, a more straightforward scene in which the child also appears. He then went on to complete Act IV, continued with Act V, and finally went back to Act II, probably composing its three scenes in sequence.

The surviving manuscripts suggest that the composition of this first version was accomplished in two stages. The first is represented by the hastily written preliminary draft, in which the music was sketchily notated.[18] The rough appearance of this draft is illustrated by Figure 1, a page from the Meyer MS (and probably dating from June 1895); it is from near the end of Act V, starting with Arkël's '[Mais la tris-]tesse de tout ce que l'on voit. . .' (VS, p. 306, bar 2) and ending with some crossed-out bars that accompany Golaud's textless sobs, which are not notated in the sketch (VS, p. 307, bar 11). On this

Figure 1   Meyer MS (Bibliothèque Nationale, Paris), Act V, fol. 17ʳ (facsimile, p. 83)

page, only one line of text is supplied (the physician's 'Elles ont raison. . .' towards the end of the second system), though rather unusually, a stage direction is indicated: *les servantes tombent à genoux* (the serving-women fall to their knees) in the left margin of the second system. Although the accompaniment is typically notated on two staves, like a piano reduction, Debussy's use of additional staves (and sometimes of contrasting coloured pencils) shows that even at this early compositional stage, he was thinking orchestrally and wished to distinguish the separate instrumental strands. This is also indicated by the orchestrational jottings, actually quite infrequent at this stage, which appear in the first system: in the left margin Debussy has written abbreviations for three solo first violins and flute ('3 1° V°' and 'Fl') and beneath the third measure of that system, specified harp harmonics ('Harpe, s[ons] harmoniques'). The final version of these bars (see OS, p. 405, bars 7–8) retained these original sonorities, despite some rhythmic changes and added doublings which made the scoring somewhat less delicate. An important difference, however, is that Debussy transferred the harp part (which states the Mélisande motif) to the oboes (the instrument associated with her), though he kept the harp sonority (without harmonics) by assigning to that instrument an independent line. This change is in keeping with Debussy's tendency throughout the composition and revision of *Pelléas* to demonstrate greater and greater consistency in his association of particular themes and timbres with particular characters, objects and places. Another such change is observable in the music to accompany Golaud's textless sobs, crossed out at the bottom of the page (Ex. 1a). Here, the orchestra contains the theme which was associated with Golaud in the earliest sketches and was retained in the final version of the opera in several key places. Initially, it was used in Act I scene 1 (VS, p. 14, bar 8) to accompany Golaud's name when he introduces himself to Mélisande; and later, it returns at several crucial dramatic points, where it is more specifically associated with Golaud's jealousy, notably at the end of Act III scene 1 (VS, pp. 138–9), the end of Act IV scene 2 (VS, p. 218, bar 12), and throughout the ending of Act IV scene 4 (starting on VS, p. 256, bar 4). But when Debussy revised this passage at the top of the next page (Ex. 1b), he substituted the theme which came to be used more consistently in connection with Golaud throughout the opera. The sketches reveal numerous instances similar to this, where Debussy substituted the 'new' Golaud motif

Example 1

a) Meyer MS, Act V, fol. 17^r, system 5, bars 2–4 (original layer, see figure 1)

b) Meyer MS, Act V, fol. 17^r, system 5, bar 2 (after revision), continuing on fol. 18^r (facsimile, p. 82), bars 1–2

c) Published version (reduced from OS, p. 406, bars 11–13)

for the original.[19] In the final version of this passage (Ex. 1c), the theme is further modified to make its presence less explicit and more subtle.

This sketch page also shows how Debussy sometimes altered the vocal rhythms and pitches in order to change the pace of the dialogue and its emphases. In addition, it contains the setting of some words of text which Debussy subsequently cut from the libretto: they are found in the last two measures of the fourth system and constitute the italicised words in Arkël's lines 'Je n'ai rien entendu. . . Si vite, si vite . . . *Tout à coup, tout à coup.* . . Elle s'en va sans rien dire. . .' (I heard nothing. . . So quick, so quick. . . *All at once, all at once.* . . She goes out without a word. . .). The cut simply eliminated a redundancy in the text.

Apart from the four scenes which he omitted entirely, Debussy made numerous cuts in the scenes which he set. While many of these may have been made before he began composing the music, many were imposed in the process of drafting and revising the score. The example just cited from Act V is one such case. Maeterlinck's text abounds in such redundant repetitions, particularly of short exclamatory phrases, and in the 1901 preface to his collected theatre works, the playwright conceded that such repetitions 'make the characters seem like slightly deaf sleepwalkers constantly roused from painful dreams'. Debussy tended to eliminate some of these repetitions (as, incidentally, did Maeterlinck in his own revisions of his play); in the following passage from Act IV scene 4, Debussy's cuts are italicised:

MELISANDE	Non, non, *non*!. . .
PELLEAS	Va-t'en! *va-t'en*! Il a tout vu!. . . Il nous tuera!. . .
MELISANDE	Tant mieux! tant mieux! *tant mieux*!. . .
PELLEAS	Il vient! *il vient*!. . . Ta bouche!. . . Ta bouche!. . .

(MELISANDE	No, no, *no*!. . .
PELLEAS	Go away! *Go away*! He has seen everything!. . . He will kill us!. . .
MELISANDE	So much the better! So much the better! *So much the better*!. . .
PELLEAS	He is coming! *He is coming*!. . . Your mouth!. . . Your mouth!. . .)

The repetitiousness which remained was further curtailed by the setting (see VS, pp. 264–5): Debussy broke up Mélisande's repetitions of 'non!' and 'tant mieux!' by interpolating Pelléas's lines between them, and in a later revision, Pelléas's repetition of 'Ta bouche!' was even changed, to 'Donne!' ('Give it!'). This latter change must have been made for the early performances: it is found in both the manuscript full score (Bibliothèque Nationale, Paris, MS 964) and the vocal score proofs used by Jean Périer, the original Pelléas, (Rés. Vma. 237), but it was never incorporated into the published scores. The overlapping of the voice parts which occurs in this passage is one of very few such instances in the opera. In his early drafts, Debussy never allowed his characters to 'speak' at the same time. As he explained in an interview which appeared in the London *Daily Mail* (28 May 1909): 'my one engrossing ambition in music is to bring it as near as possible to a representation of life itself. . . When two persons talk at the same time they cannot hear one another. Besides, it is not polite, and the one who interrupts should stop.'[20] Nevertheless, in his revisions of the score, Debussy sometimes, though rarely, allowed lines to overlap slightly, in order to express eagerness, fervour, or impatience; at the end of Act IV scene 4 (VS, p. 266) he even permitted the simultaneous singing of different texts for Pelléas and Mélisande's final impassioned exchange.

Once an entire scene or act was more or less complete in his mind and roughly sketched out in the preliminary draft, Debussy immediately wrote out the *particelle* (short score) or developed draft. This second compositional stage was not entirely an act of copying, for a great deal of refinement and spontaneous revision was also involved. Furthermore, while the completed *particelle* was assembled on 17 August 1895, pages continued to be replaced as late as September 1901 and revised even while the full score was being drafted, in January–February 1902.

Figure 2 reproduces one of the pages rejected from the *particelle* of Act IV scene 1. Beyond illustrating this compositional stage, this page contains a passage whose revisions will represent some of the types of changes through which Debussy refined his personal style of 'recitative'. (See Exx. 2a and 2b, which juxtapose the original layer of this passage – beginning with the last beat of system three in Figure 2 – with the published version.) The revisions in Pelléas's first sentence serve to emphasise the location where he wishes his last meeting with Mélisande to take place; this was achieved by (1) removing the pause that set off the phrase identifying Blindmen's Well as the proposed meeting place; (2) lengthening the second syllable of 'aveugles' and making that syllable the melodic highpoint of the phrase in order to

Acte IV, Sc. 1

Figure 2   Bréval MS (Bibliothèque Nationale, Paris), fol. 18ʳ (facsimile, p. 87)

Example 2

Bréval MS, fol. 18ʳ, system 3 (bar 4, beat 4) to system 5 (bar 5, beat 1)
(original layer, see figure 2)

a)

Example 2 (*cont.*)
Published version (reduced from OS, p. 258, bar 7, to p. 259, bar 9)

b)

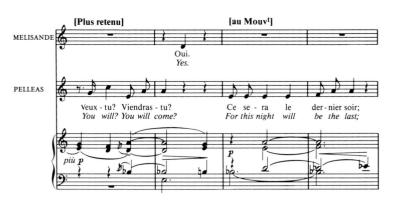

stress the name of the well; and (3) changing the accompaniment from a statement of the Pelléas motif to a theme which was specifically associated with the well in Act II scene 1. (Since Act II was the last composed, this theme was probably conceived after Act IV scene 1 was first drafted.) By eliminating the rest between Pelléas's next two lines – 'Veux-tu?' and 'Voudras-tu?' – those questions are given greater urgency. In the revision, Mélisande's affirmative reply also follows without pause, as she obeys Pelléas's prior request that she answer quickly. The pace of the exchanges is further hastened by the elimination of a crotchet rest before Pelléas's continuation. In his next line, 'Ce sera le dernier soir', stress is logically shifted from 'soir' to 'dernier' (the important point being that this evening will be their *last*), by having both the first pitch change and the metric accent coincide with that word. Changes in rhythmic durations, pitches, and metric placement also serve to emphasise 'voyager' (again, clearly the key word) in the sentence that follows, whose melody, by virtue of its expanded range and rising contour, is made more striking than the nearly monotone and rhythmically undiversified original version. Furthermore, the new melodic lines for these two sentences, both of which begin with four repeated Es and move to Fs on the downbeats for key words, create a parallelism such that the second sentence is shown to derive from the first in a melodic as well as a textual sense. Note, too, the supporting harmonies: in the original version, the stable C major triad in bar 3 and the E minor triads in bars 6 and 8 (and originally in bar 5 as well) provide harmonic resting points during the pauses between Pelléas's lines, further emphasizing the fragmented delivery of his text; in the revision, the harmonic arrival on E minor is very brief, punctuating Mélisande's 'Oui' (her agreement to the proposed meeting) on the weak third beat, while harmonic tension is maintained (over a unifying B♭ pedal) as Pelléas continues. Debussy's revision also uses melodic and harmonic means to dramatise the final, shocking line: 'Tu ne me verras plus.' In the original version, whatever tension might have been created by the pause preceding this line is nullified by the regularity of the underlying harmonic motion, which approaches this line at the steady rate of one chord per bar and moreover, with root motion following a too-predictable (and conventional) circle of fifths (F–B♭–E♭); therefore, when the harmonic shock finally arrives (bar 12), it comes at the *end* of the line, almost like a shocked reaction to it. In the revision, this line is not set off by a pause, but it is immediately and dramatically set apart from what precedes it: the accompaniment drops out on the preceding word 'dit', the chords which accompany the line are short, detached and move at an increased rate of harmonic change, and the vocal line starts after a downward leap of an octave. The rhythm of the line is also altered so that it starts on the beat, adding emphasis to its first word: '*You* will see me no more.'

This example suggests that in passages such as this, where the text is largely conversational and concerned with the communication of information, Debussy's initial concern was to establish a text delivery which was rhythmically true to the syntax of his prose libretto. The result was quite straightforward and melodically almost formulaic: each line was set off by rests and recited on a single note, with a change of pitch on the last syllable to mark the sentence or phrase ending. The revisions brought greater attention to the *meaning* of the text, introducing rhythmic, metric, and pitch changes to emphasise key words, while giving the lines more lyrical and expressive melodic profiles. In so doing, Debussy never sacrificed the essential character of his vocal style, which projected the speech patterns with clarity and naturalness. In passages such as this, the accompaniment is clearly subsidiary and subservient to the vocal parts, allowing Debussy almost total flexibility in altering the rhythms and melodic contours of the voices and in modifying the largely supportive accompaniment to correspond (though we note that certain harmonic features do remain fixed throughout the revisions). In other portions of the opera, however, where the text is more overtly dramatic or expressive, the orchestra has a more equal role, sharing in that dramatic expression, often with distinctive and independent thematic material. In parts of the earliest drafts (particularly of Act IV scene 4) the orchestra was sometimes given so much prominence that, rather than sharing, it seemed to dominate and direct the drama, contrary to Debussy's expressed views on the subject. He voiced his objections to what he called 'the application of symphonic form [and developments] to dramatic action' in his 1901 review of Alfred Bruneau's opera *L'Ouragan*:

la musique a un rythme dont la force secrète dirige le développement; les mouvements de l'âme en ont un autre plus instinctivement général et soumis à de multiples événements. De la juxtaposition de ces deux rythmes il naît un perpétuel conflit. Cela ne s'accomplit pas en même temps: ou la musique s'essouffle à courir après un personnage, ou le personnage s'assoit sur une note pour permettre à la musique de le rattraper.

(Music has a rhythm whose secret force shapes the development. The impulses of the soul, however, have a quite different rhythm – more instinctively general, and controlled by many events. From the incompatibility of these two rhythms a perpetual conflict arises. The two do not move at the same speed: either the music gets out of breath by chasing after a character, or the character sits on a note to allow the music to catch up with him.)

In the early drafts, the accompaniment occasionally took on the character of such a symphonic development (with precise, modified, or sequential repetitions – sometimes quite extensive – of a given theme, often in two- or four-bar units), and, in keeping with his critical stance, Debussy's revisions tended to eliminate or modify that effect. Example 3 juxtaposes the earliest *particelle* version of one such passage from Act IV scene 4 with the final version, as it appears in the vocal score. The accompaniment in the early version consists of a four-bar phrase and its modified repetition. The phrase itself contains internal repetitions, notably of the motif associated with Golaud's jealousy – altogether appropriate, as this is the moment when Mélisande first becomes aware that somebody is behind herself and Pelléas, and she fears that it is Golaud. In revising the passage, Debussy eliminated the impression that the characters are 'waiting' during the last bar while the orchestra finishes its second four-bar phrase: he compressed the dialogue (from eight to six bars) and reduced the orchestra's 'control' over the passage by breaking the melodic continuity of the theme-carrying bass line, by eliminating the internal repetitions of Golaud's 'jealousy' theme, and by utilising a less symmetrical four-plus-two bar structure. These observations are consistent with James R. McKay's conclusion, based on a detailed examination of the Bréval MS and illustrated by Pelléas's monologue from the start of Act IV scene 4, that 'Debussy moved from a repetitive, symmetrical, hierarchical structure towards a supple, asymmetrical texture which was sensitive to the exigencies of text and drama'.[21] One might add that the original repetitive structures were typically based on key leitmotifs, and that the revisions were not only asymmetrical but less dependent on those leitmotifs for their organisation. Rather than build his accompaniments *out of* leitmotifs, Debussy came to prefer nonthematic (or, more precisely, non-leitmotivic) accompaniments onto which his rhythmically and intervallically flexible leitmotifs could be easily superimposed. In this way, those themes could be used more for their symbolic than their structural values.

The voice parts in Example 3 reveal another tendency in the revisions. In the original version the vocal pitches were drawn almost exclusively from the accompaniment, utilising the G♭ and B♭ of the upper orchestral stave in bars 2–5, and doubling the bass line in bars 6–7. In the revision, the vocal parts take on greater independence, and, significantly, Mélisande's two lines – 'There is somebody behind us' and 'I heard a noise' – both oscillate between a pitch and the note a tone above, which suggests the 'Golaud' motif. In this subtle way, Mélisande's oscillations not only express her nervousness, but actually identify its source.

Finally, the revision also serves a long-range purpose. In the same early draft (the Legouix MS), Debussy repeated the eight bars of Example 3a in nearly identical form slightly later in the scene, at the moment when Mélisande spots Golaud behind a tree (see VS, p. 261, bars 3–10). The purpose of the musical repetition was to underline the dramatic parallel between the moment when Mélisande first becomes aware of Golaud's presence and when she actually spots him. The revision of Example 3b eliminated the literalness of the repetition without obliterating the parallel, and, appropriately, it left the later passage – the sighting of Golaud – with the greater motivic clarity and continuity; Debussy even superimposed two symmetrically placed statements of the 'Golaud' motif (VS, p. 261, bars 6 and 10) to signal the sightings. (See chapter 3, p. 75.)

The revisions shown in Examples 2 and 3 were made, not all at once, but in several stages, spread out over a number of years. Debussy was tireless and persevering in his desire to achieve the definitive setting of his text, and he continued to introduce modifications in his score even after the opera was published.[22]

The score remained in *particelle* while Debussy sought opportunities to have his opera performed. Finally, in May 1898, nearly three years after its completion, *Pelléas* was accepted 'in principle' by the Opéra-Comique, though Debussy still had to wait another three years before he received, on 3 May 1901, the written promise of Albert Carré, the company's director, that the opera would be mounted during the 1901/2 season. It then became necessary for Debussy to produce both a vocal score for the benefit of the cast and for rehearsal pianists, and a full score to serve as both a conductor's score and the source of the orchestral parts. It appears that he had already written out a vocal score, probably about a year before, around April 1900, at the request of his patron Georges Hartmann, because Debussy expected (wrongly, as it transpired) that the opera would go into rehearsal the following September. Pages from this score (from the beginning of Act IV) have survived in a private collection in Basel. Nevertheless, subsequent revisions of the opera, particularly in Act IV, made this version obsolete and a new draft was needed, at least of Acts IV and V; the manuscripts of these acts are in the Bibliothèque Nationale in Paris, MSS 17686 (Act IV scenes 1–2, Act V) and 17683 (Act IV scenes 3–4). The manuscript vocal score was given to the publisher Fromont sometime during the summer of 1901, but because the *particelle* of Act IV was revised as late as

Example 3
Legouix MS, fol. 8ʳ, bars 14–21 (original layer)

a)

Published version (VS, p. 259, bars 1–6)

b)

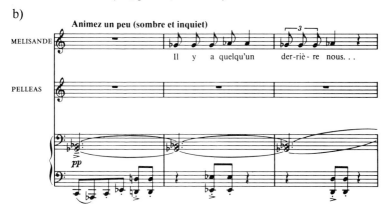

(MELISANDE   There is someone behind us,
PELLEAS   I see no one
MELISANDE   I heard a noise).

September, the final two acts could not have been submitted until then. Though the vocal score was not actually published until late April or early May 1902 (around the time of the première), the plates were engraved in time to permit uncorrected proofs to be printed for use by the singers and coaches. Those belonging to Jean Périer – the original Pelléas – have survived, though they are lacking the final act, in which Pelléas does not appear (Bibliothèque Nationale, Rés. Vma. 237).

Once the manuscript vocal score was delivered to Fromont, Debussy was free to turn his attention to the full score. A letter to

Pierre Louÿs of 2 September, which speaks of 'little Mélisande' as 'neurasthenic', and 'only able to put up with the violins if they are divided into eighteen parts'[23] suggests that Debussy may already have been working on the orchestration, while another letter, written in November, disclosed his secret intention of reorchestrating the opera.[24] But according to the eyewitness testimony of Godet, all of this was merely mental preparation (or perhaps in the form of annotations in the *particelle*), and the actual writing was done very quickly in three or four weeks early in 1902, while rehearsals (which began on 13 January) were already under way.[25] *Pelléas* was then consuming his entire time, Debussy complained to Pierre Louÿs: he attended rehearsals during the day and probably drafted the full score at night. Under considerable time pressure and 'harassed by telegrams from M. Messager', the conductor, he called upon Godet in mid-February to help him by ruling the pages, and, for the final two scenes, another friend even entered the text and vocal lines.[26] Though he worked closely from the *particelle*, Debussy revised many details of the score while orchestrating, and, besides minor rhythmic and melodic changes in the vocal parts and harmonic changes in the accompaniment, he made a number of important thematic additions to the orchestra, in particular, by adding appearances of the 'Mélisande' and 'Golaud' motifs.[27] The intervallic flexibility which he allowed in the expression of these (and other) motifs, made it relatively easy for him to work them into any accompanimental context.

The score underwent a number of significant modifications during rehearsals. Carré decided to cut Act IV scene 3 'for reasons of length' and because he felt that it held up the action too close to the *dénouement*.[28] The relatively late casting of the rôle of Yniold and difficulties the boy may have had with the part probably contributed to this decision, since the scene was restored the following season when the role was assigned to a woman. The decision to give the role of Pelléas not to a tenor, the voice for which the role was conceived, but to *baryton-martin* Jean Périer, necessitated modifying the part to suit his range. Many of the high As, G♯s, Gs (and even some F♯s) in Act III scene 1 and Act IV scene 4 were brought down. These changes were marked in the vocal score proofs from which Périer studied his role, but they were not incorporated into the published score.

About a month before the première, it also became clear that some of the interludes between scenes needed to be lengthened in order to allow the scene-shifters sufficient time to change the sets.[29] Not purely a compositional miscalculation, this resulted in part from the complexities of Carré's staging and the limitations of the Salle Favart, the home of the Opéra-Comique, whose design made set changes slow and awkward. The wings, scarcely two metres wide, were so narrow that the performers had to line up practically in single file to make their entrances. Storage space was very limited, and most of the scenery and props had to be kept at the back of the stage, rather than in the wings, making it difficult and time-consuming to transport them on and off stage. Furthermore, though built in 1898, the hall was not equipped with the most modern machinery, so everything had to be done by hand.[30] Therefore, Debussy's original conception of very rapid scene changes (or even perhaps of scene changes without lowering the curtain)[31] was simply impossible to realise under these circumstances. He had no choice but to lengthen the interludes, though he did so very reluctantly.[32]

The original, short interludes were published in the first edition of the vocal score (Fromont, 1902), which was already engraved when the expansions were requested. The expansions were inserted as added pages in the manuscript full score (Bibliothèque Nationale, MSS 961–5), and they were subsequently published in the full score (Fromont, 1904), as a separate volume in piano reduction by Gustave Samazeuilh (Durand, 1905), and in the French – English vocal score (Durand, 1907). Interlude expansions were required in Acts I, II, and IV, but not in Act V (a single scene), nor in Act III: the latter's set changes were far less complicated, since scenes 1, 3 and 4 shared the same décor. Act IV required only a single expansion (between scenes 2 and 3), not because Yniold's scene had been cut, but because the four scenes of this act had already been combined into two *tableaux* of two scenes each.

The original interludes in Acts I, II, and IV were really quite short – between ten and nineteen bars in length – and the expansions resulted in net increases of between fifteen and 45 bars each. Though he expressed resentment at being forced to extend the interludes, Debussy found ways to compose them so that they would benefit his score. For example, the expansion of the first interlude of Act I reinforces the framing function[33] of the interlude by developing the triplet motif which accompanied the closing lines of the first scene. It also signals closure by recalling the music which accompanied Golaud's entrance at the beginning of the scene. When that motif accompanied Golaud's first lines, Debussy had used the whole-tone scale, to symbolise the fact that Golaud was lost in the forest. At the end of the scene he is still lost (in that sense), but the motif is now modal, perhaps reflecting the fact that his discovery of Mélisande has given direction and focus to his life.

The first interlude expansion of Act II contributes important thematic links between the first and second scenes. By introducing the motif associated with Mélisande's wedding ring (VS, p. 73, bars 4–5), Debussy emphasised this important thematic and dramatic connection between these two scenes. He also added an anticipation of the motif which, in scene 2, was used to represent the bolting of Golaud's horse (see VS, p. 74, bar 9, and p. 77, bar 8), an event which takes place during the time frame of scene 1 but is not described until scene 2.

Perhaps even more striking is the way Debussy promoted musical unity within each act by recalling in the expansions of the *second* interludes of Acts I and II (that is, between their second and third scenes), important themes from their respective *first* scenes. For example, in the expanded second interlude of Act 1, he brought back the theme through which Golaud expressed his love for Mélisande (compare VS, p. 38, bars 10–11, and p. 7, bars 1–2)[34] and also the one he used to introduce himself to her (compare VS, p. 38, bars 14–15, and p. 14, bar 8), neither of which appears in the second or third scene. Thus, in a musical as well as dramatic way, Act I is further unified around the 'themes' of Golaud's meeting with, and love for, Mélisande – the premiss for the ensuing tragedy. Similarly, the expanded second interlude of Act II brings back the theme associated with the well in the park (compare VS, p. 103, bars 3–4 and 8–9, and p. 56, bars 1–2), which had functioned as the framing motif of scene 1 and had been heard only fleetingly in scene 2, at the moment where Mélisande recalled her meeting there with Pelléas. Now it is the set of circumstances bringing Pelléas and Mélisande together, the next fateful step in the unfolding of the tragedy, which receives musical emphasis, thus reinforcing the unity of the second act. Of course, the drama develops continuously, but there is also a musical organisation on the level of the act, which the expanded interludes promote.

We do not know the precise degree to which these expansions were 'manufactured to specification', – in other words, to what extent Debussy may, for musical reasons, have exceeded the minimum additions which the scene changes required. There is some evidence to suggest, though, that he probably wanted the expansions no longer than necessary: in a letter of 2 April 1902, he mentioned being told the previous day by Messager that 75 additional bars were needed for the Act 2 interludes; in the end he added only 52. Furthermore, cuts are marked in Debussy's own full score (now in the Bibliothèque F. Lang, Royaumont), shortening two of the longest expanded interludes: the first in Act II by eight bars, and that in Act IV by nineteen.[35]

If scenic requirements necessitated lengthening the score, censorship, in the person of Henry Roujon, sous-secrétaire des Beaux-Arts with responsibility as Inspector of Theatres, insisted that it be cut. In this era, theatres were still required to submit plays and librettos for the approval of the Commission of Censorship, and, following the controversial public dress rehearsal of *Pelléas* on 28 April 1902, Roujon ordered the Opéra-Comique to cut Act III scene 4: the scene in which Golaud forces his child to spy on his wife and half-brother. (Such an excision would have eliminated the role of Yniold altogether, since Act IV scene 3 had already been cut.) In order to save the scene Debussy agreed to make cuts in it, removing the objectionable portions, and to alter certain expressions. Two of the cuts were definitively incorporated into the score. The more notorious of the two, a passage considered extremely *risqué* at the time, was the exchange in which Golaud asks if Pelléas and Mélisande are near the bed. (The question is more scandalous than the reply because the child does not even see the bed.) Indeed, Debussy's setting of the passage drew considerable attention to the high drama of the moment, in which the precise nature of Golaud's suspicion is made painfully explicit: the momentum which had been building for several pages is brought to a sudden halt and the tempo is slowed to half its former pace as Golaud asks the shocking question. (The passage was printed in the original edition of the vocal score; see figure 3.[36] Incidentally, it is no coincidence that in bars 1–2 and 5–6 of figure 3 Yniold (naïvely?) sings the 'Mélisande' motif while defending her; although not part of the piano reduction, the motif is present in the orchestration, doubling the voice.) The second permanent cut removed a dramatic statement of the 'Golaud' motif as well as that character's closing line ('nous allons voir ce qui est arrivé!'), which clearly implied that Golaud was prepared to charge into Mélisande's room with Yniold to find out why she and Pelléas were standing against the wall, staring into the light (see figure 4).[37] Other cuts marked in the manuscript full score – all later restored – may

Figure 3   Vocal Score (First Edition, Fromont, 1902), pp. 164–5. The bars
cut following the public dress rehearsal (28 April 1902) extended
from the fifth bar on p. 164 to the seventh bar on p. 165. (For
some performances, the previous two bars might have been cut
as well.)

Figure 4   Vocal Score (First Edition, Fromont, 1902), pp. 168–9. As cut for performance, Golaud's 'Viens' was moved back one bar and the balance of his line was omitted. The orchestra played to the end of the first system of the example then cut to the $\frac{6}{8}$ section.

also have been at the censor's insistence, or may have been made voluntarily in order to avoid the audience outbursts (of both outrage and amusement) which disturbed the dress rehearsal.[38]

The manuscript full score contains signs of numerous revisions, even beyond the expansions of the interludes and the cuts imposed between the dress rehearsal and the première. Some of these changes were doubtless made while Debussy was drafting the score, but many were made following the première. The score also contains performance indications added by André Messager and Henri Busser, both of whom conducted from this score, and many of these markings were incorporated into the published score.

Since *Pelléas* proved to be a success, albeit controversial, Debussy was eager to have Fromont print a full score and orchestral parts. Hoping that the opera would make him rich, he planned to publish the score at his own expense, selling it by subscription to raise the money needed to pay for its engraving and printing. It took some time, though, to engrave the score's 409 pages, so it was not until around June 1903, months after the *second* season of performances (30 October 1902 – 6 January 1903) that Debussy, with Messager's help, was able to correct the first proofs. Debussy's 'corrections', however, included an extensive revision of the orchestration, for which the engraver was quite unprepared. Debussy had to write to Fromont to explain that the annotations in the proofs were not just corrections of mistakes, but alterations of the score, and that the engraver should simply enter them accurately, without looking for complications which went beyond his proper duties. Between July and September Debussy corrected the second proofs, which were returned to the engraver, then forwarded to the copyist at the Opéra-Comique, who made the corrections (and revisions) in the orchestral parts. A further set of proofs was pulled for use as a conductor's score during the third season of *Pelléas* performances at the Opéra-Comique (30 October 1903 – 20 April 1904), which undoubtedly offered the opportunity for finding and correcting further errors in the score. On 29 June 1904 Debussy was able to mark a final set of proofs 'ready for the press', and the score was published within two months: 27 August 1904 was the date of the copyright deposit.

Almost immediately, Debussy was beset with financial difficulties resulting from his decision to leave his wife Lilly for another woman, Emma Bardac, and he was forced to sell the copyright of *Pelléas*. Since Fromont was unwilling to pay the asking price of 25,000 francs, the copyright was transferred to Durand on 31 March 1905. Thus, in 1905 – 6, Durand issued its own editions of the opera: a vocal score printed from the same plates as the Fromont edition (though modified to carry the name and plate number of the new publisher), a separate volume of the interlude expansions to supplement the vocal score, a full score made by adapting the original Fromont volumes (replacing the preliminary pages and reprinting the first two pages of the score so that the Durand plate number would appear on page 1), and newly printed orchestral and choral parts.

These new publications did not prevent Debussy from undertaking yet another extensive revision of the orchestration, and the new changes were copied into a score in the Durand archives. Only a few of these changes are in Debussy's hand; most were entered by a copyist, who dated the corrections 25 August 1905. This copy was used to correct the printed orchestral parts and was the basis for what was to become the second edition of the full score. At first, the changes were copied by hand into the large scores in the Durand hire-library. Only later were they incorporated into the plates of the published scores: the study score (first published in 1908) was amended in 1950, but the conductor's score not until 1966, which was the first reprinting of that score since 1904! This 'second edition' represents the 'standard' *Pelléas*, which is generally heard today in the opera house. Still, it does not represent the composer's final thoughts, which are contained in his personal annotated score (Bibliothèque F. Lang, Royaumont).

The orchestration of *Pelléas* (as well as many details in the vocal parts) thus underwent numerous revisions spread out over several years: first, while the score was in manuscript, then during the correction of the proofs, and even later, following the publication of the score. No doubt many of the changes were stimulated by what Debussy heard in the theatre, for he supervised at least some rehearsals whenever *Pelléas* was performed at the Opéra-Comique (nearly every season between 1902 and 1914) and also the rehearsals for the Brussels and London premières (1907 and 1909, respectively).

Many of the revisions involved the addition of doublings, usually at the unison, but sometimes at the octave, most often using an instrument of a contrasting family to alter the timbre as well as reinforce the line. A conspicuous example of one such revision, made in Debussy's personal score, was the addition of four solo violins to double the two unison flutes in the opening of Act II. Other changes of sonority were achieved by reassigning parts to different instruments, redistributing string parts, or changing the method of production, for example, from *arco* to *pizzicato*. Pedals were reinforced or added, making explicit a pedal point which existed in the harmony but was not sustained by any single instrument. Chords were sometimes lengthened, sometimes shortened. Harmonies were enriched or altered in some places, and there were some figurational additions of a colouristic nature, including added string tremolos and trills. In a few places, key words or phrases of dialogue were further highlighted and dramatised by preceding them with strategically placed rhythmic impulses, such as *pizzicato* string chords. In some isolated instances, Debussy even added some of the opera's key leitmotifs, a practice which can be observed in every compositional stage, even following the full score's initial publication. For example, in Act IV scene 4, the rhythm of the 'Golaud' theme was added in the horns at the point where Pelléas is reassured by Mélisande that Golaud did not see her leave the castle because he was asleep. (This addition appears in the 'second edition' of the full score, p. 326, bars 3–4.) Tempo markings were also adjusted and some changes were made in the vocal lines.

Debussy's incessant refinement of his only completed opera may seem extreme, but Maurice Emmanuel explained it this way: 'It was not frivolous restlessness of the intellect, nor a sign of unhealthy indecision, but a passionate and untiring quest for the right expression. . . One could say that the orchestral text of *Pelléas et Mélisande* became definitive only with his death.'[39]

3 Synopsis

BY ROGER NICHOLS

The first scene of the first act of Maeterlinck's play was one of the four that Debussy cut, probably before settling down to compose the music. Servants washing steps may not be exactly the traditional stuff of opera, but that alone would hardly have been enough to prompt his decision, whether or not it was encouraged by Maeterlinck himself, nor would the fact that it introduces another scene change necessarily have weighed with a composer as inexperienced as he was in matters theatrical. The strong probability is rather that he instinctively homed in on the forest of Act I scene 2 as a more powerfully evocative symbol for the start of the opera and that he realised at the same time how such an opening could easily be made to absorb and reflect the two main messages of the excised scene: a premonition of important events ('Il y aura de grands événements'), and a sense of struggle against a resistant world, symbolised first by the door that has to be opened and then by the threshold that has to be cleaned ('Je ne sais pas si je pourrai l'ouvrir'; 'Nous ne pourrons jamais nettoyer tout ceci'). Furthermore, to start with the forest scene has the advantage of bringing us almost immediately into the presence of Golaud, the prime mover in the ensuing drama.

Debussy gives us a premonition of important events simply in the slow, quasi-ecclesiastical starkness of the first four bars (1), a motif identified by Terrasson[1] as that of 'The Enigma of the World' (L'énigme du monde) and, more tentatively, by Emmanuel[2] as that of 'Times Past' (Les temps lointains). Whatever its associations (and these, in any case, differ to some extent for each listener), the scoring of the motif for bassoons and muted cellos emphasises the element of darkness, progressively illuminated by the rising pitch of the introduction up to a climax in bar 18. The sense of struggle against a resistant material world comes over more through melodic and rhythmic means. The variation in bar 3 of (1) leads merely to a repeat of bar 2; and the last chord of (2), identifiable as Golaud's motif (further identified by Terrasson as 'The Enigma of Man – the masculine principle orientated towards materialism')[3] is the same as the first chord. These initial six bars are followed by a seventh consisting solely of a drum roll on A♭ (a tritone distant from the basic D modality), whose deliberate emptiness allows the listener time both

to assimilate the melodic and rhythmic failure of what he has heard so far, and to imagine ways out of the impasse – ways in which, as it were, the door may be opened and the threshold cleaned. We may compare this pause for reflection with the still bolder use of complete silence in the sixth bar of *Prélude à l'après-midi d'un faune*, which Debussy was working on at much the same time (December 1893). His way out of the impasse in *Pelléas* is to 'dynamicise' the static (2) by altering its final note, paving the way for the introduction of a third theme (3) which undoubtedly has much to do with Mélisande, even if calling it 'Mélisande's theme' has been deplored by Joseph Kerman as a 'frightful simplification' (but see plate 6 and Appendix).[4] Nomenclature aside, the theme's purely structural function is to move the music on by relaxing the rather stiff articulation of the first 13 bars. After developing (3), Debussy closes the circle by reintroducing (2) in varied form, and then (1) as Golaud enters.

This introduction is a masterpiece of compression. Into it Debussy packs not only the two messages from the excised Act I scene 1 of the play, but the naturalistic gloom of the forest, the symbolic lightening of that gloom, and the essential circularity of man's existence, looking forward to the very last words of the opera ('c'est au tour de la pauvre petite'). It is not without interest to compare his achievement here with what Wagner wrote to his wife Cosima in 1878 while composing the prelude to Act III of *Parsifal*: 'My preludes must consist of the elements, and not be dramatic like the Leonora overtures, or the drama becomes superfluous'[5] – by no means the only similarity between Wagner's opera and Debussy's.

Golaud, prince of Allemonde, has been out hunting in the forest but has lost track both of the boar he has wounded and of his own hounds. Suddenly he hears sobbing, and turns to see the unknown figure of Mélisande. He asks her why she is crying. Her only reply is to beg him not to touch her. The pattern of her evasive answers is immediately set and marked by Debussy, here as elsewhere, with abrupt changes of pace, texture and rhythm. Golaud sees, glistening at the bottom of the well, a crown given to Mélisande by a mysterious 'him' whose identity we are never told. Reasonably enough, Golaud offers to retrieve it for her but she forbids him to try, threatening to drown herself in the well if he does so. He desists, though not without muttering 'Even so, it would be easy to get it out' ('On pourrait la prendre sans peine cependant'). At this point we hear again the little C major tucket which, nearly thirty bars earlier, had depicted the glint of the crown in the water; but the original brass colouring of three muted horns is now altered to the less urgent one of two flutes and two clarinets, to indicate that for all Golaud's rational demurrers the matter of the crown is settled once and for all.

In the first trial of strength between them she, then, is the victor. This fact established, Maeterlinck and Debussy can now proceed to erect the specious outer shell of Golaud – his lineage ('Je suis le prince Golaud, le petit-fils d'Arkël, le vieux roi d'Allemonde'), accompanied by theme (4), and his appearance ('vous avez déjà les cheveux gris. . . Et la barbe aussi'; . . . 'Vous êtes un géant') – before Mélisande's questioning again begins to probe the real Golaud beneath, eliciting answers ('Je n'en sais rien moi-même'; 'Je me suis trompé de chemin') which have both a particular, literal relevance and a general, symbolic one. The undermining of Golaud's outer

authority is so complete by this stage that we may find it hard to believe his reason for refusing to let her stay alone in the forest at night: 'Vous aurez peur'. Whose fear is this in fact? Certainly nearly all the verbal action here is Golaud's, culminating in a final ambivalent remark: 'Je suis perdu aussi'.

An orchestral interlude, combining (1) and (2), takes us from the forest to another enclosed space, a room in King Arkël's castle. It may be useful at this point to set out a family tree; or rather two possible family trees:

FAMILY TREE I

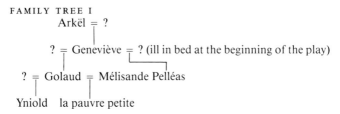

This is a commonly accepted pattern of the relationships between the characters.[6] But there is nothing in Maeterlinck's text to disallow a second pattern:

FAMILY TREE II

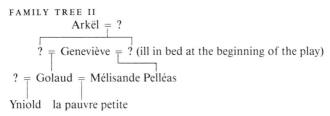

At no time in the play does Arkël refer to Geneviève as 'ma fille' nor she to Arkël as 'mon père', nor are they described as father and daughter in Maeterlinck's *dramatis personae*. One may even feel that there is a further deepening of the 'enclosed' atmosphere of the drama if we accept that Geneviève married the two sons of Arkël one after the other. Not that we should worry unduly over this – clearly neither Maeterlinck nor Debussy thought that precision here was important. As Pierre Boulez has written: 'Think for a moment of all the time and trouble that Wagner takes to explain, through Isolde, the multiple details of events that occurred before the actual action of the opera begins. . . Compared with this Maeterlinck's presentation of his characters is not so much elliptical as deliberately vague and allusive. . .'[7]

Indeed, to concern ourselves with facts is to fall into the same materialistic trap as Golaud. The scene in the castle begins with just such a factual passage: a letter from Golaud to Pelléas, read out to the blind Arkël by Geneviève, in which Golaud explains how he met Mélisande and that he has now married her. He realises that by doing so he has ruined Arkël's hopes of his making a convenient dynastic marriage and wants to know whether he is welcome to return to the castle with his new wife or not. With typical efficiency, he asks for a favourable response to be indicated by a lamp lit in the tower on the third day from the date of the letter. Debussy's fear of the factual and the emphatic is well demonstrated in the neutral tone of his setting. A literal deepening of the tone comes only with Arkël's reply, 'Je n'en dis rien', where horns and trombones underline that this is not mere laziness or lack of interest on the old man's part, but a carefully considered philosophical position of non-interference, further emphasised by trombones (though again *pianissimo*) at his statement 'Il n'arrive peut-être pas d'événements inutiles'. The appearance of (4b) in octaves on the strings suggests that this may be one of the lessons that kingship teaches. Geneviève's concern about Golaud's future is interrupted by the arrival of Pelléas. His motif (5)

is no more than a tiny snippet, devoid of rhythmic or melodic energy. It is noteworthy that both here and in the following scene Pelléas's arrival is sensed or observed by the other characters before he speaks; unlike Mélisande, he lacks any capacity to surprise people, an attribute which Debussy seizes on by deriving his motif from the last notes of the full version of (4b) at figure 30 and from the subsequent rising and falling fourth in the strings. In the cause of non-interference with fate, Arkël is quite prepared to interfere and tells him to stay: Pelléas's own father is ill and who knows what Golaud's return will bring?

Another interlude leads to the third and final scene of the first act, set in front of the castle. Mélisande, introduced by the extended (3b), voices to Geneviève her astonishment at how gloomy the environs of the castle are. Geneviève replies that one soon gets used to it; she has lived here for nearly forty years and in any case there is light to the seaward side. . . from which, of course, Mélisande has come. Debussy underlines this identification of Mélisande with light by setting '(la clar)té de la mer' to an unambiguous chord of F♯ major, echoing the G♭ major at the point in scene 1 where she tells Golaud her name; both passages are similarly underpinned by a single, pulsing note.

Pelléas joins the two women. He prophesies a storm, even though 'the sea is calm at the moment'. A ship sails out of the port to the sound of sailors' cries (6) and, when the mist clears, Mélisande recognises it as the one that brought her to Allemonde. It might seem to have been enough for Debussy to have introduced sailors' cries of any stock variety: the momentary widening of perspective of itself throws Mélisande's isolation into sharper relief. But his craftsmanship goes deeper still, and in deriving the cries from (2) he suggests not only that Mélisande has passed from one male custodianship to another but that Golaud, like the sailors, is heading blindly towards a storm. As the darkness falls, Pelléas leads Mélisande by the arm back into the castle, and the act ends on Mélisande's question to him: 'Oh! pourquoi partez-vous?' In the spoken play any competent actress would find at least a dozen ways of delivering this line to choose from. Is Mélisande merely curious? Or surprised? Or disappointed? If the latter, how much premonition should the line be made to carry considering that her next expression of interest in Pelléas, on precisely the same subject ('je pars demain'; 'non, non, non'), does not come until the tower scene in Act III? Debussy, like any good operatic composer, embraces a multiplicity of tones. The *diminuendo* in the vocal line speaks of neutral curiosity, the dissonant supertonic on 'vous' of surprise, the added sixth on F♯ major in the strings of an unacknowledged warmth of interest, and hence of disappointment.

The first scene of Act II continues the mood of innocent pleasure. Pelléas brings Mélisande to the well where he often comes to escape the midday heat. They revel in the stillness and Mélisande lies down so as to be able to look right down to the bottom of the well. Pelléas's anxiety that she may fall in is interrupted by the sight of her long blonde hair tumbling loose – a downward phrase, needless to say, but prepared by a succession of downward phrases from the beginning of the scene. From the moment Pelléas begins to question her about her meeting with Golaud, however, the phrases start to strive upwards, often urged on by (2). Mélisande begins to play with Golaud's ring, throwing it higher and higher above the water. Inevitably it falls into the well and disappears. As with Golaud and the crown in Act I scene 1, Pelléas in his turn is dissuaded by Mélisande from trying to retrieve it. What are they to tell Golaud? 'The truth', says Pelléas and takes her home, while the orchestra, for the fourth time in four scenes, plays the characters out with the opening music.

All the action so far has been enclosed and static, or at best circular. During the following interlude the focus shifts from Pelléas to Golaud, from (5) to (2), from light to heavy orchestration, and from static to dynamic action. Golaud is in bed, injured by falling from his horse at the precise moment (noon) when Mélisande dropped his ring into the well. She enquires after his health, but then suddenly starts to cry (Debussy reasonably takes the opportunity here of using the oboe to recall their first meeting). She cannot explain why she is crying, except to say it is something stronger than herself; and Debussy's use here of (5), 'très doux et très expressif', is perhaps the clearest so far of the many instances where he endows the orchestra with knowledge over and above that granted to the characters themselves – or indeed, here, what is inferrable from the spoken play; unless, of course, she is simply lying. . .

Golaud admits the castle is gloomy and (ignoring Pelléas and Yniold) that everyone in it is old, but it will soon be summer 'and then, next year' she will have a baby to console her. He takes her hands in his and Debussy accompanies this tender gesture with impossibly delicate flutterings on flutes and upper strings – a bass-less texture (Golaud himself provides the bottom line) for his baseless hopes. Then he notices that the ring is missing. At once the interrogation becomes rougher and more specific. In terror she lies, telling Golaud she dropped it in a cave by the sea and the tide came in before she could find it. Golaud insists she go and look for it at once. 'Maintenant? Tout de suite? Dans l'obscurité?' (Now? At once? In the darkness?) Golaud repeats her words by way of answer, eliminating the hesitant pauses and barbarising her sensitive prosody. Maeterlinck removed this repetition in his revised text of 1898, obviously feeling it was otiose – a clear case of music bringing an extra dimension to the spoken word, as is the sardonic laughter on *pizzicato* cellos and basses when Golaud shouts at Mélisande to take Pelléas with her: 'Pelléas will do anything you ask him. I know Pelléas better than you.'

An interlude, wonderfully orchestrated to suggest the surging of the tide, takes us to the cave where Pelléas and Mélisande have gone to look for the ring, knowing of course that they will not find it. The scene is practically a monologue for Pelléas to which Mélisande contributes only unfinished or negative phrases ('Non'; 'Allons-nous-en'; 'Je préfère marcher seule'). The music remains aimlessly atmospheric until a shaft of moonlight reveals three white-haired beggars asleep against a rock. This unwelcome contact with the 'real' outside world immediately reduces the rich orchestral texture to two bare lines on the upper strings, recalling the setting of Arkël's brutal question to Pelléas in Act I scene 2: 'Pourras-tu choisir entre le père et l'ami?' (Will you choose between your father and your friend?) The music's poise continues to be uneasy from here until the end of the act: the atmosphere surrounding Pelléas and Mélisande is a delicate one and 'cannot bear very much reality'.

Throughout the first two acts the story has been presented in the form of relationships, no scene opening on a character alone (even though Golaud thought he was alone at the very start of Act I scene 1). The two scenes omitted by Debussy at this point also open on pairs of characters: Arkël and Pelléas, and Pelléas and Mélisande. The first scene of the opera's third act begins with a decorated pedal B♮ which, as the curtain rises, is revealed as the first note of a ballad, 'Mes longs cheveux', sung by Mélisande to herself as she sits alone at a window of one of the castle towers combing her hair. The song in Maeterlinck's 1892 edition of the play, set by Debussy, was replaced at the first performance in 1893 and in subsequent editions by a more directly symbolic ballad, 'Les trois soeurs aveugles'. But since music tends anyway to accentuate any latent symbolism, and since the symbolism in this particular play is already fairly dense, it is perhaps no bad thing that the original should have been retained in the opera, allowing a few moments' respite in which Mélisande can be portrayed as a 'free child' without ulterior motives of any kind, at least so long as she is outside the magnetic field of human contact.

Pelléas comes along the path under the tower and they talk. He exclaims, for the first time, at her beauty and encourages her to lean further out of the window so that he can kiss her hand. Suddenly her hair falls over his hands and his lips, and with growing passion he ties it to the branches of the willow-tree so that she cannot escape from him. As she cries out that he is hurting her, a flock of doves is startled out of the tower. Until this point in the scene Debussy has, as it were, connived at the burgeoning of Pelléas and Mélisande's secret world by keeping the music free of motifs and therefore free from the pull of established identities and relationships. The flight of the doves brings the 'lovers' back nearer to the adult world, and Debussy marks the moment with a new version of (3) that looks to the future as well as to the past. In (7) the opening of (3) is balanced by a mirror image, but with a D♮ instead of the exactly mirroring D♯. This second bar of (7) lends itself to whole-tone harmony, which it duly receives at Mélisande's phrase 'dans l'obscurité', which in turn prepares for Golaud's entry accompanied by a new, menacing motif (8), derived

from (4(a)) (see p. 64). Debussy's motivic discretion in this scene is such that (2) appears only after the curtain has fallen on Golaud's reprimands, but the energetic motivic action in the ensuing interlude then paints with a terrible fidelity the birth of his first jealous promptings. After (2), (3) is heard first alone, then insidiously superimposed on (5), while the longed-for calm of F♯ major is twice denied by modal sideslips to D♯ minor. The triangular tensions are now established and must eventually be resolved, one way or another.

A spine-chilling reminder of (8) on muted trumpet over a timpani roll leads on to the scene of Golaud and Pelléas in the castle vaults which, as Debussy's marking 'même mouv^t' indicates, is to be heard as an extension of the feelings portrayed in the interlude. Golaud's overt reason for this grim guided tour is given in a passage cut by Debussy: he wants his brother to smell the stench of death from the underground lake. This could be interpreted as a signal to Pelléas to wake up to the deeper levels of his feelings for Mélisande and the dangers they bring with them, or he may simply want to frighten Pelléas; or could he have something more permanent in mind. . .? The composer, in a letter to Henri Lerolle of 28 August 1894, described the scene as 'full of impalpable terror', so it may be that he cut the explicatory passage in order to reinforce the impalpability. Certainly some cuts had to be made once he had decided to base the scene on the whole-tone scale – for all his notoriety as a user of this device, Debussy was in fact always sparing of it and even for this abbreviated version of Maeterlinck's text the basic whole tone outline is decorated with a large number of extraneous notes.

Throughout this gloomy scene flutes, harps and violins have all been silent. Now they bring us up to the light and the clean smell of the sea, as the midday bells ring out. Golaud warns Pelléas that last night's behaviour must not be repeated. Mélisande is delicate and will soon give birth to Golaud's child (at which point Debussy introduces (3) harmonised as it was at the end of Act I, when Pelléas first offered his arm to Mélisande – he knows better than Golaud how delicate she is). Pelléas must keep out of her way, without drawing attention to the fact.

The final scene of Act III is set in front of the castle. Golaud takes his young son Yniold on his knee and questions him about Mélisande and her relationship with Pelléas. In contrast to Golaud's tortuous harmonies, Yniold's are innocuous. He tells 'the truth' as he sees it, but it is not the sort of truth Golaud can easily understand. Pelléas and Mélisande like to have the door shut when they are together, Yniold tells him. Golaud is so determined to get to the bottom of this that he becomes impatient and Yniold begins to cry. Golaud calms him with the promise of a quiver and some arrows and the investigation proceeds. The stylisation of Yniold's rôle comes direct from Maeterlinck's text, where his part is larded with the phrase 'petit père' – in all, twenty-eight of them in the course of the scene. The irritating effect they had on sections of the early Paris audiences may be presumed to be working on Golaud too, since the 'petit père' rhythm is repeated in Golaud's outburst 'patience, mon Dieu, patience'. Golaud raises the question of whether Pelléas and Mélisande have ever kissed each other. 'Yes', says the boy, 'like this', and kisses his father on the mouth. A light goes on in the window under which they are sitting and the music modulates to F♯ major, the key of light (see chapter 5, p. 113). Golaud lifts Yniold up and asks him what he sees, as the orchestra begin the galloping triplets that will take us almost unchecked to the end of the act. Yniold in fact sees nothing except that Pelléas and Mélisande are looking at the light – the horrors are in Golaud's mind. (Here, fifteen bars in which Golaud asks whether they are near the bed were cut on the censor's instructions. As they interrupt the triplet movement and include two more invocations to 'petit père', perhaps they are no great loss.) Eventually Yniold begins to panic and threatens to scream. Golaud lets him down and they go off into the night. Here, the suppression of Golaud's original closing line, 'Nous allons voir ce qui est arrivé', printed in the Fromont vocal score of 1902, took with it a subsequent orchestral passage of eleven bars including the dotted version of (2), powerfully harmonised. It is worth noting, if without undue surprise, that Debussy here was more concerned with pace than with thematic emphasis (see chapter 4, p. 87 and Example 6). The first scene of Act IV, set in a room in the castle, continues the mood of agitation, but between Pelléas and Mélisande, although Golaud's shadow is ever-present; the prologue introduces the initial rising tone of both (2) and (4) on parallel octaves (G–A), suggesting that the two brothers are now locked together on an inflexible course. Pelléas's father, it seems, is recovering from his illness and has encouraged his son to get away from the castle; at the same time he has claimed to see in Pelléas's face a look of impending death. Pelléas and Mélisande agree to meet that evening by the well (here Debussy inverts the scene's opening semiquavers to reveal the water figuration of the well scene at the start of Act II) but, hearing voices, they now separate. After Pelléas leaves, Mélisande is joined by Arkël, who in a long, measured speech tells her that with the recovery of Pelléas's father life can at last return to the castle, and that he sees her as opening a new era in its existence.

Golaud now enters with blood on his forehead. Mélisande offers to wipe it off but he repulses her and asks for his sword. She hands it to him and he looks into her eyes, to see. . .what? 'Nothing but innocence', says Arkël, but on the word 'innocence' the strings play, a tone lower, the same ambiguous chord (major triad with added second and sixth) that concluded Mélisande's 'Pourquoi partez-vous?' at the end of Act I. These ambiguities are seized on by Golaud who starts to test the chord against others in a see-sawing movement that builds, through a terrifying passage of ever-mounting irony and rage, to a physical assault on Mélisande in which he takes her by the hair and hurls her this way and that ('A droite puis à gauche! A gauche puis à droite!'). Mélisande's theme (3), which had begun to protest, is silenced as she descends to the level of mere object. Golaud's anger, slow to mount, evaporates with unnatural and frightening speed as he realises how completely he has lost control of himself: 'je ris déjà comme un vieillard' (I'm already laughing like an old man). The scene ends with Arkël's comment, 'Si j'étais Dieu, j'aurais pitié du coeur des hommes.' One well-known philosopher has attacked this statement as being 'utterly idiotic'[8] and, in the sense that Arkël, not being God, cannot possibly know what he would feel if he were, the stricture is undoubtedly valid. But the contextual *meaning* of the sentence (as opposed to what Arkël actually says) is clearly that the breakdown of love and trust between Golaud and Mélisande is only part of a larger tragedy embracing the whole human race. Arkël's comment therefore functions as one of the periodic broadenings of perspective (like the sailors' song in Act I), which help give the drama some universal significance for the audience as well as emphasising the closed, introverted atmosphere in which the characters live and move. Debussy's music for Arkël's phrase is likewise broad, and its solemn tread and colouring of horns, trombones and strings lead naturally into the penultimate and longest interlude in the opera.

Maeterlinck no doubt intended the juxtaposition between Arkël's moralising and the struggles of his great-grandson Yniold to retrieve his ball from under a rock to be as sharp as possible – the double delivery of the message 'life is hard' over a span of four generations adds more than a little to its universality. But given that this was one of the interludes that had to be expanded (see chapter 2, pp. 52–5), Debussy seems to have turned a constraint into a virtue and developed the interlude, perhaps beyond what was practically necessary (from fifteen bars to 60), as a final opportunity for us to recollect and contemplate the horror of what has passed. It contains, unusually, not one but two climaxes. The second of these erupts after the music seems to have come definitively to rest (OS bar 2 of figure 25B), as if to underline that Golaud's anger and jealousy have now begun to trespass on the realm of the irrational. The gradual preparation for Yniold's appearance is made through a transition from the 'irrational', (because barely pitched) drumbeats of the interlude to the rational $E\flat s/D\sharp s$ of Yniold's frustrated ostinato. Yniold's scene is dominated first by this ostinato, then by the triplets of the milling sheep; and here Debussy tellingly sets Yniold's questions 'Where are they going?' to the accompaniment of Mélisande's line in Act I scene 3, 'Il fait sombre dans les jardins' (The gardens are enshrouded in night). Darkness falls and Yniold leaves. Ushered in by dark, Mussorgskyan sounds on low woodwind and strings, Pelléas comes to keep his tryst with Mélisande. Common sense tells him he should finish matters while he has the chance, and leave without seeing her. The orchestra extend Mélisande's theme, breaking its circularity, but at once proceed to repeat the new phrase – Pelléas is caught by a larger destiny. He decides he must see her just once more and prepares himself to declare everything he has so far left unspoken. Mélisande enters and the love duet begins.

Mélisande has managed to slip away from the castle while Golaud is asleep (or so she believes, though the dotted rhythms of (2) in the woodwind suggest otherwise). Pelléas tells her that he must leave the castle for ever. She cannot, or will not, guess the reason: that he loves her:

MELISANDE   I love you too.
PELLEAS   Oh, what was that, Mélisande? I could hardly hear what
             you said.

Much has been made by critics over the years of the reticence of these unaccompanied declarations, but it is difficult to see how else Debussy could have set them. Pelléas cannot claim to have hardly heard her if she has just delivered 'Je t'aime aussi' *con molto passione* over full orchestra; and if her words are to be unaccompanied then his must be too. In any case the virtual disintegration of the orchestral texture here is, from the psychological point of view, completely convincing. The orchestra acts, among other things, as a link between past, present and future; and the nearer the orchestra comes to silence (as in Mélisande's song at the beginning of Act III) the more self-contained the atmosphere. A third advantage is that this delicate, tranquil passage provides a perfect lead-in to the core of the love-scene: 'On dirait que ta voix a passé sur la mer au printemps' (It is as if your voice had passed over the sea in springtime).

This is where Debussy began his work on the opera in the autumn of 1893 and, despite the revisions that he made to the scene in 1901, echoes of Massenet are not far below the surface, even if Massenet favoured a more continuous texture than we have here. These few, traditional bars in F♯ major depict accurately and touchingly Pelléas's naïve expression of a passion new to him:

PELLEAS   You aren't lying, to make me smile?
MELISANDE   No, I never lie; I lie only to your brother.

Pelléas, far from thinking that if she lies to one man she may lie to another, hears only the beauty of her voice: for him, the medium is the message. Debussy stresses this further by allowing Pelléas – who has by far the bulk of the singing in this scene – the support of the full orchestra, while Mélisande's lines are more lightly accompanied, if at all. The sound of the castle gates closing interrupts their idyll and, as the chains fall into place and they are shut out of the castle, the fuse of (8), laid in Act III scene 1, is finally lit. The music moves into triple metre, as for the climax of Act III, and Debussy takes every advantage of Maeterlinck's interlocking threefold dramatic structure:

      (i) chains → ecstatic calm
     (ii) 'false' sighting of Golaud → ecstatic calm
    (iii) real sighting of Golaud → catastrophe

The 'false' sighting is, of course, not false at all, merely real but unacknowledged (or rather, suppressed). Debussy therefore introduces (8) at the same pitch for both sightings and, after Golaud has struck Pelléas down by the edge of the well, for the start of the orchestral coda as Golaud silently pursues Mélisande into the forest.

The final act of the spoken play opens with a conversation between the castle servants. From them we learn that after killing Pelléas and wounding Mélisande, Golaud turned his sword on himself – hence his references to his own impending death in the second scene of the play's last act, which forms Act V of the opera. It is set in a room in the castle and from large, dramatic, catastrophic gestures we move back to an intimate scale, as exemplified by the contraction of (3) with which the act opens. The sounds of flute, clarinet, harp and strings remind us of Act II and of a time when all went well, but the hesitant nature of the music they play tells us that now the time is out of joint.

Mélisande lies on the bed; Arkël, Golaud and the doctor confer in a corner of the room. The doctor has small hope of saving her but reassures Golaud that he must not feel responsible for her death. Mélisande wakes up and Arkël, somewhat nervously, tells her that

Golaud is also in the room. Mélisande, far from being afraid, is surprised that he has not come near her of his own accord. During her ensuing conversation with Golaud, Debussy contrasts Golaud's desperate, ever-ranging questions with Mélisande's calm fatalism by giving Golaud ever-ranging material, while to Mélisande he gives a calm formula, heard three times in all, its first three notes deriving from notes 4–6 of (3b). Emmanuel calls this theme (9) the theme of

'pardon'[9], but in fact its plain harmonies seem to signify as much as anything a refusal to get involved in Golaud's chromatic self-torturings: the distance between husband and wife is as great as ever.

Golaud asks to be left alone with her and from here he begins to indulge in a complex *mélange* of guilt, curiosity, jealousy and self-pity, caught by Debussy with a sure genius that defies detailed exposition; though we may once again note the appearance of urgent triplet figures as the interrogation gets under way. The goal of Golaud's search is 'la vérité'. Mélisande swears to tell the truth but, even if she does (and here we cannot help remembering her admission to Pelléas, 'I lie only to your brother'), the spiritual distance between her and Golaud deprives the concept of any common meaning. Each time the words 'la vérité' occur, Debussy sets them differently, suggesting that even for the individual 'truth' changes from moment to moment. Arkël returns and we learn from him (as Mélisande herself does) that she has given birth to her child. He holds the baby girl up for her to see. At this point the serving-women file into the room, unbidden, and range themselves along the walls. Golaud makes a brief show of authority, asking them what business they have to be there, but as they neither move nor reply he relapses into silence. Arkël refuses to leave him alone with Mélisande again, stating with brutal frankness 'Vous ne savez pas ce que c'est que l'âme' (You don't know what the soul is) as the woodwind intone (4b) for the last time, underlining the authority of this pronouncement. It may, indeed, be taken as the crux of the drama. Some are born with spiritual insight; some achieve it; some, like Golaud, search for it all their lives without even the death of those they love being able to teach them 'what the soul is', because love for them is less important than truth. As Golaud collapses into pitchless sobbing it is left for Arkël to point the way ahead. The baby girl must be removed from the death-chamber so that she can take her mother's place; it is her turn now. The circularity of the final bars, drifting down from a high chord of C♯ major and up again, summarises the failure of Golaud, who (still?) sees life as a straight-forward progress from one point to another. Even the newborn baby, the postlude seems to say, knows more than he does: that mankind is

> Rolled round in earth's diurnal course,
> With rocks, and stones, and trees.

4 *Motives and symbols*

BY RICHARD LANGHAM SMITH

> Of kin to the so incalculable influences of Concealment, and connected with still greater things, is the wondrous agency of *Symbols*. In a Symbol there is concealment and yet revelation: here therefore by silence and by speech acting together, comes a double significance.
> Carlyle, *Sartor Resartus*, 1831

When, long before Debussy considered a setting of *Pelléas*, Mallarmé, the high priest of Symbolism, had perceived 'music in the real sense'¹ in the play itself, he was not merely indulging in the fashionable and often meaningless pastime of throwing the language of one art at another. He had recently used musical terms with some precision. In his *Crayonné au Théâtre* he alludes to 'polyphony' (the interplay of themes); to 'symphonic' ideas (the development and transformation of themes); as well as to rhythm and melody. Why then does he single out *Pelléas* as 'musical in the real sense'?

He was certainly not referring to rhyme, rhythm or assonance, nor to any other of those onomatopoeic devices which are sometimes held to reflect 'musicality' in literature. In *Pelléas*, as in all works meriting the title 'Symbolist', there is a sense in which the words used create a higher level of meaning above the literal, in which to define is to destroy. Mallarmé had admired the rejection of the 'préparatoire et machinale' – the conventional scaffolding, the lyrical description. The brief scenes, where it is mainly dialogue that clothes the symbols, concentrate this higher plane of expression. Whether or not we choose, with Mallarmé, to call this 'musicality', it was surely this aspect of Pelléas which he found 'musical'. But when (to cite one example), in the last line of Act I scene 2, Geneviève reminds Pelléas to light the lamp – 'Aie soin d'allumer la lampe dès ce soir' – her comment is not musical merely in that it alludes to far more than the lighting of a lamp. It is as if she has thrown a leitmotif, as yet unexplained and undeveloped, into the proceedings. This symbol, initially simple, will develop in its own right as the play

78

unfolds, by the traditional *musical* means of insistence, repetition and transformation.

Such literary devices are thus ideally suited to be wedded to the actual musical symbolism of a more or less Wagnerian 'leitmotif' technique. Indeed, several Symbolist commentators on Wagner, taking their cue from his own ideas on the supremacy of music, put forward the view that the purely musical leitmotif was a still more perfect means of expression than the literary symbol.[2]

Wagner's ideas, as is well known, had a profound influence on Symbolist thought, largely through his 'Lettre sur la musique', quoted by Baudelaire in 1860, and through the *Revue Wagnérienne*. In this sense the way was prepared for Debussy's musical extension of *Pelléas* from the symbolist side, let alone the musical. For Baudelaire himself, acknowledged unanimously as the father-figure of Symbolist thought, had quoted Wagner's 'Lettre à Berlioz' on the subject of music and poetry:

Précisément là où l'un de ces arts [poésie et musique] atteignait à des limites infranchissables commençait aussitôt avec la plus rigoureuse exactitude la sphère de l'autre; que conséquemment, par l'union intime de ces deux arts, on exprimerait avec la clarté la plus saisissante ce que ne pouvait exprimer chacun isolément.

(At the precise point where one of these arts [of poetry or music] reached insuperable limits, there began, with the most rigorous exactitude, the realm of the other, so that as a result, through the intimate union of these two arts together would be expressed with the most striking clarity what neither could express alone.)[3]

Despite this general examination of the bonds between music and poetry, Wagner had written nothing about the leitmotif technique itself. Baudelaire, however, had noticed a 'système mnémonique' where 'chaque personnage est pour ainsi dire blasonné par la mélodie qui représente son caractère moral et le rôle qu'il est appelé à jouer dans la fable' (a mnemonic system where each character, so to speak, wears the coat of arms of a melody which represents his moral character and the role which he is called to play in the tale).[4]

Whatever Debussy said about Wagner, there are strong echoes of the leitmotivic technique in *Pelléas*, but it is rather the 'idea-leitmotifs' of the more mature Wagner of *Tristan* than the 'character-leitmotifs' of his earlier music-dramas. Debussy was surely thinking of the 'character-leitmotif' when he criticised Wagner's technique in an often-quoted journalistic interview of 1902:

Certes, mon procédé, qui consiste surtout à me passer de tous les procédés, ne doit rien à Wagner. Chez lui chaque personnage a pour ainsi dire son 'prospectus', sa photographie, son 'leitmotiv' dont il se fait toujours précéder. J'avoue estimer cette méthode un peu grossière.

(Certainly my technique (which consists of doing away with all 'techniques') owes nothing to Wagner. In his music each character has, so to speak, his own 'prospectus', his photograph, his 'leitmotif' which must always precede him. I confess to finding this method a trifle blatant.)[5]

Apart from his dislike of the over-obvious character-motifs, Debussy's essential quarrel with Wagner's technique, several times expressed, was when he found conflict between purely musical demands and those of the text. Although many of Debussy's comments on Wagner made in his journalistic articles for *La Revue blanche*, *Gil Blas* and various other outlets should be taken with a slight pinch of salt, he does take time in an article entitled 'Opéras' to step down from his lampooning pose and underline the point that 'either the music gets out of breath by chasing after a character, or the character has to sit on a note to allow the music to catch up with him'.[6]

On several occasions, Debussy did admit to finding a perfect union of these two 'rhythms' in *Tristan*, although in the journalistic articles he feels obliged to add, uncharitably, that this was probably 'by chance'. He finds in *Tristan* themes 'which do no violence to the action'.[7] reinforcing the overall impression drawn from his various writings about Wagner, that Debussy distinguished between different types of leitmotifs, tolerating the 'psychological' leitmotif, while abhorring the 'visiting-card' type.[8] The distinction seems to have been in his mind before the composition of *Pelléas*, for his ideas are already clear from the conversations he had with his teacher Guiraud, noted down by Maurice Emmanuel. 'What a bore these leitmotifs are', Debussy wrote to Guiraud, 'how sempiternally they are catapulted at one!. . .The *Nibelungen*, where there are pages which astound me, are a *machine à trucs*. They taint even my beloved *Tristan*, and it grieves me to feel detached from it.'[9] The use of the phrase *machine à trucs* (box of tricks) seems to indicate the composer's immediate distaste for the way in which motifs may destroy any sense of the unexpected in their predictable appearances. In a little-known letter to Edwin Evans, Debussy outlines his preference for a more subtle approach, and, while not denying the use of the leitmotif, stresses his avoidance of the 'slavery' of the leitmotif, which he evidently considered to taint the passages in Wagner he disliked:

Perhaps it is better that music should by simple means – a chord? a curve? – try and render successive impulses and moods as they occur rather than make laborious efforts to follow a symphonic development which is laid down in advance and therefore always arbitrary, and to which one will inevitably be tempted to sacrifice the development of feelings. . . That's why there is no 'guiding thread' in *Pelléas*, and why the characters are not subjected to the slavery of the leitmotif.[10]

Whether or not they are subjected to the 'slavery of the leitmotif', there are clearly some character-motifs in *Pelléas*. Debussy seems to have felt the need to deny this in most of the public statements he made concerning his opera, defending himself from being at all Wagnerian. Yet in an article in *Le Théâtre* of 1902, by the sympathetic critic Adolphe Jullien, Debussy provided handwritten musical examples including what he calls the 'thème initial de Mélisande' (see p. 144)[11]

In terms of its dramatic operation, Golaud's motif is the most Wagnerian, sometimes announcing his presence (in the 'visiting-card' manner) before he arrives. Mélisande's motif never does this, and that of Pelléas is less tangible still. The leitmotifs themselves, however, are only one element of Debussy's technique. Allied to their use is the employment of limited 'fields' of harmony, sometimes easily categorised – 'white-note', Dorian, added-note, tritonal, etc. – sometimes more elusive. As much as the audible motifs, and in conjunction with them, this is used to reflect and underline the interplay and development of literary themes. Such a union of motivic and harmonic technique is, of course, found in Wagner's *Tristan*. Indeed, Wagner had himself written of this in his 'Opera and Drama':

That melody which we have seen appearing on the surface of harmony, is conditioned as to its distinctive, its purely musical expression by harmony's upward-working depths alone: as it manifests itself as a horizontal chain, so is it connected by a plumbline with those depths. This plumbline is the harmonic chord, a vertical chain of notes in closest kinship, mounting from the bass note to the surface. The chiming of this chord first gives to the melodic note the peculiar significance wherein it, and it alone, has been employed to mark a distinctive moment of the expression.[12]

One need look no further than at a few transformations of the five-note motif from the beginning of the 'love' motif in that opera to see this process in action: how the mood of the motif may be altered by the application of different harmonic fields.

Example 1 Motif transformation from Act I of *Tristan und Isolde* (Wagner)

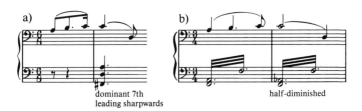

dominant 7th
leading sharpwards   half-diminished

diminished 7th

minor 9th

Several points emerge from these examples of Wagner's motivic technique. Firstly, there is a tendency (although not exclusive) for the motif to enter at the same pitch more than once. Subsequent intervals may be slightly altered, but the procedure fixes the motif in the listener's mind and projects more easily and comparatively any harmonic or textural alterations. This principle was to become an essential feature of Debussy's style. At its clearest in the *Prélude à l'après-midi d'un faune* of 1892 (where the flute theme largely retains its C♯ pitch-level while constantly changing its harmonic and orchestral colouring), the technique is also found in *Pelléas*.

A telling example underlines the coincidence of Golaud's accident in Act II scene 2. In the preceding scene, as Mélisande plays with her ring above the well, a four-note motif is heard, entering on the note C which, acting as a major ninth, is richly harmonised with a B♭ major chord with minor seventh (Example 2a). This type of harmony has already been reserved for moments of physical attraction, previously

Example 2

(VS, p. 62)

a) *en animant*

PELLEAS

Prenez garde! prenez gar - de!

B♭ major with added minor 7th and major 9th

(Take care!)

(VS, p. 77)

b) *en animant peu à peu et sourdement agité*

GOLAUD

A-t-il vu quel-que cho - se d'ex - tra - or - di - nai - re?...

dim.

p

half-diminished

GOLAUD

Je ve-nais d'en - ten-dre son-ner les dou - ze coups de mi - di.

sfz > p

half-diminished   half-diminished   half-diminished

(Did he [the horse] see something out of the ordinary? I had just heard it strike midday.)

between Golaud and Mélisande. At the end of the scene, the clock chimes twelve. Golaud, having fallen off his horse while hunting, wonders whether his horse had seen anything unusual to frighten him, and remarks that he had just heard the clock strike twelve. The motif occurs again on the same note C, but is now harmonised with an anxious half-diminished chord (Example 2b).[13]

Sometimes not one but several recurrent pitch levels are used for a motif. In the first act, the following 'Mélisande' motif, for example, has a tendency to enter on A♭ (G♯). It also tends to be associated with particular instruments, in this case oboe and flute. Entering at the same pitch, with similar timbres, emphasises the changing harmonic fields: from chromatic discord to almost resolute F♯ major. Amidst this recurrence of G♯ entries, the one entry one semitone up (on A) is thrown into heightened relief and is further highlighted (though Mélisande has not appeared in the preceding scene) by its presentation as a violin solo (Example 3c). Parallel to the semitone difference between the entries is that of a subsidiary pair, also a semitone apart, on F♯ and F♮, where the motif is extended into a more lyrical melody (VS, pp. 39 and 49).

Example 3
(VS, p. 1)

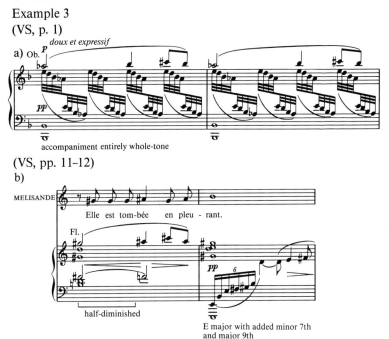

(VS, pp. 11–12)

(I was weeping, it fell in!)

Example 3 (*cont.*)
(VS, p. 37)

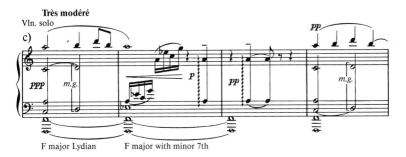

F major Lydian   F major with minor 7th

(VS, p. 54)

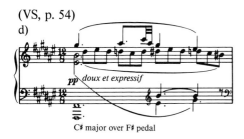

C♯ major over F♯ pedal

(VS, p. 141)

C♯ major with minor 7th, major 9th and major 13th

From here on, however, one draws contrasts rather than parallels with *Tristan*. Whereas Wagner's different harmonic fields are momentary, within a constant flow of chromatic harmony, Debussy's range far further, into modal, whole-tone, diatonic 'white-note', even octatonic areas, creating – by the range of possibilities for the presentation of any one motif – a language of extended flexibility with which to respond to Maeterlinck's interplay of themes and symbols.

We can see this procedure in operation in the first scene of the opera. At first, the opening two motifs, clear to the listener's ear, are identified with precise harmonic fields (Example 4). This opening

Example 4

(VS, p. 1)

motif Maurice Emmanuel, in his pioneering study of the opera,[14] tentatively but not inappropriately calls 'les temps lointains' (bygone ages). Not only because of *Rheingold*, first motifs tend to be associated with landscape, and it is by no means restrictive to associate this motif with the forest, embracing Emmanuel's association with agelessness.[15] This timeless association comes more from the harmony Debussy employs: a pseudo-mediaeval sounding alternation of an open fifth on D with a flattened 'antique' leading-note on C♮. Its mediaeval quality is heightened by its plainsong-like shape: a rising perfect fifth followed by stepwise movement within the fifth. In its subsequent development, 3 bars later, the pitch, the 'white-note' character and the melody are unaltered. Debussy develops *within* the harmonic field but does not alter the field itself. Instead, more white notes are superimposed to form diatonic added-note chords, but there is still no sixth degree of the scale (Example 5a). By involving no new harmonic device the immutable quality of the forest can be projected. At Golaud's entry a further reworking at the same pitch occurs, again retaining the original pitch and open fifths, but now adding the keynote B♭ (Example 5b). The threefold statement of this motif in the Prelude, and the return to the D at the end anchor the scene to a clear tonal centre; the motif occurs several times in altered versions in the middle of the scene, returning once on D shortly before the end of the scene. Again, this entry superimposes no new harmonic field, but seems to combine the added-note harmonies of its second appearance (Example 5a) with the version at Golaud's entry (Example 5b). It accompanies the world 'La nuit sera très noire et très froide' (The night will be very dark and very cold). The clear D minor which frames the scene, added to the employment of only one harmonic field, establishes from the outset

Example 5

(VS, pp. 1–2)

a)

b)   (Enter GOLAUD)

the immutability of the dark forest which, as mentioned in chapter 1, is an inescapable element of Maeterlinck's symbolic landscape.

The next motif (Example 4b) is clearly that of Golaud. Unlike the previous theme which is virtually restricted to the first scene, this motif recurs throughout the opera and is clearly associated with Golaud, thus it is potentially the most Wagnerian motif in the opera. As has been observed, Debussy's abhorrence of over-blatant uses of character-motifs was several times expressed, and he is sparing in his use of this easily identifiable phrase perhaps because it could all too easily turn Golaud into a stock-in-trade villain. In one case he cut an occurrence of the 'Golaud' motif from the first version of the inter-ludes, perhaps because he considered it too obvious. At the end of the first scene with Yniold (Act III scene 4), four bars appear in the 1902 Fromont vocal score (Example 6). In subsequent scores these bars were removed. Perhaps Debussy felt that after the emotional and physical terror of the preceding scene such a motivic underlining of Golaud's jealousy was, to use Debussy's own phrase, 'un peu grossière'.

Melodically, the motif has only two notes. Rhythmically it is also the most Wagnerian motif in the opera, having a 'sword-motif' with its characteristic dotted rhythm at the head of its second bar. In the tail of the complete motif, the energy of this trochaic 'initiative' is

Example 6

(Fromont VS, 1902)

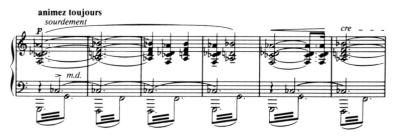

dispelled, loosening the dotted rhythm into a triplet. Quite apart from any harmonic considerations, Debussy can alter the balance of these active and passive elements. He can further activate the motif by bringing the dotted rhythm to its head, or conversely, he can dispel the motif's energy by cutting out the dotted notes altogether, repeating only the triplet tail.

Example 7

Whole 'Golaud' motif (VS, p. 1)
a)

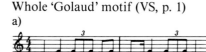

Motif devoid of 'initiative' element (VS, pp. 4–5)
b)

Je vais revenir sur mes pas (I must retrace my steps)

Increased energy by prolonging and accelerating 'initiative' element (VS, p. 17)

c)

Je chassais dans la forêt, je poursuivais un sanglier (I was hunting in the forest, I was chasing a wild boar)

Example 7 (*cont.*)

Struggling of 'initiative' element, to depict wounded Golaud (VS, p. 76)

d)

'Initiative' element only, as Golaud attacks Pelléas (VS, p. 266)

e)

In Act V Golaud's motif is almost totally without its trochaic spearhead, it does not even reappear for his relentless questioning of Mélisande. Remarkable in this act is the single entry of the complete motif in the last act, after Golaud is silent and Arkël counsels him to move away and begin again (VS, p. 308, system 2). Here, Debussy's addition of the motif gives voice to ideas unexplained in the text itself.

The application of different harmonic fields may either reinforce or contrast with these rhythmic variants described above. Golaud's motif at first has whole-tone harmonies: all the notes in the first presentation of his motif are drawn from one whole-tone scale, rendering any rhythmic energy harmonically impotent, as there is little forward-motion or tension within the limited mode. Immediately, having none of the elemental stability of the forest, Golaud's motif is more human. Restless and searching, it employs new harmonies as is appropriate to the only character who appears to be capable of self-determination in the opera. Its first transformation is with a major added sixth chord which stretches up to a chord which is itself a dissonant B♭ minor chord with a grinding major seventh and augmented eleventh. It is essentially a chord-pair (G minor and A major) which shifts over a static bass interval. But unlike the first example (4b), there is a strong feeling of movement from relative relaxation to increased tension: a progression from concord to dissonance. In this sense, this 'opening' progression may be said to be a harmonically 'initiative' device, complementing the motif's 'initiative' rhythms (Example 8).

Example 8
(VS, p. 1)

increase of tension by dissonance

The balance between tension and relaxation is entirely reversed in one subsequent statement in the Prelude, where the first chord is dominant and the second tonic, although they are enriched with added notes. It is not until later that the potential of this closing and cadential gesture (as opposed to opening and 'initiative') is realised.

Example 9
(VS, p. 22)

Debussy puts the first of these two versions (Example 8) to immediate use. There is more striving in the new harmonic device which recurs after Golaud's entry to portray his hunting (VS, p. 4):

Mais maintenant, je l'ai perdue de vue, je crois que je me suis perdu moi-même, et mes chiens ne me retrouvent plus.

(But now I have lost sight of him. I think I am lost myself and my dogs will never find me again.)

When Golaud realises the futility of his hunting and remarks 'Je vais revenir sur mes pas', Debussy retraces his own steps to the original non-progressive, whole-tone harmony of the motif: *within* the whole-tone scale, the only progress can be to another harmonic field entirely. In this quest, Golaud has so far failed. The motif not only returns empty-handed, but, as we have seen (Example 6), it has lost its dotted-rhythm 'initiative'. Devoid of its spearhead, and hesitant with a bar in-between, the tail of the motif over the inconclusive chromatic discord underlines his failure:

Example 10
(VS, p. 5)

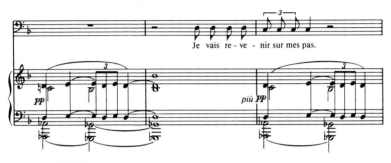

Je vais re - ve - nir sur mes pas.

(I must retrace my steps)

With Mélisande's entry into the play, the accelerated presentation of dramatic themes is complemented by further interchanges of motifs and harmonic areas. Her melodically pentatonic motif is at first projected through whole-tone harmony, at once linking her sense of being lost with that of Golaud. This quickly changes to her more characteristic harmonic association – that of the half-diminished chord. It is clearly associated with the profound *tristesse* of Maeterlinck's characters and Arkël's 'pity' for humanity. Appropriately, Arkël frequently shares a harmonic language based on this chord with Mélisande. At her first entry (in tears), Debussy's motif, clearly connected with Mélisande's weeping, is derived from two versions of the half-diminished chord, transposed up a fifth two bars later (Example 11).

In a rare technical comment about his opera, Debussy interestingly refers to his conscious treatment of Mélisande's motif to emphasise the view he held of her character:

Notice that the motif which accompanies Mélisande is never altered. It comes back in the fifth act unchanged in every respect because in fact Mélisande always remains the same and dies without anyone – only old Arkël, perhaps, – ever having understood her.[16]

Example 11

(VS, p. 5)

a)

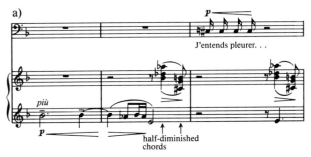

J'entends pleurer. . .

half-diminished
chords

(I hear weeping. . .)

b)

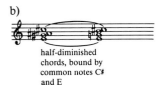

half-diminished
chords, bound by
common notes C♯
and E

Debussy's harmonic palette also includes passages based on chords with added sixths and sevenths, warm in the low register, with spacious resonance between a bass fifth and a tenor third. Frequently it also includes the major ninth. This is a somewhat more conventional language reserved for moments of physical and sexual attraction, and also emotional closeness. It first occurs when Golaud is confronted with the beauty and frailty of Mélisande: 'Oh! vous êtes belle!' (VS, p. 7).

In direct contract is a stark language of diads used for the contrary forces of jealousy, violence and death. Naturally associated with Golaud, and to symbols which pertain to him, it is used to give weight to certain events (Golaud's accident, his various questionings of Mélisande and of Yniold). It can also enhance the sense of terror in certain places and at certain moments (the grotto, the vaults under the castle, the sound of the closing gates.) But this harmonic device, frequently associated with the darker, lower register, is first used not for one of the more obvious harbingers of destiny, but for an unanswered question at the end of Act I scene 2 (Example 12), the importance of which Debussy thus underlines. Choice, which may

Example 12

(VS, pp. 36–7)

(Could you choose between your father and your friend?)

be seen as Man's attempt to interfere with destiny, is thus brought to the fore as the key to the underlying import of the opera.

With these broad harmonic fields identified, some of the subtleties of Debussy's handling of the subsequent development of the motifs may be more readily observed. The 'forest' motif, for example, may absorb Golaud's whole-tone quality (Example 13). Then again,

Example 13

(VS, p. 6)

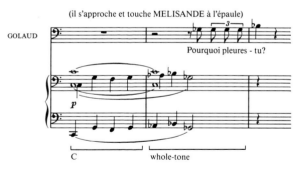

(Why are you weeping?)

though Golaud seems to retreat after frightening Mélisande, this same motif reappears, imbued now with the added sevenths associated with his first demonstration of desire for her (Example 14). When we hear the words 'Voyez, je resterai ici', the music leaves us in no doubt that this is a ploy to win her confidence. At the mention

Example 14

(VS, p. 7)

(You see, I will stay over here, by the tree)

of Mélisande's past mistreatment, the half-diminished harmony
of her initial weeping is instead projected on to the same motif.

Example 15

(VS, p. 8)

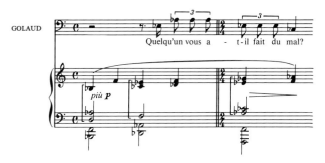

(Did someone do you harm?)

Pared down to the most economical exploitation of the moment
of transition between two harmonic fields, two chords, bridging the
two types of harmony, may distil a change of emotion. In themselves, the two chords in the following example link the half-
diminished field of Mélisande's weeping with the implied unresolved
dominant sevenths and ninths used for Golaud's sexual attraction
(Example 16).

Example 16
(VS, p. 6)

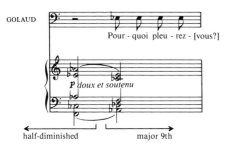

(Why are [you] crying?)

As has been seen, Golaud's motif, too, may be transformed by the application of a type of harmony originally associated with another idea, as happens to striking effect at the end of Act I scene 1 when his motif, stripped of all chromatic energy, is infused with the diatonic archaism of the Prelude, no longer harmonically 'initiative' in the sense suggested earlier. Maeterlinck's circular form emphasises the impotence of any attempt to struggle against destiny, for no progress has been made from Golaud's first line 'Je ne pourrais pas sortir de cette forêt!' to his last 'Je suis perdu aussi'. We have already observed how his first speech, up to 'Je vais revenir sur mes pas,' is a microcosm of this failure to achieve. Debussy, in one scene alone, reflects this in his manipulation of motifs and their attendant harmonies, freer now than Wagner's to absorb the fuller contrarieties of opposed harmonic languages. By employing the 'cadential' version of Golaud's motif (Example 9), Debussy not only emphasises how Golaud has gained nothing from his strivings in the forest in which he is lost. The additional superimposition of 'white-note' harmony on to Golaud's motif also underlines the inevitable supremacy of the timeless forest, ultimately more powerful than any human will that ventures therein.

It is a development of the implied dominant-ninth added-note vocabulary which is used not only for Golaud's desire for the young Mélisande, nor only for the growing love between Pelléas and Mélisande, but also – most expressively – for moments of particular understanding between Arkël and Mélisande. Arkël remarks that those close to death 'need to touch with their lips the brow of a maid or the cheeks of a child.' The music responds with a passage based on chords of the ninth, *très expressif*, and a repeated motif delicately orchestrated in octaves on the oboe and bassoon, which is later accompanied by the special sonority of *divisi* violas and cellos. Relative stability of key, non-existent between Golaud and Mélisande, is allied to this harmonic language, as it is several times between Pelléas and Mélisande. Only Golaud's disturbance of the scene arrests a resolute cadence in the E major of the key-signature.

Example 17

(VS, p. 205)

ARKEL

Laisse-moi te re-gar-der ain-si,   detout près, un moment. . .

E major: II (half-diminished)

ARKEL

on a tant be-soin de beauté aux côtés de la   mort. . .

f soutenu et expressif   *sf*   *più p*

I   V   I   V   V

(Let me look at you from close to for a moment: one needs so much beauty in the face of death. . .)

It is naturally for the love-music between Pelléas and Mélisande that this harmonic language is developed to the full. Debussy here has no need to curb his instinct for the repeated two-bar phrase which infuses the warmest moments with a cradling security. Pelléas's vocal lines stretch the recitative, curving and arching above

the monotone declamation which characterises the loveless characters of the drama. Parallels can be drawn with the love-music from
Act II of *Tristan* – not only in some of the chord-pairs, but also in
some of the syncopated rhythms.

Most *Tristan*-like, although to entirely different effect, is the technique in which the expectancy of resolution from a dominant is used
for the two prolonged love-scenes. As we shall see in chapter 5, the
idealised goal-key of many of these dominants is F# major, prepared
for in Act III scene 1 as Pelléas covers himself in Mélisande's hair.
It is prepared for and hinted at, but as yet frustrated, in the subsequent interlude and again introduced in the final love-scene when
Pelléas symbolically asks Mélisande to come into the light. It is
finally achieved after Mélisande has 'broken the ice with red-hot
irons' by declaring her love for Pelléas.

Apart from the love-language, and posing a threat to it, is the
sense of mystery. By introducing oblique answers, unanswered questions, unexplained events and coincidences, Maeterlinck maintains
this throughout the play, and Debussy heightens it further. In Act I
Mélisande's attendant sense of mystery is overlaid with a sudden
treble pedal, Lombardic in rhythm, imparting an eerie question-
mark over her evasive reply 'Je commence à avoir froid. . .' (I begin
to feel cold. . .) (VS, p. 18). Similar devices recur, and this side of
Mélisande, who deals in symbols when she seems to know something
which nobody else can perceive, comes to a head in the final act as
she approaches death.

Inversely, statements of extreme importance can literally be underlined with pedals, as happens frequently in the case of Arkël.

Example 18
(VS, p. 32)

(There are perhaps no events which are pointless)

It is the interludes which Debussy exploits as the main opportunity for a musical shaping of events. Here, themes are most fully transformed and developed. More importantly, 'pure' motifs may be introduced, unattached to any expressed idea. Reserving musical development for the interludes is evidently Debussy's solution to the problem he saw in most opera:

I have never allowed my music to precipitate or retard the changing feeling or passions of my characters for technical convenience. It stands aside as soon as it can, leaving them the freedom of their gestures, their utterances – their joy or their sorrow. [17]

In the first interlude, the importance of Golaud's theme, now diatonic, has been discussed. Chords that follow (Example 19a) are taken up again in Act II scene 2 when the domain of Allemonde is again under discussion (Example 19b). Thus, the interludes can link passages in time by introducing a new idea (less of a motif, here) which will be taken up again later.

Example 19

(VS, p. 22)

a)

(VS, p. 20)

(It is true that the castle is very old and dark. . .)

Most striking in the first interlude is a motif highlighted on trumpets which emerges from the middle of the texture to predominate over it. It is a passage worth quoting in the full score. Note how Debussy uses the trombones to give weight to the motif as it emerges from the texture, making a crescendo to help it on its way, but retracting at the last to enable the motif to sing clearly over the other remaining instruments (Example 20). It is clearly a motif of great import, as it precedes Arkël's first entrance and recurs as he utters profundities about destiny (Example 18). It has also appeared in a far less prominent way as Golaud proudly announces that he is a prince and 'le petit-fils d'Arkël', suggesting that the motif has something to do with the character of Arkël himself. But a final recurrence suggests that this is Debussy's supreme motif for giving weight to Maeterlinck's most important themes, far beyond a mere character-motif. Emmanuel's categorisation of it as the 'destiny' motif is apt, but does not adequately explain all its appearances (Example 21).

It is thus in the interludes that literary symbolism first extends to the purer plane of entirely musical symbolism. If Maeterlinck's 'theatre of the half-expressed' poses questions rather than provides answers, then Debussy may be said to have the final hand in the interludes, where motifs are introduced and developed without specific reference to visible events in the play. More conventionally operatic is Debussy's use of musical material to enhance the atmosphere of mystery and sadness which pervades the play. Mystery is above all created by harmonic means. 'Vagrant' progressions or chord-pairs with allegiance to no clear tonal centre are used to portray particularly mysterious moments, often providing a void in which a literary symbol may resonate. As has already been suggested, harmonic developments of the half-diminished chord are the main means of expressing the profound sadness of the play, distilled in the frequent references to weeping. Golaud first remarks 'J'entends pleurer', at his initial meeting with Mélisande, and at the end of the opera she dies, 'her eyes full of tears'. When Pelléas enters, he too has been in tears, and Yniold (who has to be bribed not to cry) remarks that the couple frequently 'weep together in the darkness' (pleurent dans l'obscurité). Even Golaud, no cardboard villain, is not impervious to Mélisande's emotional frailty and is tender in response to her until he discovers the loss of the ring. Only in Act V, however, does he allude to the theme of weeping himself: 'J'ai tué sans raison! Est-ce que ce

Example 20
(OS, p. 29)

Example 21
(VS, p. 303)

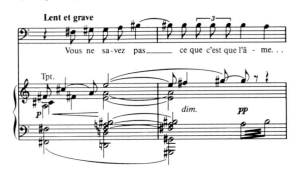

(You do not know what the soul is. . .)

n'est pas à faire pleurer les pierres?' Mélisande's tears well up in Act II scene 2, and Debussy's initial response to her weeping in the first act is further developed, drawing further extensions of a language based upon the half-diminished chord (VS, pp. 81–2).

Perhaps it was the profound *tristesse* of *Pelléas* which caused Debussy to develop, further than any other composer, such harmonic extensions of the half-diminished chord which operate in many different ways, sometimes in parallel, sometimes rootless, and in other cases having their own half-diminished dominants and subdominants. It is Arkël who extends the theme of weeping into that of pity for the human condition, and Debussy complements this with a further development of his half-diminished language. His telling words at the end of Act III scene 2 draw from Debussy an extension of Mélisande's weeping music, now more fully orchestrated and intensified with double dissonances.

Example 22
(VS, p. 220)

Such is Debussy's technique with the characters, themes and external events of the play, but what of his response to the actual symbols of Maeterlinck's drama? Two broad types of symbol may be distinguished: firstly, the local or momentary symbol, alluded to in the text – a ring, a crown, doves, three beggars, a window. Secondly, there is the extended symbolism which is frequently elemental – light and dark, warm and cold, or the various types of water-imagery which recur throughout the play. To these, the local symbols – *shining* rings and crowns, lamps, light flooding through windows – may serve as adjuncts. Broadly, the first of these normally draws from Debussy a leitmotif or passing acknowledgement, while the second necessitates a more extended level of response.

Local symbols in the play are rarely totally isolated and Debussy takes some care to forge appropriate links with more recurrent motifs as well as to avoid too obviously pictorial a representation. Not that there is inevitably a concrete symbol to be depicted. As Mélisande first looks into the well with Pelléas she remarks 'Oh! Oh! J'ai vu passer quelque-chose au fond de l'eau!' Debussy gives a touch of the 'love-key' of G♭ major, leaning upwards with a Lydian C♮, and the symbol, unexplained but lightly underlined, is gone.

Example 23

(VS, p. 65)

(Oh! oh! I can see something moving at the bottom of the water. . .)

More concrete are the symbols of the lost crown and ring. A tiny horn-motif is heard as Golaud sees the crown at the bottom of the well, but more important is the first use of the key-area of C major. It is reiterated when Golaud thinks of trying to retrieve it. The key returns when Mélisande retreats from Golaud's prickly beard, reminding her (one is tempted to surmise) of Bluebeard, from whom she may have acquired the first crown (see chapter 1, p. 2).

It seems that particular chords are associated with certain crucial themes in the opera. A polarity straddling the opposite poles of the circle of fifths seems to be established, with C major representing Mélisande's previous life, as well as underlining themes of darkness in the play; and G♭ (or F♯) major links the aspirations of her new-found love to Pelléas. Such connections of key are, of course, nothing new, going back as far as Monteverdi, perhaps further. But in Debussy's harmonic language in *Pelléas* the establishment of keys is rare. If there are dominants – the most fundamental way of establishing a key – they rarely resolve. It is thus more a case of pausing on chords, or highlighting them within the forward flow.

The loss of the ring is also underlined in a subtle way. The downward harp gesture as the ring falls into the water is in fact the very first chord associated with Mélisande, a half-diminished chord on A♯ (Example 11). Thus, in a sense, the circular, non-progressive key-structure, which we have seen to parallel Golaud's being lost within the forest, is also found to accompany the first episode in Mélisande's life – from her initial meeting with Golaud to her (perhaps deliberate) loss of her wedding-ring. As the ring falls, the failure of this unfulfilled episode in Mélisande's life is thus underlined.

Example 24

(VS, p. 67)

In another way too, this scene harks back to the first act, resolving unresolved tensions. When the ring is finally lost all that remains is a 'circle of water'. Root-position chords fan out in a circular motion, resolving on to D major for the first time in the opera whose first scene was so strongly in D minor. A sense of resolution is felt: a reworking of the original meeting by the well, but now with more promise of fulfilment (VS, p. 69).

More extended are the recurrent images of water throughout the play. To all of these, Debussy responds with pictorial motifs and orchestral contrasts. But he also takes care to link them to human themes within the play. The well has a grace-note motif which recurs many times, momentarily stilling the harmonic movement. Its chord of the minor seventh and major ninth links the motif with its human relevance, for it is a part of the love-language of Debussy's harmonic associations, and while the well was once miraculous in that it 'cured the eyes of the blind', the well's magic is now that of the Pre-Raphaelite 'Well at the World's End' in that it primarily nurtures love.

The sea is less trustworthy: 'Nous aurons une tempête cette nuit. . . et cependant elle est si calme maintenant' (We shall have a storm tonight. . .yet it is so calm now). Debussy's means of expression is utterly simple: a G♯ minor chord, sustained for a whole bar on the wind, and underlined with a pianissimo timpani roll (see chapter 5, Example 7). The threat of the storm is expressed with a whole-tone scale, filled in with a chromatic step – a language which recurs in the darkest waters of all, the castle vaults, where stagnant waters exude the 'stench of death'.

The light and spume twice provide relief and sharp contrast to the underground darknesses: the precarious (and no doubt symbolic) path between the two lakes of the underground sea-caverns, where Pelléas and Mélisande search in vain for the lost wedding-ring; and more acutely still, the vaults of the castle. For this, a pure whole-tone language will not suffice, and intervening semitones are introduced, dissonant against the monochrome of the whole-tones. As will be seen in chapter 5, the elemental contrasts of water are related to the more extensive central thematic interplay of dark and light within the play.

Another way in which Debussy adds to the literary symbolism of the play is by introducing Golaud's motif at times when he is neither present nor mentioned. At its most conventional the device communicates the sense of Golaud spying in the background. But Debussy does not always use the device in such an obvious way: when, in Act I scene 3, the ship is seen on the sea and there is talk of imminent storm and shipwreck, fragments of Golaud's motif lurk in the background, suggesting a possible link between the appearance of the symbolic ship in danger and Golaud himself.

Appearances of musical motifs are by no means always so tangible. To take one motif of particular interest, first appearing as Pelléas first enters in Act I scene 2, designated by Emmanuel as the 'Pelléas' motif. Its simple fourths allow it many transformations in terms of harmony. It links with Mélisande's initial motif in that it is at first based on half-diminished chords, softening into dominants as Arkël welcomes Pelléas with the words 'Viens un peu plus près que je te voie dans la lumière' (Come a little closer so that I may see you in the light). In the following scene, the motif attracts far more straightforward harmony – a single chord – and is here interspersed with an F♯ major chord, connected with the light from the sea, and later to play an important role in the love music. Already it is clear that it is no mere character-motif. This is confirmed in the final love-scene, as complex chromatic chords accompany the motif at the point where Pelléas gives voice to his confused feelings: 'Je vais fuir en criant de joie et de douleur'. By the time Mélisande enters, the motif has become condensed, and is accompanied by an intensified form of the love-language, where thirteenths are added to the norm of the ninths, and the chords are inverted so that they are founded upon a warm, close-position fourth. It is in this position, and at the same pitch, that the motif floats across Mélisande's mind as Golaud asks her if she had ever loved Pelléas (Example 25).

Many of Debussy's motifs transcend clear explanation; indeed Emmanuel, before giving us his 'convenient labels' for the motifs, affirms that 'L'auteur n'est pour rien dans ces désignations' (The

Example 25
(VS, p. 287)

(I loved him. Where is he?)

composer is not responsible for these labels).[18] They are neither the pure character-motifs Debussy objected to in early Wagner, nor are they specific enough to be tied to themes as in later Wagner. Maeterlinck's text, after all, is far more fully developed in its own right than any Wagner libretto. In this they complement the Symbolist aesthetic in that they embody the oft-repeated Symbolist view of pure music as an ideal above even the verbal symbol. The French Wagnerian Téodore de Wyzewa even went so far as to claim that the silent reading of a textless musical score was the final distillation of the ideals of Symbolism.[19] Whilst textless pieces such as Debussy's *Préludes* may complement this ideal from the opposite angle, his play of musical motifs and symbols in *Pelléas* perfectly complements Maeterlinck's 'theatre of the unexpressed'. W. B. Yeats, writing two years before the first performance of Debussy's *Pelléas*, typifies the view of music as an extension of symbolism:

Metaphors are not profound enough to be moving, when they are not symbols, and when they are symbols they are the most perfect, *because the most subtle outside of pure sound*, and through them one can best find out what symbols are.   W. B. Yeats, 'The symbolism of poetry', 1900

5 Tonalities of darkness and light

BY RICHARD LANGHAM SMITH

Vous avez allumé les lampes,
   Oh! le soleil dans le jardin!
Vous avez allumé les lampes,
Je vois le soleil par les fentes,
Ouvrez les portes du jardin!

   Les clefs des portes sont perdues
Il faut attendre, il faut attendre,
Les clefs sont tombées de la tour,
Il faut attendre, il faut attendre,
Il faut attendre, d'autres jours. . . .

D'autres jours ouvriront les portes,
La forêt garde les verrous,
La forêt brûle autour de nous,
C'est la clarté des feuilles mortes,
Qui brûlent sur le seuil des portes. . . .

   Les autres jours sont déjà las,
Les autres jours ont peur aussi,
Les autres jours ne viendront pas,
Les autres jours mourront aussi,
Nous aussi nous mourrons ici. . . .

Maurice Maeterlinck, 'Lied', published in the first number of the literary review *La Conque*, founded and edited by Debussy's close friend Pierre Louÿs in 1891.

By the year 1902, when Debussy's opera was first performed, the Symbolist movement was already in decline. Maeterlinck had moved on, and critics could view the movement with a certain detachment. André Beaunier concluded that literature had divided into two main types:

There are essentially two types of art of which one consists of direct expression, and the other proceeds by symbols. A symbol is an image that can be used to represent an idea, thanks to secret correspondences that we do not know how to analyse.[1]

107

While Beaunier's clear-cut division may apply to a poet like Mallarmé, in whose writings *direct* expression frequently finds no place, it can hardly be said to apply unequivocally to Maeterlinck's *Pelléas*, where external events are charted with the utmost clarity and simplicity, whatever else is alluded to in the dialogue. Indeed, it is difficult to imagine any opera in which some semblance of a plot would be entirely absent.

The first two scenes of the opera contain some narrative element, although one or two symbols which will recur are thrown into the proceedings, and there are passages of dialogue which allude to themes (the sense of being lost; darkness; cold) rather than to purely external events. The lamp mentioned by Golaud in his letter to Pelléas, read out by Geneviève in Act I scene 2, forms an important link between the narrative content of the first two scenes, and that of the third which is in a more symbolic vein. In the context of the letter, the lamp is a clear sign rather than a symbol. If the lamp is lit, Golaud is welcome with his new bride. But by the time Geneviève highlights the lamp in the last line of the scene – 'Aie soin d'allumer la lampe dès ce soir, Pelléas' – we conclude that more is at stake than a mere sign. We have moved to a different plane of expression, where Beaunier's 'direct expression' recedes, and a symbolic framework begins to make itself apparent. This framework is essentially based on the polar opposites of darkness and light.

The transfer to this higher plane of expression is signalled by a new manner of language whose lack of narrative continuity commands a different nature of response. Oblique answers increase: 'Why is it going away tonight?' asks Mélisande, referring to the ship; 'One can hardly see it any longer. . . Perhaps it will be wrecked. . .' Pelléas answers: 'The night falls very quickly.' Unconnected and seemingly unusual statements further invite the listener to adopt a different receptive attitude: 'The ship is in the light', remarks Mélisande. Negatives and references to the unspecific also abound: 'Nothing can be seen any longer on the sea. . . It is already far away.' In terms of punctuation, ellipses (suspension points) are the graphic way in which these loose connections are communicated, giving a pause for the listener to reflect on the deeper significance, and in the case of the opera, a moment for prolongation into music. Tzvetan Todorov puts it nicely when he suggests that in dialogue of this nature Maeterlinck 'asks his readers to dream over insignificant sentences'.[2]

As has been noted in chapter 1, the characters themselves describe the elements of Maeterlinck's landscape: the dark forests and the light of the sea on the other side. These elements of darkness and light return many times during the course of the play, developing and deepening their resonance with each subsequent entrance. Geneviève is the first to remark that they are '*looking* for the light' – 'Nous aussi, nous cherchions la clarté' – a theme which is to become crucial in the symbolic unfolding of this theme in the play.

This dark and light symbolism is never left undeveloped or simplistic. Immediately, complexities are introduced. Although it is 'a little more light than elsewhere', remarks Geneviève, 'the sea is none the less dark'. A ship with its own lights enters the discussion. 'Les lumières sont très hautes' – (Its lights are very high) – remarks Pelléas, adding further to the symbolism by observing that it will soon be seen as it enters the 'band of light', ('Nous le verrons tout à l'heure quand il entrera dans la bande de clarté. . .'). Geneviève then remarks upon the mist which is preventing clear vision. Pelléas thinks it is lifting, Mélisande thinks she sees a little light she has never before seen. 'It's a beacon', surmises Pelléas, adding that there are 'others which we haven't yet seen'. Night falls quickly, and in the dark Mélisande is able to see other lights. Pelléas concludes that they are the 'other beacons'. Without examining the complex explanations of such symbolism offered by interpreters of Maeterlinck, we can distil from the scene that Geneviève, Pelléas and Mélisande fear the dark, seek the light, are prevented from clear vision by the mist, and are beginning to perceive beacons lighting the way.

In a rejected fourth scene to the first act, this idle discussion about the light and dark was further developed. A manuscript now in the Pierpont Morgan Library in New York contains a completed scene where Arkël, Pelléas and Geneviève wait, in the depths of night, for a boat to arrive. It is striking in developing an image of terrifying darkness paralleled only by the scene in the castle vaults. A fierce wind – 'like a bar of iron' – threatens to extinguish the lamp which is guarded by a sentinel, Claudius. Ideas which reappear elsewhere in the play are common in the scene: either Maeterlinck incorporated them elsewhere in the play or he intended the scene to underline further structural connections. There is talk of midnight sounding, reflecting the stress on the chimes of midday which occurs in Act II, and later Pelléas remarks, perhaps a little prematurely, that he pities everyone that he sees: 'J'ai pitié de tous que je vois. . .' Geneviève is further developed as a female sage, complementing Arkël's prophetic utterances, as she had begun to do with her comments on the lamp in scene 2. Advising the fatigued Pelléas to rest, she remarks that women are better at 'watching' than men: 'les femmes veillent mieux que les hommes'. But light and dark remain the principal elements of the scene:

PELLEAS	De quel côté y a-t-il une clarté dans le ciel?
VOIX DU VEILLEUR	Du côté où le soleil va se lever. . .
PELLEAS	Il fait noir par ici – c'est étrange – il n'y a pas d'étoiles de ce côté.
(PELLEAS	In which direction is there light in the sky?
VOICE OF THE SENTINEL	In the direction where the sun is going to rise.
PELLEAS	It is dark over here – it's strange – there are no stars on this side.)[3]

If we take the ideas of *Le Trésor des Humbles* as our guide, this banter is clearly of great import. Maeterlinck's belief in the wisdom of the old man with the lamp has been referred to in chapter 1. Lamps and beacons, and light and dark, are common in *Le Trésor des Humbles*, giving us pointers to the frame of reference of this aspect of the symbolism of *Pelléas*. In the essay on 'Mystic Morality', a passage dealing with Man's unsuccessful attempt to voyage into his own soul uses imagery strikingly reminiscent of that of *Pelléas*:

We believe we have dived down to the most unfathomable depths, and when we reappear on the surface, the drop of water that glistens on our trembling finger-tips no longer resembles the sea from which it came. We believe we have discovered a grotto that is stored with bewildering treasure; we come back to the light of day, and the gems we have brought are false – mere pieces of glass – and yet does the treasure shine on, unceasingly in the darkness.[4]

In the essay 'On Women' our own destiny is seen in terms of a 'circle of light':

For indeed we can never emerge from the little circle of light that destiny traces about our footsteps. . .

In this context Pelléas and Mélisande's constant moving in and out of circles of light in Act IV scene 4 come to mind.

But it is in another essay from *Le Trésor des Humbles* – 'La vie profonde' (The Deeper Life) – that references to light and dark are perhaps at their most pertinent as regards *Pelléas*. The essay begins with a reference to Man's search for the ideal:

It is well that men should be reminded that the very humblest of them has the power to fashion, after a divine model that he chooses not, a great moral personality, composed in equal parts of himself and the ideal, and that if anything lives in fullest reality, of a surety it is that.[5]

This regeneration is seen by Maeterlinck in terms of dark and light:

We can be born more than once: and each birth brings us a little nearer to our God. But most of us are content to wait till an event, charged with almost irresistible radiance, intrudes itself violently upon our darkness and enlightens us in our despite. We await I know not what happy coincidence, when it may so come about that the eyes of our soul shall be open at the very moment that something extraordinary shall take place. But in everything that happens is there light; and the greatness of the greatest of men has but consisted in that they had trained their eyes to be open to every ray of this light.[6]

Profound love is seen as the agency of this renewal:

If you have loved profoundly you have needed no one to tell you that your soul was a thing as great in itself as the world; that the stars, the flowers, the waves of night and sea were not solitary; that it was on the threshold of appearances that everything began, but nothing ended, and that the very lips you kissed belonged to a creature who was loftier, much purer, and much more beautiful than the one your arms enfolded. You have beheld that which in life cannot be seen without ecstasy.[7]

Expressed in the above passage is the idea of love leading to an ideal far above itself. This, too, is a theme which may well be one interpretation of the quest for light pursued by the protagonists of Maeterlinck's play. A subsequent passage leads us into further developments of the ideas of 'Le tragique quotidien'. It seems that love itself can be intensified by a receptivity to the symbols of everyday life, again notably the light:

And yet we are in a world where the smallest events assume, spontaneously, a beauty that ever becomes purer and loftier. There is nothing that coalesces more readily than earth and sky; if your eyes have rested upon the stars, before enfolding in your arms the woman you love, your embrace will not be the same as though you had merely looked at the walls of your room. Be sure that the day you lingered to follow a ray of light through a crevice in the door of life, you did something as great as though you had bandaged the wounds of your enemy for at that moment did you no longer have any enemies.[8]

As in the symbolism of the play, the contrarieties of dark and light in the essay are not left undeveloped. There are those, concludes Maeterlinck, for whom illumination comes more in the dark:

Which of us has not met, more than once, along the paths of life, a forsaken soul that has yet not lost the courage to cherish, in the darkness, a thought diviner and purer than all those that so many others had the power to choose in the light?[9]

Bearing in mind this recognition of the agency of love in the search for the 'deeper life', we may interpret a passage in Act III scene 1 in terms of these extracts from *Le Trésor des Humbles*. Pelléas is now searching for the light not, 'du côté de la mer', but in Mélisande herself. More specifically, he mistakes her hair for a ray of light:

MELISANDE   J'arrange mes cheveux pour la nuit. . .
PELLEAS   C'est là ce que je vois sur le mur?
            Je croyais que tu avais de la lumière.
            ['Je croyais que c'était un rayon de lumière' in the original text.]

(MELISANDE   I am arranging my hair for the night. . .
PELLEAS   Is that what I see on the wall?
             I thought you had a light with you.)

Again, further complexities are added to the symbolism, for while Pelléas mistook Mélisande's hair for the light itself, it also prevents him from seeing the light:

PELLEAS   Je ne vois plus le ciel à travers tes cheveux.
          (I can no longer see the sky through your hair.)

These words find an interpretative echo in 'The Deeper Life' as Maeterlinck warns:

And if the sky is hidden from you, 'does not the great starry sky', asks the poet, 'spread over our soul, in spite of all, under guise of death?'[10]

In the love-scenes, darkness and light are again brought into the action of the play. Pelléas and Mélisande hesitate, not knowing whether to seek the light and shun the dark, or vice versa. In their scene by the well, Act II scene 1, Mélisande pursues the shining object in the depths of the well. Pelléas, however, knows a lime-tree where the sun never penetrates: 'Il y a un tilleul où le soleil n'entre jamais.' At the beginning of the final love-scene a similar confusion occurs. Pelléas is afraid of the external world, Mélisande craves the light:

PELLEAS   Viens ici, ne reste pas au bord du clair de lune. . . Viens ici, nous avons tant de choses à nous dire. . . Viens ici, dans l'ombre du tilleul.
MELISANDE   Laissez-moi dans la clarté. . .

(PELLEAS   Come, do not stay on the edge of the moonlight. . . Come, we have so much to say to each other. . . Come, under the shade of the lime-tree.
MELISANDE   Leave me in the light. . .)

Further into the act, after they have declared their love, it is Pelléas who craves the light:

PELLEAS   Nous sommes déjà dans l'ombre – Il fait trop noir sous cet arbre. Viens dans la lumière. Nous ne pouvons pas voir combien nous sommes heureux. . .
MELISANDE   Non, non; restons ici. . .Je suis plus près de toi dans l'obscurité. . .

(PELLEAS   We are already in the shade. It is too dark under this tree. Come into the light. We cannot see how happy we are. . .
MELISANDE   No, no; let us stay here. . .I am closer to you in the darkness. . .)

By the last act, the light is no longer sought after. Instead, the sunset is perceived by the fading Mélisande. She cannot recognise Golaud because she has the evening sun in her eyes. (C'est que j'ai le soleil du soir dans les yeux.) Finally she asks that the window be left open 'until the sun is in the depths of the sea'; 'It goes down slowly', she observes, asking 'Is it the beginning of winter?' She fears the cold, especially the 'great cold':

ARKEL   Veux-tu qu'on ferme les fenêtres?
MELISANDE   Non. . .jusqu'à ce que le soleil soit au fond de la mer. – Il descend lentement; alors c'est l'hiver qui commence?
ARKEL   Tu n'aimes pas l'hiver?
MELISANDE   Oh! non. J'ai peur du froid! J'ai si peur des grands froids. . .

(ARKEL   Do you want the windows closed?
MELISANDE   No. . .not until the sun has gone down to the depths of the sea. It is going down slowly, does that mean it is the beginning of winter?
ARKEL   Don't you like the winter?
MELISANDE   Oh no! I am afraid of the cold. I am so afraid of the great cold. . .)

At this point the dark–light symbolism expires, giving way to the final events and the pronouncements of Arkël.

Debussy responds to this symbolic framework with a system of keys, preparations for keys, and different modal scales. Complementing the sense in which Mélisande herself represents an ideal, Debussy reserves the sharp-key area of F♯ major, with its dominant preparation of C♯ major, for the gradually increasing sense of striving for this ideal which occurs in the early part of the play. The procedure works in several ways. In the broadest way, frustrated or unconsummated preparations for F♯ major occur in the first three acts, frequently to mirror some aspect of the light-imagery, or to suggest the rising desire for union with Mélisande. These preparations are consummated only in the final love-scene between Pelléas and Mélisande (Act IV scene 4) where the dominant finally resolves into a new motif, clearly in the aspired-to key of F♯ major.

Example 1

(VS, p. 245)

(It is as if your voice had come over the sea in the spring! I have never heard it until today)

Debussy achieves this aspiring for the F♯ major 'light' by several means, not only the occasional unresolved C♯ major dominant seventh. Indeed, it is absorbed into the whole structure of the work, first appearing cadentially at the end of the first act (where, in the third scene, the aspiration for the light first becomes a prominent theme). The diagram (Example 2) shows the stepwise movement at the beginning and ends of the first three scenes, leading to the F♯ major resolution at the end of the act.

Example 2 Tonal progression to F# major in Act I

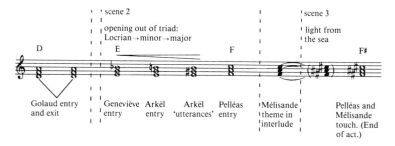

Within this rising structure, local hints of the key-area of F# (sometimes spelt as G♭) occur at pertinent points in the text. Most obvious, as a means of aspiring to the key, is the use of the unresolved dominant. Since Mélisande is the agent through whom man may achieve 'the light', it is logical that the agency of the dominant chord should at first be associated with her. Can it be fortuitous that the first occurrence of the chord of C#, with a dominant seventh, is at the moment of Golaud's first attraction to Mélisande? (See chapter 3, Examples 16 and 14.) Golaud has a glimpse of the light as he looks into Mélisande's eyes, but it is passing and irresolute in that it has minor versions of its dominant and subdominant, and is immediately dispelled into whole-tone harmonies at the words 'Pourquoi avez-vous l'air si étonné?' (Example 3). At his rebuffed attempt to hold Mélisande's hand, the key-area of F# is

Example 3
(VS, p. 16)

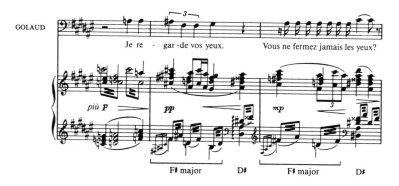

Example 3 (*cont.*)

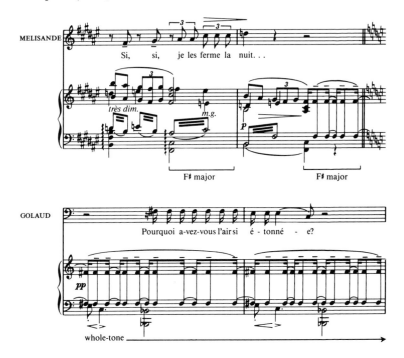

(I am looking at your eyes, You never close your eyes?
Why yes, I close them at night.
Why do you have such an astonished air about you?)

again introduced, underlining the parallel to the accepted offer of a hand made by Pelléas at the end of scene 3. The frustration of Golaud's unsuccessful attempt at physical contact with Mélisande is portrayed with F♯ *minor* (VS, pp. 20–1). These two instances are the closest to the 'light' that Golaud ever gets.

In scene 3 the light-key of F♯ is again in evidence, here it is set against a background of 'white-note' neutrality alternating with whole-tone chords. Immediately the polarity of the dark–light symbolism is thrown into relief, and it is intensified by contrasts of orchestration and register. The notes F and A are common to the 'white-note' chords and used for the remarks Mélisande and Geneviève make about the darkness of the forest and the gardens.

The same notes are also found in the whole-tone chords a few bars later, at Geneviève's words 'Il y a des endroits où l'on ne voit jamais le soleil.' (There are places where the sun is never seen.) The two notes act as double leading-notes to the F♯ major triad which, a few bars later, accompanies the mention of the 'light' for which they are searching: 'Regardez de l'autre côté, vous aurez la clarté de la mer.' (Look the other way, you will have the light from the sea.) The F♯ major chord is projected high in register, with a distinct change in orchestration, and is also an opening out from the minor third (F♯–A♮) of the preceding minor chord, its characteristic third having been kept in the middle register. All this helps to highlight the burst of F♯ major for 'la clarté de la mer'.

Example 4

(VS, p. 41)

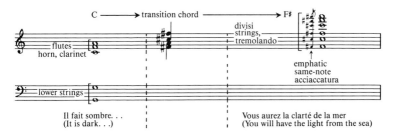

This basic cadential device is reworked to conclude the act, the white-note chords recurring at Geneviève's observation that it is time to go back. Mélisande sees the other guiding lights out to sea. Pelléas asks for her hand, but her hands are full of flowers. He touches her for the first time, supporting her by the arm, and again we move into F♯ major, though the resolution is (deliciously) delayed by changing chords over the tonic pedal, and finally left hanging as Debussy delicately ends the act with unresolved, though sensuous, added sixth and ninth colouring the 'light' chord of F♯ major (VS, p. 54).

In addition to the device of the extreme sharpward tonality of F♯, Debussy introduces a further device, also one with a sharpward pull, to communicate Mélisande's leading of Pelléas towards the light. It first occurs in her own motif at its appearance in the interlude between the second and third scenes in Act I. The device is a Lydian one, leaning sharpwards in that it sharpens the fourth degree of the scale, providing a semitonal leading-note to the fifth, and thus increasing the upward pull within the characteristic fifth of the scale. Mélisande has not appeared in scene 2, although she has been discussed. As has been observed in chapter 4 (p. 85, Example 3c), Debussy highlights the appearance of her motif in this interlude by placing it a semitone above the normal entry note of G♯. Starting on A, and thrown into relief by rare orchestration on the solo violin, it is accompanied by an F major chord. The B♮ thus becomes a Lydian note in this harmonisation, thrown into relief by its natural prominence in the motif itself.

In the next scene, the one touch of F♯ major (though spelt as G♭) comes when Mélisande sees something shining in the depths of the well. (See chapter 4, Example 23, p. 102.) Debussy again introduces a Lydian device to project the idea of aspiration. Here, a chord-pair occurs, consisting of a G♭ major chord and its supertonic A♭, chromatically altered to the major. It is again a Lydian device, now a respelt version of the aforementioned 'light' key.

Example 5

chord-pair   Lydian scale from which it is derived

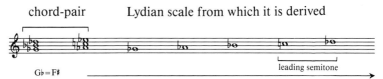

J'ai vu passer quelque chose au fond de l'eau (I can see something moving at the bottom of the water)

The most striking development of this Lydian leaning towards the light, again in F♯, is in Act II, scene 3, as the moonlight floods the entrance to the grotto after the acute darkness of the cavern. Pelléas cries out 'Oh. . .voici la clarté!' (Here is the light!) A momentary motif, *doux et expressif*, is introduced on the flutes and oboes, characterised again by a prominent C♮, the Lydian note of the 'light' key. Debussy makes much of the moment, flooding the texture with crossing harp *glissandi* and shimmering strings, its light gleaming all the more brilliantly as the bass is entirely withdrawn. Few other moments underline the light–dark polarity so vividly (Example 6).

Layers of darkness within the play are also projected by recurrent musical devices, but whereas a clear tonality seems to be associated with the light, chromatic discord and obscured tonal centres are used

Example 6
(OS, 1948 version, pp. 144–5)

(Oh! Here is the light)

to trace the references to the dark. Several of these harmonic languages have been introduced in the opening scene of the opera – the whole-tone chords and other devices in some way based upon the tritone. In Act I scene 3, a sudden tritonal shift, and more opaque orchestration accompany Pelléas's remark that, despite the light, the sea is none the less dark. While devices which pull upwards, scalically, or sharpwards through the circle-of-fifths, are used to portray the light, falling-devices take us down into the darkness.

Example 7

(VS, pp. 43–4)

(We were [also] looking for the light. Just here, it is a little lighter than elsewhere, but the sea is still dark.
We shall have a storm [tonight])

Further into the same scene, as the ship is seen sailing in the darkness towards the band of light, a Phrygian device – the first of many – is introduced. The off-stage chorus is based on a chord of G, with added minor seventh. Underpinning this is a bare tritone, sounded on *tremolando* strings *sur la touche*. It is the diametrical opposite of the Lydian device used for the light in that its semitone, from the first to the second degree – the flat supertonic – pulls down to the lower note of the characteristic fifth (Example 8). As Pelléas remarks that the night falls very quickly, the chorus sing a bare tritone before the music recapitulates.

Example 8
(VS, p. 45)

(Something is leaving the port.
It must be a large ship. . .)

b) scale

Phrygian supertonic

Not only harmonic and modal devices underline the dark and light of the scene, but also the orchestration. Debussy employs the obvious parallel of high sounds for light and low sounds for darkness. As the sea swells at the phrase 'Entendez-vous la mer?. . . C'est le vent qui s'élève', many unusual effects are introduced – oboes and cor anglais in octaves; combinations of simultaneous *arco*, *tremolando* and *pizzicato* in the strings, underlined with touches of *pianissimo* timpani. Only a study of the orchestral score can show all these, but the listener can clearly perceive Debussy's portrayal of darkness and light.

For the deepening layers of darkness which are presented as the play unfolds, Debussy develops and intensifies existing ideas rather than introducing a string of new motifs. In this way the long-term development of Maeterlinck's symbolic structure is respected. In Act II scene 3, the triplets which had represented the darkness of the forest and later the gardens in Act I are retained, as are the tritones of what was the whole-tone scale. Now they are starker, often bare, or with a touch of half-diminished harmony. The springboard chord for the sinister oscillating chords portraying the darkness of the grotto is C major, the extreme opposite (in terms of the circle-of-fifths) from the 'light' key of F♯ major. This association of the note C with darkness becomes increasingly frequent. As a whole, the chords of this scene further intensify the tritonal portrayal of darkness by extending the tritonality of the whole-tone scale (based on three interlocking tritones) into the octatonic scale (based on four).[11] This, too, will further develop as the opera proceeds (Example 9).

The octatonic scale used in this way effectively combines major and minor (and in Example 9 the false-relation clash of the two is exploited). It also has the potential to combine the Lydian and Phrygian modes and thus may be exploited in several ways. In Act II scene 3 Pelléas has forgotten his lantern and thinks that the 'clarté' will be sufficient to guide them. Darkness and light are again heavily featured in the conversation. The grotto is full of 'ténèbres bleues', but by lighting a lamp one can fill the vault with stars. There is no danger, remarks Pelléas, for they will stop, the moment they no longer can see the light from the sea. ('Nous nous arrêterons au moment où nous n'apercevrons plus la lumière de la mer. . .') The eerie image of the white-haired beggars sleeping in the darkness draws a Phrygian mode from Debussy (Example 10), in direct contrast to the Lydian flood of light in Example 6.

Example 9
(VS, p. 105)

(It is so dark that the entrance to the grotto cannot be distinguished
from the rest of the night)

Version of octatonic scale from which the chords in Example 9a are
derived

Example 10

(VS, p. 111)

Example 10 (*cont.*)

(What is it?
There are. . . There are. . . (indicating the three beggars)
Yes. . . I've seen them too. . .
Let's go!. . .)

The C major–F♯ major contrast is most apparent at a moment where light and dark are again confused. Blinded by the light of Mélisande's hair, Pelléas can no longer see the light of the sky.

Example 11
(VS, p. 130)

(I can no longer see the sky through your hair)

Another case where the note C seems to be associated with darkness occurs after Mélisande has 'flooded' Pelléas with her hair. As Golaud approaches, references to the darkness (l'obscurité) increase. First of all, remarks Mélisande, her doves will lose themselves in the darkness: 'Ce sont mes colombes, Pelléas. . . Elles se perdront dans l'obscurité.' As it is realised that Golaud is approaching, the tonal centre falls to the C, now in the form of a pedal-point, while chords which seem to be dissonances *resolving* onto nearby whole-tone chords occur.

Example 12
(VS, p. 137)

(It [Mélisande's hair] is caught in the branches in the dark. Stay still! Stay still! It's dark)

The nadir of the symbolism of darkness is Act III scene 2, the scene in the castle vaults. To depict the dark, noxious air, later described by Pelléas as 'des ténèbres épaisses comme une pâte empoisonné' (thick darkness like a poisoned paste), Debussy almost exclusively uses the whole-tone scale but with the dark-key note of C as the recurrent pedal-point, and a C minor chord as the departure point (VS, p. 142). But a passage of more extreme dissonance is yet to be heard – perhaps the most extreme in the opera. The bass pedal-points on which the scene is constructed have moved upward, by way of E♭ and E♮, through the dark–light axis of C–F♯, as Pelléas realises that Golaud himself, forcing Pelléas into the dark, has control of the light (Example 13).

Example 13
(VS, p. 146)

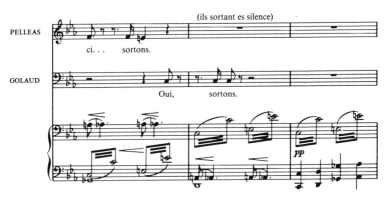

(Yes, it's the lantern. . . You see, I was moving it to throw light on the
walls. . .
It's stifling here. . . Let's go out)

After this scene the music reverts to C before moving, in the opera's second moment of emergence into the light, to an area of F♯ which now has the attendant major harmonies and the Lydian devices of the 'light' language. Admiring the roses, Pelléas remarks that it must be nearly midday and that they are already shaded by the shadow of the tower. Golaud observes to Pelléas that Geneviève and Mélisande have already sought refuge in the shade. It is at this point that Golaud delivers his warning to Pelléas not to repeat his 'children's games' with Mélisande. A Phrygian cell of three notes, descending to C, is heard on cellos, basses and bassoons. The following interlude (VS, p. 158), typically echoing and summarising contrarieties seen and to be seen, moves to the motif which first announced Pelléas and was present in the first discussions of darkness and light in Act I scene 3. A transitory *tierce de Picardie* on F♯ major throws into relief the C tonality of the next scene, now clearly Phrygian with its D♭, which is to begin the scene where Golaud forces Yniold to spy on Pelléas and Mélisande. This repetition of a tonal centre of C, combined with a Phrygian device, links the scene tonally with his earlier forcing of Pelléas to 'smell the stench of death'.

Our feeling from these two scenes is perhaps that Golaud understands something about darkness and light that the other characters do not, for in this scene, Yniold's mention of Pelléas and Mélisande 'continually weeping in the darkness' particularly enrages Golaud, and Yniold has already suggested that they quarrel about the light. The symbolism extends to the level of the *mise-en-scène*, for as Yniold reminds Golaud of his grey hair and beard, Mélisande lights her lamp, and the music moves at once into F♯ as the stage direction reads 'The window under which they are sitting lights up for a moment and its light falls on them [Golaud and Yniold].' Yniold, too, wants to go into the light, but Golaud wishes to remain in the darkness. When Yniold is finally lifted up to the window he tells us that Pelléas and Mélisande are looking at the light. Although the scene has advanced the external action of the play in showing us Golaud's increasing jealousy, it is clear that we are witnessing an extension of the discontinuous symbolic dialogue which was first presented to us in Act I scene 3, and that we must adopt the appropriate attitude of receptivity.

In Yniold's soliloquy scene, where he has lost his golden ball and attempts to move a rock, the symbolism is pushed still further. 'The sun has gone', Yniold remarks, 'and the lambs. . . are afraid of the darkness.' As he utters 'Il n'y a plus de soleil', a sustained horn note C cuts through the texture, echoing its previous associations with the darkness, and the note returns later, now thickened with bassoons as he cries 'Oh, oh, il fait trop noir', in his penultimate line.

The briefest of interludes connects this to the final love-scene, thus approached with the idea of the young lambs going to the slaughter still resonating. Pelléas appears at once, aware now that he is playing around the snares of destiny (J'ai joué, en rêve, autour des pièges de la destinée). The first hint of 'darkness' and 'light' symbolism is accompanied by two bars of the anticipatory C♯ (though spelt in flats), here functioning strongly as a dominant of the 'light' key of F♯ (Example 14). We are at once reinstated into the circle of the 'light'

Example 14
(VS, p. 236)

(Do not stay there on the edge of the moonlight)

key. Debussy's tonal structure for the scene is in part based on recurrences of this dominant preparation which occur at the important landmarks in the text, themselves preparations for the declaration of love. Firstly, there is Pelléas's touching of Mélisande:

Example 15
(VS, p. 239)

(My poor Mélisande, I am almost afraid to touch you)

Secondly, there is Mélisande's recalling of their past times together:
(Example 16). Thirdly, there is Pelléas's question 'Do you know why
I have asked you to come here tonight?', though here, the dominant
dissolves into a half-diminished as Pelléas announces that he will be
leaving imminently (Example 17):

Example 16
(VS, p. 241)

(We came here a long time ago. I remember. . .)

Example 17
(VS, p. 242)

(It is perhaps the last time I will see you. . . I must go away for ever!)

After the declaration of love, Debussy is respectful of Maeterlinck's 'great silences of love', adding only the barest music to the couple's subsequent dialogue. It is then that the resolution into F♯, which has become the key of light and love, is fulfilled. As it moves to a passage over a dominant pedal another Lydian device is used to project Pelléas's ecstasy. In this case it is melodic rather than harmonic, with a pedal-point on C♯. It is achieved by chromatically altering the F to a double-sharp at the words 'On dirait qu'il a plu sur mon coeur'. Though not Lydian in the sense that a mode with a sharpened fourth is used over the tonic (in this case F♯), the dominant pedal-point itself acts as a temporary bass for a rising and falling transposition of the characteristic augmented fourth of the mode:

Example 18
(VS, p. 246)

(It is as if it has rained on my heart. . .)

A few bars later, a similar Lydian phrase, with the sharp fourth over the note E, is used further to portray Pelléas's ecstatic outbursts:

Example 19
(VS, p. 250)

(I have found you! I did not think that there was [such a beautiful woman on earth])

Although it was Act IV scene 4 – the act in question – that Debussy composed first, it is in the final part of this act that the harmonic fields and keys are at their least stable. Before the hand of destiny is explicitly evident from the text, it is clear from the instability of Debussy's music that Pelléas and Mélisande's declaration of love is not the final *dénouement* of the opera. A later discussion of light and dark causes the rich chords previously associated with the shade of the *tilleuls* to deliquesce into half-diminished chords. 'We are already in the shade', remarks Pelléas, 'It is too dark under this tree. Come into the light. We cannot see how happy we are.' At the final word 'heureux' we have neither Lydian devices nor keys of light. instead, the half-diminished language of Mélisande's *tristesse* infuses the harmony. A few bars later, after the last, now momentary and unresolved, hint of F♯ major, Mélisande, the 'forewarned', remarks 'Si, si, je suis heureuse, mais je suis triste. . .' (Yes, yes, I am happy, but I am sad. . .); and at once the noise of the closing of the castle gates is heard. Paradoxes and opposites abound in text and music from here onwards. 'Il est trop tard', cries Pelléas. 'Tant mieux!' answers Mélisande (It is too late – So much the better!). Just as C♯ dominants prepared for the F♯ major beginning of the love-scene, dominants of the 'dark' key accompany this exchange, the resolution (in C major) occurring a few bars later as the couple move into the darkness: 'Ah! qu'il fait beau dans les ténèbres!' The darkness is now of a dual significance. Not only is it a haven for the declared love of the hopeless pair, but in the very next bar Golaud makes his presence felt, bringing with him the inevitable threat of a violent retribution. What was the initial love-scene theme in F♯ major is now heard in the 'dark' key of C major (VS, p. 258).

As Golaud falls on Pelléas with his sword, a highlighted, but as yet unrepeated, key from the first 'light and dark' scene (Act I scene 3) is heard. At the first mention of the darkness of the sea, contrasting with the light for which everyone was searching, a sustained G♯ minor wind chord had been heard, contrasting with the scintillating *tremolandi* of the 'clarté' (see Example 7, VS, p. 44). Two bars later it had portrayed the threat of the storm. Is it fortuitous that the symbolic tempest of that scene erupts in reality in the same key at this point in the opera (VS, pp. 266–7)?

The pall of darkness which hangs over the last act of the opera is at once announced by an intensification of the Phrygian and octatonic elements which have been developing throughout the opera. By the time of Pelléas's forebodings at the beginning of the final love-scene, Mélisande's theme is itself completely infused with this scale, and the five notes of the opening of Act V are drawn from the same mode. In the following example only the A in the vocal part does not belong to an octatonic scale of which the first two notes are G♯ and B♭, thus Mélisande's theme, and its harmonic field are totally octatonic, absorbing the quadruple tritonic tension of that scale:

Example 20

(VS, p. 235)

(And I have not yet looked at her look. . .)

Dominants of the 'dark' key of C accompany Arkël's references to Mélisande's sleep, while irresolute dominants of the 'light' key are used as Mélisande asks whether the sun is setting. Later, as she is blinded by the evening sun, a hint of the Lydian scale of E♭ remains (VS, p. 279). The 'great window' has been opened, and Mélisande does not wish it to be closed until the sun has gone down to the depths of the sea. Her final reference to the light is still accompanied by the C♯ dominant of the 'light' key, but it now has a new, Lombardic rhythm buried within, perhaps signifying the onset of winter to which she alludes. A similar rhythm, we may recall, is later used not only for Debussy's 'winter' *Prélude* 'Des pas sur la neige' (Footsteps in the snow) but also is a key rhythm in 'La mer', and 'Sirènes' from the 'Nocturnes' for orchestra. The associations with winter and the sea seem to have been deeply ingrained (Example 21).

This is the effective end of the light–dark symbolism within the play, though not of the conflicts of Debussy's musical structure by which it is mirrored. There is a further reference to the 'light' key, expressing a degree of hope as Arkël shows Mélisande that he can look after the child (VS, p. 298). Chromatically descending motifs, Phrygian devices, whole-tone passages and octatonic fragments

Example 21
(VS, pp. 295–6)

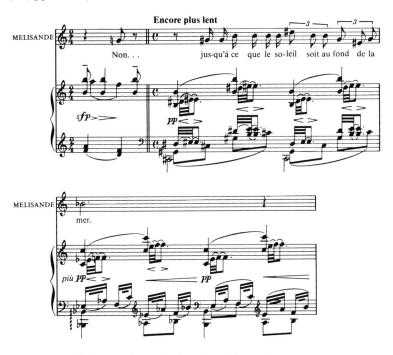

(No, not until the sun is in the depths of the sea)

continue to permeate the scene. Interspersed with them are preparations for the final resolution into a key which, in its own right, has
barely featured in the entire opera: C♯ major. The overall tonal
progression of the opera is thus of a progression sharpward (through
the circle-of-fifths) towards this, the sharpest key, highlighting the
sharp key of F♯ (one sharp less) and finally pushing one key further.

Preparation for the resolution into this key is made in three principal ways during the final act. Firstly, the notes are contained within
the opening cell, drawn from the octatonic scale, several times
repeated at its original pitch. Secondly, moments of the dominant
seventh of the final key of C♯ occur at various points during the
scene. These preparations bring to the fore certain telling statements uttered by Mélisande. The first accompanies her response to
Golaud's question asking whether or not he pardons her. It ends on

the dominant of the resolution-key of C♯ (Example 22). Precisely the same preparation occurs as Mélisande asks whether she is going to die (VS, p. 290).

Example 22

(VS, p. 282)

(Yes, yes, I forgive you. . .)

During Arkël's statements which immediately precede the end of the opera, G♯s become more frequent in the bass. As he reflects on her life, 'C'était un petit être si tranquille', her motif is heard over a dominant preparation for the final cadence, and the bars immediately preceding the final chord of C♯ also begin with a conventional dominant.

The third way of leading to the final chord of C♯ is via the note C, already seen as a crucial note and tonal centre, and enharmonically the leading note of the resolution-key. Appropriately, several motifs in the final act centre on this note, already associated with the dark. They include Mélisande's own motif (VS, pp. 292–3), and the long section where the servants silently enter the room; a scene ending on a C–D diad – the upper and lower leading-notes of the final C♯ (VS, p. 299, penultimate bar). The last motif too, is based on C, resolving on to the final C♯. It is led to by a previous statement on F, but harmonised with a G, its own dominant. The progress to the final note is thus prepared (VS, pp. 309–10).

The final C♯ passage itself resolves another contrariety in the modal scheme, for both Phrygian descent and Lydian ascent act upon the C♯ which persists in every bar of the postlude. A descending phrase is heard first and repeated, approaching the C♯ through the flattened supertonic – the characteristic Phrygian note – of D♮ (Example 23).

Example 23
(VS, p. 310)

After some deliberation, Debussy chooses a Lydian approach to the final chord. In a letter to Henri Lerolle of June 1895, a more conventional ending was given (Example 24a). If we assume it represented Debussy's thoughts at that time, it shows that the Lydian ending, with its F double-sharp and the penultimate bar repeated (Example 24b), was later added, at some time when the opera was closer to its final form.[12] For whatever reason the original version was altered, Debussy's final version relates more nearly to a resolution of the Lydian and Phrygian scales which we have seen to play an

Example 24

1895 ending

a)

Example 24 (*cont.*)

Final ending

b)

important part in paralleling the most important and fundamental symbolic plane of Maeterlinck's drama.

   Thus far the connections drawn have concentrated exclusively upon certain relationships between keys and modes and their associations with symbols, characters and events in the opera as it stands. No attempt has been made to discover the stage in Debussy's conception of the opera at which these key-schemes became conscious, and how he projected and altered them in the various stages of composition. A fascinating section of an article by Carolyn Abbate[13] throws some light on this question. Study of the 'Meyer' manuscript drafts for Act V leads her to conclude that the whole of this act 'evolved backwards from the final cadence', thus the 'goal' key of C♯ seems to have been clear in the composer's mind from the outset. In the second folio of the manuscript,[14] Mélisande's initial vocal entrance in Act IV scene 4 is first drafted. One of the composer's shorthand methods for indicating key-changes in the early drafts (especially where the labour of writing out a complicated key-signature can be by-passed) is simply to write out the name of the new tonality. At this point in the manuscript is a clear 'Fa ♯'. After employing this tonality in association with Mélisande in this final love-scene (the first Debussy composed), he continued to do so in a similar way throughout the composition of the opera. Carolyn Abbate also notes E♭ (or D♯) as a complementary key to the F♯, used for Pelléas's responses to Mélisande's F♯ major leads. This key, we may remember, alternated with the F♯ in the crucial scene of Act I scene 3, where the foundations of key-association were laid (Example 25).

Having traced clear key-associations in the early sketches, Carolyn Abbate assesses Debussy's subsequent methods as regards the refine-

Example 25

(VS, pp. 41–2)

Example 25 (*cont.*)

GENEVIEVE

Ah!   c'est Pellé - as. . .

([You will have the light] of the sea.
There is a noise underneath us. . .
Yes, someone is coming up towards us. . . Ah! it's Pelléas. . .)

ment of the key system he has established: 'Once Debussy allowed
textual imagery to control a pattern of tonalities, then the important
subsequent revisions and recompositions, in all the drafts for the
scene, took the form of defusing the reflexive, sometimes even trivial,
musical responses to the text. . . Put another way, Debussy was
obscuring the traces of the system.'[15]

Whether this is the case, or whether, as Marie Rolf has suggested,[16] these obscurities were deliberate attempts to reflect the
ironic twists of Maeterlinck's play, *Pelléas* was not Debussy's first
attempt at underpinning an opera with a scheme of two tritonally
opposed keys to depict dramatic conflict. In his earlier opera *Rodrigue et Chimène* (as yet unpublished), he had blatantly used precisely the contrast of C and F♯ that we have observed in *Pelléas*.
It occurs both harmonically and melodically in the opening Prelude.
In Example 26, one imagines the upper stave to represent brass
instruments cutting through a fully orchestrated texture of strings
and wind.

Whatever the similarities, *Rodrigue et Chimène* was in concept a
traditional opera where *Pelléas* was revolutionary. But there can be
little doubt that although Debussy was ultimately dissatisfied with
it, *Rodrigue et Chimène* was an important milestone in the composer's assimilation of the techniques involved in writing a large-
scale dramatic work. Here, faced with a hack libretto blatantly
devoid of poetry, heavy with over-obvious images and rhymes,
Debussy must have reinforced his conviction that his ideals lay in a

Example 26 Prelude to *Rodrigue et Chimène*

work where refined verbal expression would be complemented by a subtlety of musical expression. If, by the time of *Pelléas*, Debussy was 'covering his tracks' by disguising too-easily perceived key-devices, it was very possibly his failure with *Rodrigue et Chimène* that persuaded him of the necessity to avoid blatant methods at all costs.

Clearly, though, a key-scheme, which one might justifiably put forward as another Wagnerian feature, was in Debussy's mind from an early stage in the gestation of *Pelléas*. The two overall features of this scheme seem to have been present from the outset – the sharp-ward procedure to a 'goal' key of C♯, and the use of keys from the opposite side of the circle-of-fifths to represent forces pulling against this forward progression. We may express the forces represented by this tonal conflict in different ways – life and death, love and venge-ance, hope and failure. Maeterlinck's way, however, resided in the elemental forces of darkness and light. Whatever links a large-scale harmonic analysis may reveal, the overall resolution is into a key-area that has hardly been asserted as a tonic at any point in the opera.

6 *Pelléas in performance I – a history*

BY ROGER NICHOLS

When Debussy had put the finishing touches to his initial version of the opera in August 1895, he thought immediately of its future. 'Now at once my anxiety begins', he wrote to Henri Lerolle; 'how will the world behave towards these two poor creatures?' Nearly seven years were to pass before he had his first answer to that question, but during that time *Pelléas* led a fairly eventful underground existence.

There were two groups of people whose support Debussy was above all anxious to secure: friends, and influential members of the Parisian musical establishment. It was unfortunate for him that, partly because he was young and partly because he was no great respecter of authority, these two groups barely overlapped. The mobilisation of friends like Raymond Bonheur, Robert Godet, Etienne Dupin and Pierre Louÿs could therefore be seen, quite apart from the pleasure it afforded of hearing their good opinions, as merely a tentative step towards the other, more directly relevant, objective.

Friends like these also helped sustain Debussy's morale, either when he began to doubt the viability of his opera or when he began simply to give up hope of ever seeing it performed. Pierre Louÿs, for example, who had organised a private reading *autour du piano* of scenes from *Pelléas* as early as May 1894, was urging Debussy eighteen months later to make what Louÿs called 'a symphonic suite' from the opera for performance in London.[1] This referred to an offer made to Debussy by the actress Mrs Patrick Campbell to write incidental music for performances of the Maeterlinck play; Debussy refused and the commission was passed on to Fauré. In the autumn of 1896 Ysaÿe suggested the performance of extracts from the opera in the concert hall. Debussy again refused, saying 'If this work has any merit, it lies above all in the connection between the movement on stage and the movement in the music. . . Pelléas and Mélisande must appear as they are. People will have to take them or leave them

140

and, if there has to be a fight, it will be worthwhile.'[2] In both cases Louÿs and Ysaÿe seem only to have strengthened the composer's contrary resolve by their well-meaning suggestions. Later, Louÿs was moved by a desperate letter from Debussy to offer straightforward encouragement: 'Whatever troubles you may have, this thought must dominate everything: you must continue with your work, and you must get it known. . . It's not by giving music lessons that you will be assured of a livelihood, it's by doing everything to get *Pelléas* performed. You think of practical negotiations as beneath you, but I think you may be mistaken. . .'[3]

No doubt shyness played a part in Debussy's unwillingness to say the right things to the right people, in addition to his fears about how the world would behave towards his creation. The private performance for a small company of friends, with Debussy singing each role in turn, was as public an exposure of *Pelléas* as he really felt inclined to give.[4] His reticence had its advantages. Certainly, when *Pelléas* was finally performed no one could accuse him of having indulged in machinations or self-seeking publicity. Instead, the work was seen to have arrived simply from the force of enthusiasm travelling along the underground network and, as Debussy had perhaps always hoped and expected, from an influential person eventually being caught up by the current. This was André Messager, who had risen to fame in the 1890s with light operas like *La Basoche*, *Les P'tites Michu* and *Véronique*, and who had been appointed chief conductor and musical director of the Opéra-Comique when the new building opened in 1898. He had admired Debussy's music since hearing *La Damoiselle élue* in 1893, and it was through his prompting that Albert Carré, the director of the Opéra-Comique, came to Debussy's lodgings to hear extracts from the opera, first in May 1898 and again in April 1901. On the second occasion two scenes, it appears, were enough to convince Carré, and on 3 May he sent Debussy his written promise to perform *Pelléas* the following season.

The first of Debussy's problems was not long in arriving. Even if he and Carré had not yet applied their minds to matters of casting, Maeterlinck had. Specifically, he wanted his mistress Georgette Leblanc for the part of Mélisande. According to Leblanc, Debussy was delighted with the idea and they had four or five rehearsals.[5] Even so, when the cast list was announced in *Le Ménestrel* on 29 December the part of Mélisande had been given to the young Scot-

5   *Pelléas et Mélisande*, watercolour by Maurice Denis illustrating a limited edition of the play. Denis was closely associated with Debussy and illustrated the cover of the first edition of the composer's cantata *La damoiselle élue*.

tish soprano Mary Garden, and from that point on Maeterlinck's hostility to the opera was unyielding. There was also the problem of finding a boy to sing Yniold;[6] in the event the young Blondin did not join the cast until 5 March, seven weeks after rehearsals began on 13 January 1902.

These brought in their train the difficulties many a new work has had to suffer before and since: inexpertly copied parts, hostility from the orchestra, and incomprehension from some of the cast who may not have taken altogether kindly to the composer's injunction, as reported by Mary Garden, to 'forget, please, that you are singers'.[7] Patiently Messager coaxed and persuaded. Less patiently, perhaps, Debussy nonetheless involved himself in the preparations, being present for 69 days of rehearsal for the première,[8] as well as casting a critical eye over Jusseaume and Ronsin's designs – of this last activity he wrote to Carré, 'Let's hope God will support me in this new trial of strength.'[9] After the sudden demand by Messager for some of the interludes to be lengthened (see chapter 2, p. 52) came the climax of Maeterlinck's long drawn out campaign of antagonism, a letter to *Le Figaro* published on 14 April.[10] In it he complained that his choice of singer for the part of Mélisande had been ignored and that the text had suffered 'arbitrary and absurd cuts' which rendered it unintelligible, and finished by saying 'In a word, the *Pelléas* in question is a piece that is now strange to me, to which I feel almost an antipathy; and as I have been deprived of all control over my work, I am reduced to hoping that it will be an immediate and resounding flop.'

The following day's copy of *Le Figaro* carried a statement from Carré that he 'detested rumours circulating about a work before it had been given and would reply to M. Maurice Maeterlinck after the première'. But as the *Société des auteurs* had found in Carré's favour over Maeterlinck's deprivation of control, presumably Carré thought the matter was now at an end. The dress rehearsal took place on the afternoon of Monday, 28 April. The cast was:

Pelléas	Jean Périer
Golaud	Hector Dufranne
Arkël	Félix Vieuille
Yniold	Blondin
Le médecin	M. Viguié
Mélisande	Mary Garden
Geneviève	Mlle Gerville-Réache

6   Debussy's own handwritten examples illustrating an article on Pelléas published in *Le Théâtre* of 1902. Character themes are identified by the composer despite his admitted abhorrence of the leitmotif. Debussy appends the words 'Thème initial de Mélisande' to this example.

7   Jean Périer, the first Pelléas

8 Jusseaume's original set for Act II scene 1

The conductor was André Messager, the producer Albert Carré, the scene designers Lucien Jusseaume and Eugène Ronsin, the costume designer Bianchini, the stage manager Albert Vizentini, the chorus-master Henri Busser.

Some resistance to the work was to be expected from the older *habitués* of the Opéra-Comique, but no one was prepared for what did happen. 'People began to laugh. . .We hadn't the faintest idea what was going on, and we were all suddenly paralysed on the stage. Here was a drama of pure poetry and tragedy, and people were giggling and chuckling as if they were at the Folies Bergère.'[11] The cause of the hilarity was a 'programme du spectacle' distributed at the door, which gave a salaciously slanted resumé of the plot: in Act I scene 3 'Pelléas, Golaud's brother, takes a walk with his little sister-in-law in the shade of the garden. Ho, ho. . .' Hard though it is to believe that Maeterlinck would have thus sabotaged his own play, in whatever form it was being produced, Mary Garden is categoric that he was indeed the author of this pamphlet.[12] Further outbursts from the audience were provoked by Garden's foreign accent in phrases such as 'Je n'ai pas de *curages* [courage]' – 'curages' being the dirt that gets stuck in drains – and by Yniold's repeated 'petit père' in Act III scene 4. But as Marcel Dietschy reminds us,[13] the police were not called in and the performance went through from start to finish, so by Parisian standards this dress rehearsal must be classed as a fairly restrained affair.

The première took place two days later. Whereas the dress rehearsal had excited an atmosphere of levity, now the opera's supporters in the upper galleries, the 'initiates' like Ravel, Léon-Paul Fargue and Maurice Delage prominent among them, made their presence felt as they looked down in more than one sense on the frowning critics and *mélomanes* in the stalls. Messager remembered the occasion a quarter of a century later as being 'certainly not a triumph, but no longer the disaster of two days before. . .From the second performance onwards, the public remained calm and above all curious to hear this work everyone was talking about. . .The little group of admirers, Conservatoire pupils and students for the most part, grew day by day. . .'[14]

The press, predictably, was divided in its opinions. Some critics, like Henri de Curzon,[15] inveighed against the music's Impressionism: 'one can certainly find cause for discussion and dislike in the brutal realism of a Charpentier but at least it's robust, healthy music. M. Debussy's is disappointing, sickly and practically lifeless.' Others, like Eugène d'Harcourt,[16] realised something of Debussy's stature but felt he had not lived up to his abilities because of being tied to a system which involved 'sacrificing music to vague conceptions and dangerous compromises'; while Pierre Lalo wavered until worked on by Paul Dukas and others; he then, on 20 May, delivered a panegyric in *Le Temps* for which Debussy was always to remain grateful, even when Lalo later expressed serious reservations about *La mer.*

Debussy's fellow-composers were similarly divided. Dukas, a close friend, wrote a eulogistic article[17] including several swipes at the facts of operatic life: 'I don't think either M. Maeterlinck or M. Debussy was particularly well-known. Whether they are now, or whether the future has unalloyed glory in store for them, I don't know. But one has to admit neither of them has done anything to deserve it. It is unpardonable not to be aware after all this time that success in Paris is determined almost exclusively by routine, snobbery and self-advertisement.' In the other camp, the director of the Conservatoire, Théodore Dubois, forbade students of the institution to attend performances, and Saint-Saëns, Debussy's implacable enemy, claimed later on in the summer that he had not gone on holiday as usual, but was staying on in Paris 'to say nasty things about *Pelléas*'.[18]

More interesting perhaps than any of these are the opinions of Gabriel Fauré, and of one of Paris's profounder thinkers about music, Vincent d'Indy. Fauré's view of *Pelléas* was understandably coloured by his own incidental music to the play for Mrs Patrick Campbell's London performances in 1898, and we should be wrong to hold against him permanently the off-the-cuff remark quoted by the Princess Edmond de Polignac, who accompanied him to the opera's première: 'If that's music, then I've never understood what music is.'[19] A more considered opinion is to be found in a letter of early May 1902 to Albert Carré: 'I remain opposed to Debussy's procedures, but I applaud his opera nonetheless. It has given me, in more places than one, the real *frisson* of true feeling which I abandoned myself to completely!'[20] The dichotomy between Debussy's unacceptable procedures and his abandon-inducing music probably worried the 57-year-old Fauré because he knew that he himself was now too old to start rethinking his own procedures, and that his music might, as a result, be in some sense impoverished.

Vincent d'Indy was less worried about procedures. Indeed, he castigated the critics for failing to see beyond them to the heart of the opera,[21] in line with his belief that 'the worst listeners to music are those who've learnt harmony'.[22] His review, written a good month after the première, was unparalleled at the time for its insights into what was new in *Pelléas* and what was the logical outcome of tradition. The crux in understanding the opera was 'to find in *Pelléas et Mélisande* not what one had come to look for, but what the composer had intended to put in it'. But while he stressed its novelty of form and character, he was among the first to see what it owed to Wagner and, more arguably, to the *stile rappresentativo* of early seventeenth-century opera. He was also perceptive enough to be able to penetrate the work's densely symbolic texture: 'the composer has in fact simply felt and expressed *human* feelings and *human* sufferings in *human* terms, despite the outward appearance the characters present of living in a mysterious dream.'

Messager conducted the first three performances, on 30 April, 2 May and 3 May, but was then called away to Covent Garden whose musical directorship he shared with that of the Opéra-Comique. He was replaced on the rostrum by the chorus master Henri Busser, making his first appearance as conductor; and here began the first in a long litany of complaints from the composer as *Pelléas* started to deviate from its initial pattern of performance. Busser, according to Debussy,[23] 'paid no attention whatever to the singers and threw chords at their feet without the least concern for harmonic propriety', and as the run of fourteen performances approached its end in June, the composer commented to Godet[24] 'It's time it did, I may say: it's beginning to sound like a repertory opera! The singers are improvising, the orchestra's getting heavy. . .' Still, all but two of the fourteen performances made a profit so Carré billed a revival for October, when Lucien Rigaux took over as Pelléas, Jeanne Passama as Geneviève and Suzanne Dumesnil as Yniold. This last change, though contrary to Debussy's wish to have Yniold played by a boy, encouraged Carré to put back the scene with the sheep (Act IV scene 3) which had so far been omitted from all performances; 'Debussy' wrote Messager to Carré, 'will be so pleased!'[25]

From 1902 until 1914 *Pelléas* was given at the Opéra-Comique in every season except two (1905/6 and 1909/10) and reached its hundredth performance there on 25 January 1913. From letters and memoirs we get glimpses of Debussy's frustrations in his search for a *via media* between the perils of underfamiliarity and over-

9 Maggie Teyte, who took over the role of Mélisande from Mary Garden in 1908

familiarity. To Hector Dufranne, the original Golaud, he wrote on 26 October 1906: 'I hope you will forgive my irritability during the *Pelléas* rehearsals, which leads me to express myself more vigorously than I really meant to. . . You and Vieuille are almost the only two who have maintained your understanding of my artistic aims in *Pelléas*.'[26] Maggie Teyte, who took over the rôle of Mélisande from Mary Garden in 1908, relates that 'when Debussy was told of my nationality, he exclaimed: "Quoi? Encore une Ecossaise? (What? Another Scotswoman?)" This may account for his next remark, which was "I will have Mélisande as *I* want her!"'[27] One must make allowances here for a small element of soprano rivalry since, in fact, Mary Garden was the only one of the four Mélisandes known to him about whom he seems not to have made disparaging remarks. Maggie Teyte although earning his high approval by and large, was accused on one occasion at least of 'exhibiting about as much emotion as a prison door'[28] while her successor, Marguerite Carré, brought 'a furious zeal to the task of portraying Mélisande as a kind of melancholy washerwoman'.[29] Of the men, Louis Azéma (Arkël) and Ghasne (Golaud) were categorised as having 'that robust lack of understanding characteristic of the opera singer',[30] Périer was generally agreed to be getting better and better, 'the reason, I'm sure, being that he's entirely given up singing what I wrote',[31] and 'A Monsieur Boulogne [?] regularly allows you a choice of two notes with every one he sings.'[32]

The first foreign production of *Pelléas* was at the Théâtre de la Monnaie in Brussels on 9 January 1907. Debussy took an active part in the rehearsals which, like the vocal performances mentioned in the previous paragraph, fed his talent for literary venom: the bell in Act V gave a C instead of a G so that 'it sounds rather as if it's dinner time in the castle',[33] while 'the woodwind were thick and noisy, the brass on the other hand stuffed with cotton wool'.[34] But entertaining though it is for us, at a safe distance from Debussy's temper, to read the chronicle of his troubles in the staging of *Pelléas*, he tells us little about how any particular producer saw the opera or about the *mise en scène*, except when things went wrong (as in Brussels, with 'dungeons so realistic no one can get into them!'),[35] or about the work's effect on audiences. In this respect the testimony of others tends to be more illuminating.

The next foreign premières after the one in Brussels were given in Frankfurt (19 April 1907), New York (Manhattan Opera House,

19 February 1908, with the cast of the Opéra-Comique) and at
La Scala, Milan (2 April 1908, under Toscanini), all without benefit
of the composer's participation. The impact of Toscanini's performance can be gauged to some degree from two separate sources.
Edward Lockspeiser records[36] what was possibly a verbatim account
from someone who attended it: 'The audience. . . were either hostile
or indifferent. At the conclusion most of them hurried away without
either approving or condemning the work, and the cast embarrass-
ingly appeared before a mere handful of people whom Toscanini
himself applauded with the encouraging words, 'Molto intelligente,
molto intelligente!' The other source is a review by the composer
Ildebrando Pizzetti.[37] He wrote it in May, leaving time for the immediate hullabaloo to die down, of detractors condemning the opera
as 'a triumph of aberration' and of supporters moved by snobbery to
praise every new thing to the skies regardless. For Pizzetti, *Pelléas*
pointed the way that opera should go in the Latin countries – that is,
he heard in it not the least echo of Wagner, whose influence he,
(like Debussy) deplored. Apart from some reservations about the
rôle of the singers, the only criticism he had of the performance itself
was that some of the scenery was too realistic for the drama it was
serving. He felt that a designer like Gordon Craig was what the opera
really needed. Certainly, the news of the performance that reached
Debussy in Paris was that *Pelléas* in Milan had been a success after
some demonstrations of discontent during Act III scene 2 (the scene
in the vaults).[38]

   The opera had three more foreign premières in 1908, in Prague
(Czech première: 28 September), in Munich (9 October) and in
Berlin (6 November), and two more in 1909, at the Teatro Costanzi in
Rome (28 March) and at Covent Garden (English première: 21 May).
A description of the Rome performance was given by a critic for the
Frankfurter Zeitung:[39] 'It was a catastrophe of sorts. The audience
started talking loudly and exchanging sarcastic remarks, and it soon
became impossible to hear a single note of the music. At the end, the
orchestra counter-demonstrated by wildly cheering the conductor.'
Even if the conservatism of Italian opera audiences is hardly news,
this was an interesting reversal of the opera's reception in Paris where
it was to a large extent those 'who had not learnt harmony' who
supported it against the cavils of the critics and professionals.

   The opera's English première at Covent Garden was the second
and last foreign production in which the composer played any

part. There were the usual frustrations – of the producer, Debussy wrote 'I've rarely had such a strong desire to kill anybody'[40] – but the orchestra actually earned his approval, as did the conductor Cleofonte Campanini, who 'understands the work fairly well – a little too extrovert – but at least it's warm and alive'.[41] Even so, the state of the dress rehearsal was not such as to override Debussy's habitual antipathy towards attending performances of *Pelléas*, and he spent the evening in his room in the Royal Palace Hotel, Kensington.

From 1909 until the outbreak of the First World War Debussy continued to attend rehearsals at the Opéra-Comique, but otherwise he rather kept his distance from the opera. He did not go to performances, partly because he disliked the attendant publicity and partly, no doubt, because he still treasured his vision of *Pelléas* above the reality. Neither did he bombard conductors and singers with advice. If men like Pierre Monteux or D.-E. Inghelbrecht came to ask his opinion he was happy to give it, but in general he seems to have acquiesced in the fact that the future of *Pelléas* was now necessarily beyond his immediate control. As he wrote to his publisher on receiving the news that *Pelléas* was to be given at Nice and Cannes in 1912, 'I realise it's a necessary cog in the glory machine, but I'm also thinking how ridiculous such performances are where everything is brought down to the scale of the participants! (performers and public). Still, one has to put up with the things one can't change.'[42] The only performances that might just have tempted him to attend were those conducted by his friend André Caplet in London in 1913, but one of his wife's many strategic illnesses prevented him. 'Naturally, I'm very upset', he wrote to Caplet,' and have lost all hope of hearing *Pelléas* as I wrote it.'[43]

What precisely '*Pelléas* as Debussy wrote it' was remains a subject of scholarly conjecture because of his many revisions to the score, but there is no real debate over the nature of the theatrical experience it offered to those who saw it in the pre-war years. This was to a large extent escapist. Jacques Rivière, the editor of the *Nouvelle revue française*, described it as 'a miraculous world, a cherished paradise where we could escape from our troubles. . . We knew the secret door and the outside world had no more hold upon us.'[44] The highly stylised nature of Maeterlinck's text also made the opera a tempting target for spoofs. Stravinsky later remembered that 'in the intermissions of *Pelléas*, the people in the foyers were making fun of the *récit* style and intoning little sentences à la *Pelléas* to each other'.[45] Marcel Proust (who, though he never attended a performance of the opera, knew it by listening to relays on the 'théâtrophone') left among his papers a short pastiche in which, for example, the lines from Act IV scene 1 reportedly spoken by Pelléas's father, 'Tu as le visage grave et amical de ceux qui ne vivront pas longtemps' (You have the solemn, kindly expression of those who will not live long) are given a less philosophical slant as 'Vous avez, Pelléas, le visage grave et plein de larmes de ceux qui sont enrhumés pour longtemps' (You, Pelléas, have the solemn, tearful expression of those with a long-standing cold).[46]

These two qualities of being escapist and easily caricatured meant that in the brittle, post-war Parisian climate *Pelléas* could readily be written off as no longer relevant. We are told[47] that Debussy himself was becoming bored around 1914 with the naturalism of Jusseaume and Ronsin's sets and looked forward to some more imaginative *décor*. But the only change *Pelléas* underwent in the immediate post-war period was an adaptation of the rôle of Pelléas for the tenor Fernand Francell for the 1919 Opéra-Comique production, of which René Chalupt wrote, 'M. Messager conducted the work with greater perfection than ever, but the new version of the part of *Pelléas* for tenor makes one regret the old. . .'[48] The extent to which the opera was showing its age is well captured in a review by Charles Tenroc, the editor of *Le Courrier musical*, of a gala performance at the Opéra-Comique on 24 December 1920:

Debussy's dramatic inspiration makes it easy for his interpreters to express the feelings of far-away events, of undulating lines, of the softened sensibilities which belong to these evanescent, dreamlike characters. Every interpreter these days can manage such things. So much so that the shading à la Cézanne or simply the taffeta-like vocal lines are exaggerated to the detriment of the expressive vigour which the composer's palette in many places contains. Everything is misted over with a touching but plaintive charm, and muffled by an intimate vapour to the point of being depressing. We can smell the perfume of roses, but they're dried flowers now. In a word, the piece no longer has the spark of youth.[49]

Although this may recall the aesthetic stance of Jean Cocteau in *Le coq et l'Harlequin* ('Enough of clouds, waves, aquariums, water nymphs and nocturnal perfumes'), Tenroc was a mature critic, quite capable of making up his own mind, and his strictures concern a problem at the heart of *Pelléas*, that of charting a course between over-refinement on one hand and bluster on the other. The ossified condition of *Pelléas* in the 1920s was not improved, either, by Marguerite Carré's determined tenure of the part of Mélisande. If she gave it the allure of 'a melancholy washerwoman' in 1913, we have no reason to suppose that her interpretation was transformed by age, even if her husband's standing in the musical world did much to inhibit uncomplimentary notices.

The first move towards any reinterpretation of *Pelléas* came at the Opéra-Comique in January 1930 with the new *décor* by Valdo-Barbey. Three years earlier Valdo-Barbey had expressed surprise that *Pelléas* should still be presented in a setting 'analogous to those of *Faust, Rigoletto, Samson et Dalila* and other operatic favourites'.[50] He explained that he would like to follow the 'true admirers of *Pelléas*' who had come to regard it as a work of pure classicism, thus suggesting that there was a body of opinion to support Tenroc's unsympathetic view of the current performing style. In particular Valdo-Barbey insisted that the *décor* must be unfussy. 'In this work' he wrote, 'more than in any other it is essential not to distract the attention from the words and the music' and to this end the designer must concentrate that attention 'on the mathematical point of the scene'. In Act I scene 2, for example, where Geneviève reads out Golaud's letter, 'it is towards the *window* that all the lines of the scenery must converge. . . the scenery all round it must be *suggested* rather than spelt out by useless decorative exactitude'. This emphasis on the symbolic import of natural objects – the trees, the window, the bed, the terrace, the tower, the vaults – was at one with Maeterlinck's verbal technique, which similarly infuses mundane entities with unusual significance, just as the blend of nuances of lighting with a solid frame for the action and firmly held backcloths matched both the delicacy and the strength of Debussy's music. No doubt this was Valdo-Barbey's intention, but at least one souvenir of what he actually produced relates less to such subtleties than to his use of colour: 'A Mediterranean setting, with the castle of Allemonde installed on the Côte d'Azur, bright sunlight, white walls, dark blue sea. And in the middle of it all M. Roger Bourdin in a crimson doublet.'[51]

Bourdin had taken over the rôle of Pelléas for the 1927 revival, when Mary Garden and Hector Dufranne returned to join Félix Vieuille. Dufranne and Vieuille were still singing their original rôles in the 1932 revival, thereby further reinforcing the 'timeless' aspect of the opera despite Valdo-Barbey's efforts at renewal. In general

Pelléas fared even less well in the 1930s than it had in the 1920s. There were several revivals at the Opéra-Comique between 1930 and 1942 but of the new singers only Henri Etcheverry as Golaud made any impact, while in 1933 Inghelbrecht wrote of a contemporary conductor telling his theatre directors that *Pelléas* 'could be enjoyed only by snobs and pederasts'.[52] Perhaps the situation might have been improved if *Pelléas* had been an opera which could be performed by amateurs, who can sometimes make up in enthusiasm and imagination for what they lack in technique. As it was, the performance at the Théâtre des Champs-Elysées on 20 June 1933 stood as an awful warning: Mme Ganna Walska, supported by the dollars of her American industrialist husband, rendered Mélisande to such effect that with the death of Pelléas (in the person of Pierre Bernac) the audience abandoned hope, and Mélisande's own demise was played to a totally empty house.

Outside France the situation was no better. In the whole decade there were only two productions at Covent Garden: in 1930 with Bourdin, Maggie Teyte and John Brownlee, and in 1937 with Golaud being played by Vanni-Marcoux who had sung Arkël at the English première in 1909; and only one at the New York Metropolitan, in 1933 with Ezio Pinza as Golaud. Neither Rome nor Milan heard the opera at all during the 1930s. Edward J. Dent, writing in 1940, could truthfully say '*Pelléas et Mélisande* seems to have fallen into complete oblivion', giving as a reason that 'the strain of listening to this rather long opera, almost all in subdued tones, never knowing what the harmonies of the music are, never knowing what the characters are really supposed to be thinking and doing. . . is to some people unbearable'.[53]

With the outbreak of war and the German occupation of Paris in June 1940, the French might seem to have had other things on their mind than the revival of a 40-year-old opera. But it would not be going too far to say that at the Opéra-Comique on 22 May 1942 *Pelléas et Mélisande* was not just revived but reborn. It is not easy to put one's finger on the reasons with any certainty. The conductor, Roger Desormière, was not a Debussy specialist, and apart from Etcheverry as Golaud and C. Gaudel as Yniold all the artists were new to their rôles. Neither the production nor the *décor* (by P. Lavalley) aimed at being revolutionary, and on paper one would put this down as just another of the 437 performances given at the Opéra-Comique between 1902 and 1970. That this was emphatically not

10 Irène Joachim as Mélisande and Louis Guénot as Arkël in the 1942
Opéra-Comique production

11 One of Valentine Hugo's designs for the 1947 Opéra-Comique production

the case may have been due to any or all of four factors. Firstly, to the casting of the two title rôles – Jacques Jansen as Pelléas and Irène Joachim as Mélisande. Neither had what one would call a 'great' voice. Instead they were both intelligent, dedicated and profoundly musical, perhaps what the composer had in mind when he told the original cast to forget that they were singers. . .Secondly, advice was on hand not only from Georges Viseur, who had worked as a repetiteur on the original production, but also from Mary Garden, who was a friend of Irène Joachim's family. Thirdly, the opportunity to work on this most French of French masterpieces allowed a clear conscience to performers who elsewhere were continually beset by doubts as to what did or did not constitute collaboration. And, last but not least, the imprisonment of Mélisande's free spirit in the gloom of the castle held obvious parallels (Allemonde as Allemagne?).

Whatever the reasons, this 1942 production (four members of which appear on the first complete recording of the opera, made in that year) answered Charles Tenroc's criticism in finding the 'spark of youth' that had been missing, and Jansen and Joachim were the Pelléas and Mélisande for a whole generation of opera-goers, last appearing together at the Opéra-Comique in 1955.

The next attempt at renewal was more radical, in the sets designed by Valentine Hugo for the Opéra-Comique production of 1947. These caused a furore among audiences and performers alike because they were the first to explore a symbolism that bore no relation whatever, as Valdo-Barbey's had done, to the material objects of the drama. The curtain, lowered for the interludes, was painted with what one critic called 'a madman's face and a twisted hand undulating in arabesques of gelatinous ectoplasm',[54] while Act I opened on a forest without trees and the terrace of the castle was dominated by an enormous spider's web. This underlining of the opera's kinship with 'the theatre of cruelty' was understandably resented by a public only just recovering from Nazi occupation, and Debussy's heir, Mme Gaston de Tinan, tried to have the production banned, the first of several such post-war attempts. Some years later, however, the influential critic Claude Rostand came to its defence, claiming that of all the *Pelléas* designers whose work he had seen 'only Valentine Hugo came close to the truth, but her intentions were totally destroyed by the efforts of the Opéra-Comique work-shop, by those responsible for the lighting, by the production and

12 Jacqueline Brumaire as Mélisande, Pierre Mollet as Pelléas and Solange Michel as Geneviève in André Boll's 1959 Opéra-Comique production

by the hostility of some of the singers.'[55] 'Hostility' was perhaps understandable from that quarter, since the set had to be simplified merely so that the singers could find some space to act in, but Mme Joachim agrees[56] that the lighting left much to be desired. This aspect seems to have been improved upon when the production came to Covent Garden in June 1949, even if not enough to please the reviewer from *The Musical Times*, who also complained about two other areas of notorious difficulty: 'Mélisande's hair (Act III scene 1) belonged to parody – such an outrageous profusion of tow or jute, like nothing Mélisande had hitherto been wearing. The child Yniold was represented by a well-grown young woman in bouncing spirits. Violent, ruddy light shone at midnight and in caves.' The sets, however, had by now been toned down to such an extent that he found them 'well-worn and rather wishy-washy'.[57]

There was therefore relief in many quarters when the Opéra-Comique revival of 1952 turned to a reconstitution of Jusseaume's sets which were familiar and easy to work with and, by their naturalism, seemed to be aimed at emphasising that 'the frenetic search for detailed symbols is Symbolism's most bitter enemy'.[58] But now that Mme Hugo had at least broken the ice, producers and designers from the mid-1950s onwards began to approach *Pelléas* rather more imaginatively, some of them at least being careful to remember that singers do have to move and make themselves heard. In 1955 André Boll designed the opera for two performances by the Wagner Society of Amsterdam, and these sets were transferred to the Opéra-Comique for Boll's 1959 production, conducted by Inghelbrecht, with Pierre Mollet as Pelléas and Jacqueline Brumaire as Mélisande. Pierre Dominique remembered the set as consisting of 'several cubes of pseudo-cement. . . the action taking place between the buffers and the public conveniences on some suburban railway platform'.[59] This was not so much the theatre of cruelty as the theatre of brutality, deliberately demystifying (and demistifying) the opera and presenting it as a contemporary story. The overall problem, though, was that under Inghelbrecht's exacting baton the music remained firmly in the traditional mould.

A rethinking of the total opera on modern lines was not to come for another ten years. In the meantime, 1962, the centenary of Debussy's birth, was marked by *Pelléas* performances worldwide. Since 1942 the Opéra-Comique production had travelled extensively on the continent and in Britain, almost absolving foreign opera houses from the duty of mounting their own performances. At the New York Metropolitan in 1959, Victoria de los Angeles had sung Mélisande with George London as Golaud, but on this side of the Atlantic only an occasional non-French name interrupted the roster (such as Elisabeth Schwarzkopf as Mélisande at La Scala in 1953, under de Sabata's baton). The 1962 productions to a large extent broke with this pattern, and indeed Paris's own centenary version only just squeezed into the centenary year (on 14 December), some ten months after the opera had been given in Austria, Germany, Italy, England, the U.S.A., Brussels, Buenos Aires and (more humiliating still) by French provincial theatres in Lyons, Strasbourg, Marseilles and Metz. As so often in Paris, the problems were political rather than musical, stemming mainly from a quarrel between André Malraux and the administrator of the two opera houses as to whether *Pelléas* should be moved from the Opéra-Comique to the Opéra. In the event, it was given at the Opéra-Comique under Manuel Rosenthal, with Denise Duval as Mélisande, Henri Gui as Pelléas and Gérard Souzay as Golaud, but haste and ill-temper took their toll, and Rosenthal's vigorous conducting was not relished by some of the old guard.

Outside Paris, Ansermet conducted a French cast at the Rome Opera and Serge Baudo an international one at La Scala, but the most interesting productions took place in the French provinces, at Lyon and Marseille. The Lyon version was produced by Louis Erlo, a disciple of Wieland Wagner, and marked the introduction of the greatly simplified, indeed stark, settings characteristic of Bayreuth at that period. The problem of Mélisande's hair falling from the tower was solved simply by omission, leaving Pelléas to bring off some awkward make-believe, but Poulenc for one liked the production, saying that the business with the hair had always made him uncomfortable. Once again Mme de Tinan entered the lists to try and ban the production (though again unavailingly) but, whatever the level of its success or failure, the entry of a Wagnerian element into the history of *Pelléas* performance was a pointer to the future and, perhaps, an indication that Debussy's comments about his own work, while never to be ignored, should not necessarily be taken at their face value.

The Marseille version (which went on to Metz and Strasbourg and in 1963 replaced the centenary production at the Opéra-Comique) was designed by Jean Cocteau, who claimed to have based his sketches on childhood memories of the 1902 production (he was not quite 13 at the time), working 'quickly and with my eyes almost closed'.[60] The designs were painted on gauzes in large, black outlines. The Jusseaume/Ronsin originals were recognisably a basis but one critic, while regarding the *décor* as 'a very acceptable modernisation of the traditional sets', found it 'a little cold, without much atmosphere'.[61] The critic Jean Hamon was rather more vigorous. For him the general ugliness of the production was exemplified in 'the two drop curtains, one of which seems to have escaped from a publicity poster for St Tropez, the scenery for the well (a baroque irrelevance), as well as that for the bedroom which has no poetic mystery about it. Who will give us a *Pelléas* in which the *décor* is simply suggested by lighting and drapes? Who will efface himself to leave room for the dream? M. Cocteau is too egocentric for that.'[62]

This was not, of course, the first time Cocteau found himself accused of egocentricity, but to talk of a designer 'effacing himself' and of 'leaving room for the dream' merely went to the other extreme from an over-profusion of symbols, allowing the audience to bask in the music without involving themselves in the drama. Cocteau's treatment of the original sets as part of the collective unconscious of twentieth-century opera-goers seems, in any case, less egocentric than an intelligent acceptance of fact, while the absence of atmosphere or mystery, deplored by the two critics above, was in part due to Cocteau's inimitable way with line, from which a certain sardonic objectivity was rarely absent.

The performance history of *Pelléas*, as outlined so far, has been concerned almost entirely with the *décor*, for the simple reason that no thoroughgoing attempts were made in nearly 70 years either to reinterpret the drama or to find a new approach to Debussy's score. Whether this reflected the supreme excellence of the established tradition or plain idleness on the part of producers and conductors must remain a matter of conjecture, but certainly the first really new approach to the music, when it did come, made a considerable stir.

The occasion was the 1969 Covent Garden production conducted by Pierre Boulez and produced by Vaclav Kaslik with *décor* by Joseph Svoboda. Boulez had submitted the '*Pelléas* tradition' to unsentimental scrutiny and had not been impressed with what he found. In one of the most perceptive of all articles about this work he gave his opinion that it was 'the very height of nonsense to associate this opera with a kind of celestial boredom, a pale, remote,

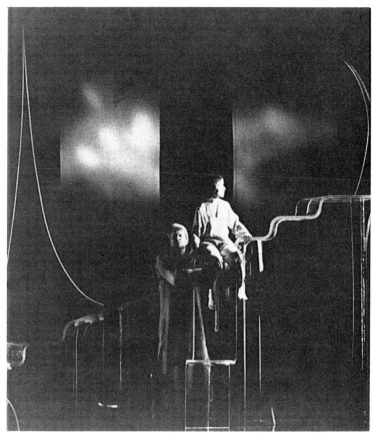

13   Frantz Petri as Golaud and Elisabeth Conquet as Yniold in Louis Erlo's
1972 production at the Opéra de Lyon

"distinguished" poetry and an imagination that is not so much exquisite as tired, even exhausted. People who use words like "mystery" or "dream" when speaking of *Pelléas* are in fact emptying them of all real significance and indulging in an imagery that is insipid, bland, mock-modest, and in fact plain silly.'[63] Boulez's determination to avoid 'celestial boredom' led him, not to *a priori* posturing or displays of egocentricity, but to a re-examination of the score, which convinced him that a faithful reading allowed for greater contrasts of dynamics, tempo and mood than tradition had countenanced. Critics retorted that he had Wagnerised Debussy; to which Boulez replied in turn that Debussy was already Wagnerised (despite the composer's own protestations) and that the vocabulary of *Pelléas* was deeply indebted to that of *Parsifal* – a thesis which, though amply documented since,[64] was in 1969 fairly close to being heretical. Further details of Boulez's approach find a place in the following chapter, but its historical importance can be compared with that of Valentine Hugo's 1947 *décor*: it released the music (and hence, to a large extent, the drama) from a tradition whose value can be judged more accurately from a critical distance than from a blindly dependent proximity.

The Opéra-Comique made no attempt to come to terms with Boulez's vision – their 1969 production, revived the following year, saw Jacques Jansen both playing Pelléas and producing, with recreations of Jusseaume's sets – but the innovative spirit has not been lacking elsewhere, notably in the productions of Jorge Lavelli at the Paris Opéra in 1977, of Harry Kupfer at the London Coliseum in 1981, and most recently in the 'authentic' *Pelléas* conducted by John Eliot Gardiner at Lyon in 1985.

Rumours began to circulate about Lavelli's production some months before it appeared in March 1977, the work's first performance at the Paris Opéra. Mélisande was supposed to be wearing blue jeans, it was to be set in a replica of a Métro station. . . and Mme de Tinan was on the warpath once more. In the event the most unpopular element was Maazel's conducting, while Lavelli's thoughtful reconsideration of what was and was not essential to an understanding of the drama cleared away a good deal of dead wood. He stressed the strength of Debussy's dramatic intuitions and 'an implacable dynamic which is motivated by the developing relationships between the characters'.[65] The surrounding scenery was of secondary importance to the vitality and interest of the characters themselves, so that for the tower scene of Act III scene 1 Mélisande stood behind a simple, high-backed chair. The castle was omnipresent but only in the form of a maquette three metres high, and the sense of vertigo essential to the vault scene was captured by suspending a walkway from one side of the stage to the other. At the very end of the opera the castle was entirely surrounded by water: 'Mélisande lies on her bed like a little boat lost on the ocean; she is returning to nature.' Perhaps Lavelli's most striking innovation was to leave the curtain up throughout the performance and have the props moved in full sight of the audience by women in black who then reappeared in the final scene as the castle servants, 'silent, distant witnesses of situations ritually prepared by them' – an economical way both of demystifying the action and of embodying the malignant fate which seems to lie in wait for the characters' best intentions. It also did something towards restoring the unity weakened by Debussy in omitting the scene with the servants at the very start of the play.

A more immediate symbol of fate was provided in Harry Kupfer's production at the London Coliseum in 1981 by a large, black bird (Poe's raven?) which hovered over the stage. Kupfer had already used the bird in a production in Dresden in 1978 (the opera's première in that city). There it loomed over romantic ruins, but for London the ruins were replaced by two brightly lit, movable greenhouses, an abstract setting more in keeping with Kupfer's view of *Pelléas* as less a fairy story than an allegory whose 'atmosphere is very close to Thomas Mann's *Der Zauberberg* (The Magic Mountain), with its metaphors of the illness of the time and its men and women reluctant to leave the isolation of the sanatorium.'[66] Kupfer's most radical departures from tradition were to dispense with all naturalistic props (except a small drinking-fountain 'such as one might find in a motel lobby'[67] clipped on to the side of one of the greenhouses), to imprison Arkël in a wheelchair and, at the end of the opera, to lower the black bird on to the adult characters, leaving Yniold to come towards the footlights with Mélisande's baby in his arms. The London critics were sharply divided between expressions of enthusiasm and outrage, Peter Conrad approving Kupfer's practice of 'bringing works forward into a future which they may not have known about but which they predict and indirectly cause',[68] while Felix Aprahamian lamented that those responsible 'had read too much. Not, unfortunately, the play or the score'.[69] But the orchestral playing under Mark Elder was widely praised, as in general was

14 Eilene Hannan as Mélisande and Robert Dean as Pelléas, with one of the 'mobile, self-propelled greenhouses', in Harry Kupfer's 1981 production at the English National Opera

Hugh Macdonald's translation, which aimed at good, clear English even where this meant altering some of Debussy's note values.[70]

The most recent performance of interest up to the time of writing has been John Eliot Gardiner's 'authentic' version, first given in Lyon in 1985 and brought to the Edinburgh Festival later that year. While the production had little to teach anybody, Gardiner's reliance on Debussy's autograph manuscript rather than on the published full score as emended in 1966, was certainly thought-provoking, his contention being that Debussy had been forced by the technical inadequacies of the Opéra-Comique and its orchestra not only to lengthen interludes against his will but to strengthen the orchestral texture, making it coarser and less intimate. The removal of the extra passages from the interludes was easily done (and had already been tried in a Camden Festival production in London in the 1960s, in one conducted by Gunther Schuller in Cambridge, Massachusetts in 1969, and in Kupfer's in 1981). But to restore Debussy's 'original' orchestration was more problematic. Indeed David Grayson, while being sympathetic to Gardiner's spirit of enterprise, has concluded that 'a performance of the manuscript score with the original interludes is a version of the opera which never existed – until 1985'.[71]

Clearly the last word has not been said on this subject, any more than it has on the essence of *Pelléas et Mélisande* and the messages it can, or even should be asked to convey. Various lines of thought as to what might go towards the making of that impossibility, 'the perfect Pelléas', are pursued in the following chapter.

7 Pelléas in performance II – ideals and enigmas

BY ROGER NICHOLS

In May 1902 Debussy gave Albert Carré, the producer of *Pelléas*, a copy of the vocal score with the dedication 'A Monsieur A. Carré, et plus encore à l'artiste qui sut créer l'atmosphère de rêve inoubliable sans laquelle *Pelléas et Mélisande* n'auraient pu vivre' (To Monsieur A. Carré, and still more to the artist who was able to create the unforgettable dream atmosphere without which *Pelléas et Mélisande* would not have come to life).[1] Debussy, then, was himself responsible to some extent for perpetuating the 'dream' tradition which surrounded *Pelléas* completely for the first thirty years of its existence and sporadically thereafter. But what exactly did Debussy understand by an 'atmosphère de rêve'?

It may be easier for us to grasp the answer if we look rather at what Debussy was reacting against: specifically, Wagner and *verismo*. Of the two he seems to have preferred Wagner, although he gave his opinion on many occasions that Wagner was a dangerous model for French composers (the debt *Pelléas* owes to Wagner, and to *Parsifal* in particular, is evidence not so much of a conscious preference as of an unconscious empathy). For *verismo* he had little time. He wrote to Messager on 29 June 1903 about the latest winner of the Prix de Rome, Raoul Laparra, 'The distinguished candidate who got the prize this year strikes me as being Leoncavallo's best pupil. Ye gods, what music! And all the artistic sensitivity of a pork-butcher.'[2] He was just as outspoken in his condemnation of Charpentier's *Louise*, in which low-life *verismo* found a home in Montmartre: 'it was a necessity, I think, for this work to be written, performed and applauded. It fills to perfection the need for vulgar beauty and imbecile art proclaimed by the many. . .'[3]

Debussy, we may remember, was talking about founding a Society for Musical Esotericism as far back as September 1893, exactly the time when he was starting work on *Pelléas*, and nothing in the ensuing nine years induced him to look more favourably on operas which

169

served up slices of 'real life'. The inverted commas are necessary because for Debussy this kind of life was not real. At least Wagner's music dramas made no pretence of aiming at reality, and in any case improbabilities in the stories had a habit of being carried over the chasm of disbelief by Wagner's genius as a composer. For Debussy, reality lay not in surface action but in interior reflection. This is what he meant by 'rêve' (possibly influenced by Mallarmé's use of the word to denote the artist's aspiration to a representation of the ideal), and it is clear from everything he wrote about *Pelléas*, as well as from the meticulous revisions he made to the score over many years, that he saw the realization of this dream as stemming only from the greatest professionalism and hard work. His complaints to Messager about Busser's conducting contain the phrase 'En somme impression vague et fuligineuse' (All in all, a vague, foggy impression),[4] which accords only too well with Busser's own view of the score, as expressed in an unpublished letter to the conductor Paul Taffanel: '*Pelléas* est assez difficile à mener sans accroc mais c'est si intéressant. . . On est baigné dans des harmonies et des sonorités. . . violettes – ne trouvez-vous pas?' (*Pelléas* is quite difficult to get through without mishap, but it's so interesting. . . One is bathed, don't you find, in violet harmonies and sounds?')[5]

The acting in these early performances would have been sharp and direct. In the words of Garry O'Connor, the biographer of Maggie Teyte, 'Various forms of naturalism flourished at the time, from an extreme Zola-esque crudity to the delicate performances of Antoine's *Théâtre Libre*, and the enchanting performances of Chekhov, and it was these daring innovatory practices in the straight theatre on which Debussy drew heavily for *Pelléas*.'[6] Maggie Teyte herself, describing the 1908 production nearly 50 years later, said 'The characters were so *strong*. It was very misty, and dark, and sombre and all that, but the *men*. . . Golaud (Dufranne), he sings and uses his voice like Klingsor.' Modern performers, she felt, had 'taken out all the blood.'[7] The naturalism of Carré's *mise en scène* can be verified from the production books still extant.[8] In Act I scene 1, for example, the well is placed downstage right and the scene begins with Mélisande crouched on its upstage edge, facing the audience, who are thus immediately in a position of dramatic superiority over Golaud – he, entering upstage left, has to find his way through the trees, so that her weeping can realistically catch him by surprise. And the realism extends further, to the gap after the words 'une petite fille qui pleure au bord de l'eau' (a young girl weeping at the water's edge): on the two *pizzicato* string chords Carré had Golaud cough to try and attract Mélisande's attention (as marked in the vocal score). This realism did not, however, in any way militate against the hallucinatory quality of the drama as a whole, because the 'atmosphère de rêve' depends far less on words or movements than on the lighting, and above all on Debussy's music.

It can fairly be stressed, then, that the true 'dreamlike' atmosphere of *Pelléas* derives not from any vagueness or sloppiness, but rather from a feeling of being inescapably enclosed. In capturing this atmosphere the accurate definition of the 'dark' and 'light' elements discussed in chapter 5 is obviously crucial – one critic has even called it 'as important as accurate note values'[9] – both in the general contrast between scenes and in the moments of particular illumination, like the wonderful F♯ major passage in Act III scene 4 where Mélisande lights the lamp in her room (fifth bar of figure 56 in the full score). It is perhaps as well, though, for any producer to bear in mind that the overall level of lighting in the Lugné-Poë production of the play, which Debussy saw in 1893, was sombre. Henry Fouquier, reviewing it in *Le Figaro*, wrote somewhat unkindly that 'the more obscure something is, the happier are the real Symbolists, who get irritated when people start understanding things', and continued: 'M. Maeterlinck's literary procedures are visually represented by the *mise en scène*. The stage is always in darkness, or in half-light at the most.'[10] Whether Debussy intended this gloom to be carried over into the operatic production is, of course, another matter, but we must imagine that his one and only experience of the play in the theatre left at least some lingering impression. He would surely have approved too of Carré bringing in Henri Rivière, who was famous in Paris for the shadow-plays he put on at the cabaret *Le Chat noir*, patronised by Debussy. The impresario Gabriel Astruc recalls in his memoirs that André Antoine offered Rivière the use of his Théâtre Libre, with 'a group of real technicians and a lighting board. . . Albert Carré, who was at this performance [of *Le juif errant*] realised its importance and later asked Rivière to oversee the lighting of *Pelléas* and of *Hänsel und Gretel*.'[11] Astruc's own view was that on a large stage much of Rivière's magic was lost. Did Debussy also instinctively carry over into his vision of *Pelléas* some of the intimacy of those *Chat noir* shadow-plays, for which he may well have provided a piano accompaniment? The evidence, at all events, suggests that imaginative lighting is historically justified, and no producer needs to feel inhibited in his use of gauzes, cycloramas, laser beams etc., as long as these are deployed in accordance with the text, and as long as the result is to concentrate and involve the eye of the spectator and to intensify the sensation of his being almost imprisoned against his will in the hermetic world of Allemonde.

The part played by Debussy's music in creating the 'atmosphère de rêve' hardly needs underlining. As Joseph Kerman wrote, 'in the play, the sense of fatality is projected first by dialogue and action, which Debussy left alone, and second – more strongly – by the poetically induced mood. Debussy could induce mood better than Maeterlinck or anyone else. By abandoning himself to mood-painting, his greatest strength, Debussy not only preserved Maeterlinck's guiding dramatic conception, but deepened it in directions unknown to verbal imagery.'[12] This deepening can therefore be left to the music (in the hands of a sympathetic conductor); dialogue and action can be allowed to remain natural and unemphatic, apart from the scenes of Golaud's violence which thereby strike us all the more powerfully, as manic deviations from the norm.

It would however be simplistic to say that the orchestra totally takes over the rôle of fate, releasing the characters to get on with their everyday concerns as best they may. As Kerman says, a sense of fatality emanates from the dialogue and does so however gently it is played. Nor is the dialogue as monochrome as it may at first appear. One of the main difficulties for a conductor has been identified by Pierre Boulez as the ability to differentiate, without loss of continuity, between the moments of reflection and of action, in passages that he terms '*modulations*, which move rapidly, sometimes with hardly a change in the vocal or instrumental style. . . This grafting of the poetic moment on to the dramatic, a sort of instantaneous efflorescence, proves to be the chief characteristic of *Pelléas*. . .'[13] Boulez mentions Mélisande's hair in this respect, pointing out that, for all its power as an erotic symbol, when Golaud uses it to drag Mélisande across the stage it 'is not a poetic transposition at one remove from reality but is clearly an instrument of torture necessary to the dramatic climax of the scene'.[14]

The older tradition of *Pelléas* conducting perhaps underplayed the importance of these 'modulations' in the interests of preserving continuity: Inghelbrecht, for example, claimed in 1933 that 'the most usual mistake made these days in playing Debussy's music is to make the instruments *enter*, as in a Saint-Saëns or Beethoven symphony, whereas for the most part they should *insinuate* themselves'.[15] The Inghelbrecht tradition was the one Boulez was determined to subvert in the 1969 Covent Garden production and in the recording he made the following year, where orchestral attack is the order of the day. We may think here of Richard Strauss's comment on being taken to see a traditional *Pelléas*, that it lacked *Schwung*, that is 'swing, flourish, verve, zest, momentum', what we might vulgarly call 'oomph'. Boulez's performance certainly has *Schwung*, but some critics have found this a small gain to set off against a loss of mystery; not that Boulez sets any store by such a thing (see chapter 6, pp. 163–4).

Personal opinions aside, there is a cyclic, repetitive, monotonous aspect to *Pelléas* that cannot be ignored, with its roots in Poe and Laforgue and branches stretching forward to Debussy's 'La Soirée dans Grenade' and the *Epigraphes antiques*, as well as to Ravel's 'Le gibet' in *Gaspard de la nuit*, to *La Valse* and *Boléro*, and to many works by Satie. This monotony forms a necessary component in what one might call *Pelléas*'s 'double life': reflection balanced by action, monotony by excitement, universal symbolism by local realism and, not least, what the characters feel, balanced by what they simultaneously say and do. Although Debussy claimed, in the letter to Edwin Evans published as an appendix to this volume, that expressing what a character feels and what he actually says are 'two contradictory operations' that cannot be simultaneously reconciled, in fact his practice flies in the face of this assertion. All we can say is that Wagner uses the technique in a far more thoroughgoing, and at times heavy-handed, manner. The tensions of this double life lie at the heart of the opera. To miss them or fumble them is to turn *Pelléas* into a one-dimensional melodrama. Maggie Teyte referred to an 'undercurrent of violence and terror' in the work[16] and it is vital that this current stays 'under' for as long as possible, heard and felt only by what is most intuitive in us. In a review of the 1981 English National Opera performance, Peter Conrad wrote that 'orchestrally, the work is Debussy's enforced stifling of Wagner. . ., dramatically. . . it's about the punitive silencing of its characters, who aren't permitted the operatic liberty to sing out loud about what they feel.'[17] Such a claustrophobic view accords well with the visual obscurity of the original 1893 production of the play. But the real point is surely that Pelléas and Mélisande and Golaud all do, eventually, admit to at least part of what they really feel – with catastrophic results.

Further light may be shed on the 'meaning' of *Pelléas* by looking at the individual characters. Within the overall 'atmosphère de rêve' two of them, Mélisande and Golaud, stand apart as being active, rather than passive like Arkël, Pelléas and Yniold (Geneviève, even if not a nonentity like the doctor or the shepherd, is still not a well enough delineated character to merit individual discussion). It may at first sight seem surprising to describe Mélisande as active, especially if the reader has in mind a vision of her as a 'princesse lointaine'. She is that, of course, but this is not to deny the 'activity' of her personality which operates on all the characters in the drama, quite apart from any intentions she may or may not have. Her activity is instinctive and unwilled. She brings love and light to the gloomy castle not as an act of mercy but because that is her nature. For all her apparent frailty, she is on the side of life. Maggie Teyte wrote that 'when Mélisande sings "Ne me touchez pas", she has to move about. You have to feel this constant nervosity. She has a kind of shimmering quality.'[18] Perhaps the sharpest comments about Mélisande's impact on the royal family of Allemonde have come from Virgil Thomson, and they are worth quoting at some length:

The characters in *Pelléas et Mélisande* are correct, well-to-do French people. They don't talk about their business much; but they own property, wear good clothes and seem to be running some sort of kingdom. They have strong passions, kind hearts, good manners and an intense family life. They understand about love and approve of it. What they cannot deal with is any vagueness on the subject. Mélisande's attractiveness for them seems to be due partly to the fact that she has no family ties (they can thus adopt her completely) and partly to the fact that her affections and her amorous tendencies are both powerful and imprecise. She fascinates them; they never know what to think of her. She keeps them guessing not through any plan but simply through the fact, astounding and incredible to them, that she has no plan, no conscious motives of any sort.

This lack of project, of intention on her part does not prevent her from acting with utter straightforwardness. Her one interest in life is being loved; she demands love from everybody and gets it. She pays willingly any price asked and suffers cheerfully all the consequences involved, early marriage, childbirth and death. She will do anything to avoid not being loved. She lies about a ring she has lost; she submits to a thorough beating from her husband; she refuses to hold a grudge against anyone at any time. Her famous remark at the end of the flagellation scene reveals how egocentric is all her sweetness. 'I am not happy here' is her whole comment on the incident. A lonely girl with a floating libido and no malice toward anyone can cause lots of trouble in a well-organized family.[19]

It may even be that Mélisande has made a career of causing trouble, in her apparently submissive fashion. Paul Dukas, whose opera based on Maeterlinck's *Ariane et Barbe-bleue* was produced at the Opéra-Comique in 1907, identified the Mélisande of *Pelléas* with one of Bluebeard's wives similarly named by Maeterlinck. If this identification is valid, then Mélisande's passage from one sombre, oppressive castle to another begins to take on an almost masochistic tinge and we are perhaps less surprised at how uncomplainingly she suffers Golaud's physical abuse. From experience, she understands his violence better than he does – certainly better than Arkël, who can only suppose that Golaud must be drunk. Is Mélisande one of 'les avertis' ('the warned ones' or 'the old souls'), 'the children prepared for an early death' of whom Maeterlinck wrote in *Le Trésor des Humbles*? Similarities of language between the chapter 'Les avertis' in that book and *Pelléas* (see chapter 1, p. 25) suggest that this may well have been how Maeterlinck saw her; in which case Debussy was right in thinking that she does not change,[20] not because she is stubborn or stupid but because she has all along known what she needs to know. At the same time, on the level of day-to-day existence, she is not going to throw her life away, and will lie to Golaud out of an instinct for preservation in the short term – another instance of 'double life' in the opera. No one has ever suggested that Mélisande is an easy rôle to play. But what she emphatically is not is a 'femme–enfant', still less a 'femme–objet', pushed around by others. As Thomson says, she will pay any price to achieve her end, though whether that is to be loved or to bring love, or both, is open to question. But, quite without meaning to be, she is a strong character and must be played and sung as such.

If in her case strength is masked by superficial weakness, Golaud presents a precisely contrary picture. As outlined in chapter 3, his strength is only skin deep. Beneath is a maelstrom of fears and uncertainties: about his status (the over-prompt appearance of the 'royal' motif [4b], as he introduces himself to Mélisande, is Debussy's ironic commentary on this – a deliberate reversion to Wagner's 'visiting card' technique); about finding his way out of the forest; about how to cope with the famine; and increasingly, about whether Mélisande is faithful to him or not. His only way of keeping his fear in abeyance is to do things, and therein lies his weakness, especially when he attempts 'to understand and rationalise Mélisande – to comprehend the incomprehensible. . .'[21] He is not a bad man, and his clothes and gestures in the early scenes should suggest not merely normality but chivalry and nobility. It is his struggle to know what cannot be known that pushes him over the edge. Violence is not his usual way of behaviour, as we can tell from his shocked realisation, after his attack on Mélisande, that he is 'laughing like an old man', as well as from his remorse in the final act. Debussy showed a clear understanding of Golaud's character when he asked Hector Dufranne to 'exaggerate, even, Golaud's poignant misery. . . to get over clearly all that he regrets not having said and done. . .'[22] It is this thought, that he might by saying or doing something differently have averted the tragedy, which will surely haunt Golaud to the grave. On the other hand, there is at least the hope that now he will be moved to examine himself more closely and to realise that 'la vérité' is not the ultimate spiritual goal.

Of the three passive characters, Arkël is by some way the most interesting, though his traditional status as the bringer of wisdom, the wounded (half blind) Fisher King, has more recently come under attack. Boulez regards him as 'another frightened person trying to reassure himself by reassuring others'.[23] Bernard Williams acknowledges that Arkël has a poor record as a prophet, but finds revealing his comment 'nous ne voyons jamais que l'envers des destinées' (we see only the reverse side of destiny). He takes this as being closely interwoven with the opera's message 'that to many questions that we are driven by our fears to ask about ourselves and others, there are no answers; and that [it] is essential to the life of the feelings to recognize that fact.'[24] Golaud, of course, believes that every question has an answer, as long as you put it loudly and clearly enough. To this extent Arkël is wiser, as he is in his distrust of action. There is no reason, however, to regard his quietism as cynical or as demonstrating a lack of care for others. On three separate occasions, writing to Félix Vieuille, the first Arkël, Debussy stressed the character's goodness and humanity,[25] and there seems no cause to doubt Arkël's affection for Mélisande, who has by instinct reached a state of acceptance to which he has come, it would seem, only through a lifetime's struggle. Even if his prophecies are wrong or – like the new era he sees opening up with Mélisande's arrival – likely to be fulfilled only obliquely through her child, his scene with Mélisande in Act IV touches on an area of emotion which, when we hear it, we realise has been missing from the opera so far: of love unmixed with sex, fear or jealousy. And, as often, Arkël in this scene is responsible for a modulation between action and reflection when he kisses Mélisande, with the words 'les vieillards ont besoin, quelquefois, de toucher de leurs lèvres le front d'une femme ou la joue d'un enfant' (old men sometimes need to place their lips on a woman's forehead or a child's cheek). He thus turns a simple, particular act of tenderness into a more general reassurance that life does indeed go on, as the last words of the opera would have us believe.

About the character of Pelléas there is less to be said. He is young, unformed, unknowing, the archetype of an 'inaverti'. Such strength as he has comes from his passion for Mélisande, but on the very brink of the love-duet in Act IV he is still able to say 'Je ferais mieux de m'en aller sans la revoir' (I would do better to leave without seeing her). It may seem unduly dismissive to designate Pelléas simply as the vehicle through which Mélisande's love can enter Allemonde, but the essence of any such vehicle is that it should not at any point impede. The singer of the rôle of Pelléas therefore has the unenviable task of being not only a psychological cipher but one who is never allowed to put a foot wrong. He must look good, move well and sing perfectly. Inghelbrecht remembered how Jean Périer, at Pelléas's first entrance, 'gave it an admirable definition by simply coming forward to the front of the stage, without any gesture, holding in his hand the letter from his friend Marcellus. . .'[26] Any actor will confirm that this kind of simplicity is one of the hardest things to bring off. A further difficulty in casting the rôle is to find someone who can cope with the low Cs and Ds in the first three acts and then rise confidently to the high G♯ and even an A in Act IV. Traditionally the part has been thought suitable for a *baryton-martin*, a high-lying baritone with a light top register, but they are rare birds and, as mentioned in chapter 6, as early as 1919 Pelléas's line was being adapted for the tenor Fernand Francell, since when other tenors such as Raoul Jobin and Eric Tappy have followed his lead. But there is no escaping the fact that Debussy accepted Périer, who was more of a medium baritone than a *baryton-martin*, and who also sang an adapted version of his part, omitting some of the high notes (see chapter 2, p. 52). All in all, the casting of Pelléas remains one of the major difficulties in putting on the opera, even if we may think Jacques Jansen goes too far in claiming that 'one has to be French to sing the rôle well'.[27] On the other hand, to have to listen to this or indeed any of the rôles sung in bad French is surely a penance fit for Dante's inner circle of malefactors.

The part of Yniold at once raises the problem of whether to opt boldly for a boy, as Debussy wanted (with the risk of unconvincing singing or acting), or to settle for a woman (with the risk of unconvincing hips). As with the part of Pelléas, the choice will always depend to some extent on who is available, but certainly it is possible for a boy to make a success of the rôle, as Christoph Wegmann did in Gian-Carlo Menotti's La Scala production, which came to the Théâtre des Champs-Elysées in June 1985. To be concerned about ill-concealed hips is no flippant objection either, since Mélisande must have the monopoly of female sexuality on stage. For the spying scene in Act III too, the impact is immeasurably greater if Yniold's gestures and exclamations are truly boyish, something few actresses can achieve. As with that of Pelléas, the part of Yniold calls for no depths of interpretation. He is the personification of innocence, the ideal against which we can judge Mélisande's lack of that quality. She may not be guilty of sexual impropriety with Pelléas, but as an 'avertie' she is not innocent in the full meaning of the word. To be convinced of this by the presentation of Yniold is to understand, moreover, the symbolic force of Arkël's half-blindness when he says of her eyes 'Je n'y vois qu'une grande innocence' (I see there only a great innocence). Yniold's struggles to extract his ball from where it is wedged behind a heavy stone obviously mirror his father's struggles with life in general, and one of the enigmas Yniold leaves us pondering is 'What will he turn into? A Pelléas or a Golaud?' Perhaps we should not take too seriously Debussy's reference to him as 'le petit ignoble' for his part in Golaud's spying activities (the pun was probably too nice to resist). At least Yniold's heart has not yet been hardened by living in Allemonde. At the end of his last scene he greets nightfall with the words 'Oh! oh! il fait trop noir. . .', a condition which Golaud and Geneviève have long ago learned to accept.

In a sense one of the most important characters, who is both seen and yet unseen, is Mélisande's baby daughter. For any producer to have a coherent view of the opera, he has to decide on the meaning of the last line of all, 'C'est au tour de la pauvre petite' (It's the turn of the poor little girl). The word 'pauvre' may suggest that Kerman is right in seeing the pointlessness of action as the opera's theme.[28] A slightly different slant on the same viewpoint comes from Robin Holloway who takes the theme to be human isolation:[29] action is pointless because, although it may impinge on others to the extent of terminating their lives, it can never reach the soul. Alternatively, there is the more optimistic interpretation of the line which lays stress less on 'pauvre' (the little girl will have a hard life, but then don't we all?) than on 'au tour': life is a self-renewing process and with that renewal comes the possibility that Mélisande's daughter may achieve what her mother could not, that one day Allemonde will be filled with light, love and self-awareness. A third, narrower interpretation of the opera might possibly see it as a feminist tract, with Mélisande fighting for liberation in a male-dominated world and Geneviève as the archetypal unliberated female who, after her dramatic function is exhausted in Act I, presumably returns to supervising the kitchen and making sure that Golaud's bedroom is properly dusted. In this case Arkël's use of the word 'pauvre' would suggest that he is sympathetic to women's 'lib', as he has been to Mélisande throughout the opera.

The evidence for a pessimistic view of the meaning of *Pelléas* lies plentifully to hand. The etiolation of the orchestral texture in Act V is impossible to ignore, and indeed Holloway goes so far as to say of the whole opera that it 'has musically the thinness and emptiness of the essential nihilism of its subject-matter'.[30] But there are at least one or two pointers towards a more optimistic interpretation. Even though in the first scene of the opera the F♮ of the basic D minor is implied rather than stated, it is not hard to believe that in such a carefully constructed work as *Pelléas* (where, as has been shown, 'tonalities of dark and light' play an important part), the re-emergence of this F♮ in the final bars, enharmonically altered to E♯, is deliberate, minor third becoming major third. A second pointer towards optimism, or at least away from pessimism, is that at no time in the text of either play or opera does Mélisande say she is unhappy ('malheureuse'). In Act IV scene 2 she admits 'je ne suis pas heureuse', but her only use of the word 'malheureuse' comes earlier in the scene in answer to Arkël's gentle enquiries when she says specifically 'je n'étais pas malheureuse'. As mentioned in chapter 2, only mocking laughter from the audience at the dress rehearsal forced a temporary change from 'je ne suis pas heureuse' to 'je suis si malheureuse'. The nearest she comes to admitting she is unhappy is in Act IV scene 4, immediately before the castle doors are heard closing, when she says to Pelléas, 'Si, si, je suis heureuse, mais je suis triste.' If she is neither happy nor unhappy, or both simultaneously (and if she is telling the truth), then perhaps the most likely explanation is that she is in some neutral, Zen-like state of acceptance, an 'avertie' who remains at the deepest level untouched by what happens to her; in which case her death is not the tragedy it may at first appear, but a way for her soul to progress to another, higher plane of existence as well as a powerful impulse for Golaud to start out on the painful path to self-awareness. On this interpretation, happiness is an irrelevance for either of them.

For the producer and cast of a production of *Pelléas* to come to some measure of understanding about how the characters are to be played is clearly important, but no less important is for them to go on from there to refine to the last degree the reactions *between* the characters. Maeterlinck was not alone in recognizing the value of what is not spoken. Marcel Proust wrote, in *A la recherche du temps perdu*, that 'truth does not need to be spoken to be manifested and one can perhaps grasp it more firmly, without waiting for words or even taking account of them, in a thousand external signs, even in certain phenomena that are invisible, analogous in the human world to what atmospheric changes are in the physical one'.[31] Such atmospheric changes are operated to a large extent by Debussy's music, but the singers can also contribute through glances, smiles, frowns and gestures. Arkël, for instance, being at least half blind, surely has the keen hearing which the visually handicapped learn to develop. He must therefore react when another character comes on stage and, difficult though it is, some plausible movements must be found for him during Golaud's attack on Mélisande – it is not enough for him to go into a trance for no reason and suddenly emerge from it to exclaim 'Golaud!' In Mélisande's case, symbolism and realism can be brought into a profitable conjunction. Mélisande-as-feminine-symbol demands an aura of otherness, through lighting, costume, shoes (it was the custom at the Opéra-Comique for her to wear flat, 'English' shoes so that she could shimmer in the way Maggie Teyte describes) and possibly even through accent, as with the first two Mélisandes. Mélisande-as-human-being, on the other hand, has to act in accordance with the exigencies of the text. At the very end of Act I, for instance, Joachim and Jansen would observe the following scenario: when Pelléas offers her his arm to help her descend the path, she glances at him as he does so; he says 'Je pars peut-être demain' (Perhaps I have to leave tomorrow); she stops momentarily to ask 'Oh! Pourquoi partez-vous?' (Oh! Why are you leaving?) and again glances at him; but as he turns towards her for the first time, she looks away – all this so that Pelléas, in Act IV scene 4, can truthfully say 'Et je n'ai pas encor regardé son regard' (I have not yet looked closely into her eyes). Needless to say, it is also necessary for the two to maintain a polite distance from each other throughout Acts II and III, but the plot accommodates this quite easily, and indeed, by preserving this distance until the love duet in Act IV Pelléas and Mélisande make Golaud's earlier suspicions seem all the more unreasonable.

This realistic approach can be summed up in the words of the great French baritone Lucien Fugère, who impressed on singers that the operatic public would judge them by their ability to tell the story.[32] Some of Debussy's many revisions to the vocal line were directed more towards realism than towards any abstract musical end. In Act II scene 2, when Golaud is interrogating Mélisande about the loss of the ring, she has to invent on the spur of the moment a likely place where she might have mislaid it: 'You know. . . You know. . .the cave on the edge of the sea?':

Vous savez bien. . .   Vous savez bien   la grotte au bord de   la   mer?. . .

In Debussy's sketch draft the first 'bien' was set to a crotchet, a reading which, through an apparent copying error, found its way into the 1904 full score. But in the short score and all editions of the vocal score Debussy altered that to a quaver followed by a quaver rest, so that the first 'bien' is just a prevaricating noise, while the second carries all the conviction she can muster (the cave, you know it *well*). In other words, this change of note-value gives meaning to the silence between the two phrases.

Mary Garden used to say of *Pelléas* 'every scene is crucial'. That being so, it demands of an audience unremitting concentration, and perhaps not the least of a producer's tasks is to try and make the audience's job easier. One way not to do this is to overload the opera with extra symbols. It may be as well to quote Georgette Leblanc who in 1933, now as Maeterlinck's ex-mistress, wrote of the Symbolist era as one when 'people wove garlands round the simplest things, surrounding them with an artificial mystery and complicating them with absurd significations which buried their true meaning. They would have attributed profound intentions to a mechanical carpet-sweeper.'[33] For Charles Koechlin, too, 'the high points of the opera – the scene of Golaud's jealousy, the conversation by the well and the touching duet between Arkël and Mélisande – are devoid of symbols.'[34] Even if we may not agree entirely with him over the scene of Golaud's jealousy (Act IV scene 2), where the symbolic value of Golaud's shouts of 'Absalon!' and of his making the sign of the cross with Mélisande's hair cannot be denied, Koechlin's point is surely that neither of these moments requires any inordinate amount of thought or interpretation. The symbols are there in the music and in the text and, as long as the audience understand the text, they probably have enough symbolic content to manage without the addition of ravens or wheelchairs. As to whether *Pelléas* should always be given in French, that must remain a matter of taste. Andrew Porter has defined the problem with his customary acuity: 'It may well be that the operas most closely tied to particular speech rhythms and inflexions – Monteverdi's, Mussorgsky's, Janáček's, Debussy's – gain most by translation even as in another way they lose most. The paradox arises from the fact that the more nearly a musical line is inspired by its words, the more imperatively must those words be understood, and used.'[35] But if *Pelléas* is nonetheless to be given in French, no trouble taken to perfect the diction can be too great, as the music example quoted above demonstrates.

When Albert Carré first gave public notice of his intention to mount *Pelléas* at the Opéra-Comique, he foresaw that it would need an inordinate amount of rehearsal,[36] and Mary Garden wrote later that 'no opera I know of, at least of our time, was given such infinite study and attention'.[37] The impact of *Pelléas*, deriving from the accumulation of a thousand tiny details, depends on their fitting perfectly into the whole: it is the work of a miniaturist operating on a grand scale.

For singers, players and conductors of *Pelléas*, though, even hard work is not enough. Just as much of the interior action goes on in the spaces between the characters, so the truth of the music lies a long way behind the notes. While the Golaud of the stage play has been criticised as a cardboard villain, the Golaud of the opera has never, indeed could never, be found guilty of such a charge. Through the understanding invested in Debussy's music, Golaud becomes far more than what he says or does. In him live the fears and anxieties of every man who has ever been, including, one may surmise, Debussy himself. This tapping of the collective unconscious occurs also throughout in the portrayal of Mélisande, who not only rises to a higher plane of existence with her death but even before that is seen as the denizen of the tower, where she moves as easily as do the rest of the characters on the floor below: a Blessed Damozel leaning out from the gold bar of heaven. The various levels at work in the opera – of action, of staging, of understanding – posit the existence outside its confines of an ideal, transcendental world which we, the audience, barely glimpse and even then only through the medium of the music as it soars out beyond the reach of words. This world is evoked most powerfully in the last act, above all in the final bars where the voices are silent, and in the final chord whose spacing (with three low flutes playing a close-position major triad) bears an unmistakable resemblance to that of the final chord in *La Damoiselle élue* and whose tonality of C sharp major transcends the F sharp major of earthly light and love. When Debussy, during the composition of *Pelléas*, wrote of 'the value of silence', he may have been thinking not so much of silent bars in the music as of the 'silences of the soul' which lie behind the utterances of the characters and which gave him room, as he predicted in the conversations with his teacher Guiraud, 'to graft his dream' on to that of the poet. No more persuasive testimonial exists to Debussy's extraordinarily firm grasp of the unconscious mind than Maeterlinck's later admission to Mary Garden that thanks to her performance of Debussy's music he 'entirely understood' his own play for the first time,[38] an admission confirmed by his statement to an American reporter that 'the spirit of the play had been enhanced and beautified by the musical setting of Debussy'.[39]

For performers, to reach the depths of *Pelléas* requires long and patient searching. Irène Joachim recalls the occasion in the 1950s when the Opéra-Comique production, with herself, Jansen and Etcheverry and with Desormière conducting, came to Dublin. At the beginning of the last act Etcheverry as Golaud sang his phrase 'J'ai tué sans raison! Est-ce que ce n'est pas à faire pleurer les pierres!' (I killed without cause. Is it not enough to make the stones weep?) with such passionate desperation that both Desormière in the pit and Joachim on her deathbed found themselves in tears. Having supper after the performance, they told Etcheverry of the effect he had produced. 'Good!' he said, 'I've been trying to do that for fifteen years.'

Appendix

Before the English première of *Pelléas* at Covent Garden on 21 May 1909, the critic Edwin Evans gave a lecture on the opera at the Royal Academy of Music and to prepare himself for this he apparently wrote to the composer asking for some guidelines. An incomplete translation of Debussy's reply was published by the *New York Times* in its obituary of the composer on 5 May 1918, but the original text has so far remained unpublished. The letter now forms part of the Frederick R. Koch Foundation Collection, on deposit in The Pierpont Morgan Library, and we are grateful to the Foundation and to Dr J. Rigbie Turner for permission to reproduce it here:

80, Avenue du Bois de Boulogne

18.IV/09

Cher Monsieur,

à réfléchir, il m'est assez difficile de vous parler de Pelléas et d'en souligner les parties caractéristiques, excusez donc ce qui va suivre:

Avant tout vous ferez bien d'écarter du débat la question de savoir si il y a ou si il n'y a pas de mélodie dans Pelléas. . . Il faut décidément comprendre que la mélodie – ou lied – est une chose et que 'l'expression lyrique' en est une autre! Il est par trop illogique de penser que l'on peut faire tenir dans une ligne mélodique *arrêtée*, les nuances innombrables par lesquelles passe un personnage, cela est non seulement une faute de goût, mais une faute de 'quantité'.

Si dans Pelléas la trâme symphonique tient, en somme, peu de place, c'est pour réagir contre cette néfaste esthétique néo-wagnérienne qui prétend rendre, en même temps, le sentiment exprimé par le personnage, et les réflexions intérieures qui le font agir. . . A mon avis, ce sont deux opérations contradictoires, au point de vue lyrique, et qui ne peuvent, à être réunies, que s'affaiblir l'une par l'autre. Il vaut peut-être mieux que, par des moyens simples, – un accord? une courbe? – la musique s'essaie à rendre les états d'ambiance et d'âme successifs, cela à mesure qu'ils se produisent, sans s'astreindre à suivre, péniblement, une trame symphonique prévue et *toujours arbitraire*, à laquelle on sera nécessairement tenté de sacrifier la

184

trâme sentimentale; mais on aura réussi un beau développement symphonique. . .! encore une fois ça n'a rien à faire dans le drame lyrique; au surplus,
c'est esquiver une difficulté à trop bon marché. C'est pourquoi il n'y a pas de
'fil conducteur' dans Pelléas et que les personnages n'y subissent pas
l'esclavage du 'leit-motive', comme un aveugle l'est de son caniche, ou de sa
clarinette! – Remarquez que le motif qui accompagne Mélisande ne se trans-
forme jamais; il revient en tous points semblable au 5ème acte, parce que en
réalité, Mélisande est toujours pareille à elle même, et meurt sans que
personne – peut-être le vieil Arkel? – l'a jamais comprise.

Il faut insister sur la simplicité dans Pelléas – j'ai mis douze ans à en
soulever tout ce qu'il pouvait s'y être glissé de *parasitaire* – Jamais je n'y ai
cherché à y révolutionner quoique ce soit. . . seulement on a pris l'habitude
de traîner la musique dans des 'mauvais lieux' ou bien d'en faire un jeu que
personne ne peut comprendre sans un dur entraînement.

J'ai essayé de prouver que des gens qui chantent pouvaient rester humains
et naturels, sans avoir jamais besoin de ressembler à des fous ou à des rébus!
Cela a d'abord gêné les 'professionels' et aussi le simple public qui, habitué à
être ému par des moyens aussi faux que grandiloquents, n'a pas compris tout
de suite qu'on ne lui demandait qu'un peu de bonne volonté – Il importe très
peu que l'on pénètre dans le secret des moyens employés. C'est une curiosité
aussi blâmable que ridicule, et pour tout dire, complètement inutile.

. . . Voilà, cher Monsieur, tout ce que je trouve à vous dire. . . le reste
appartient à l'anecdote sur quoi je suis mal documenté.

Avec ma sincère sympathie, trouvez ici mon remerciement pour votre aide
précieux – Présentez, je vous prie, mon respectueux souvenir à Madame
Evans.

Claude Debussy

80, Avenue du Bois de Boulogne

18.IV/09

Dear Sir,

On reflection, I find it rather difficult to discuss *Pelléas* and to point to its
salient characteristics, so please excuse what follows:

First of all you will do well to eliminate from the discussion the matter of
whether there is or is not melody in *Pelléas*. . . It must be clearly understood
that melody – or song – is one thing and 'operatic expression' another! It is
totally illogical to think that a *fixed* melodic line can be made to hold the
innumerable nuances through which a character passes. That is not only a
mistake of taste but a mistake of 'quantity'.

If in *Pelléas* symphonic development does not, on the whole, find much of
a place, it is a reaction against that pernicious neo-Wagnerian aesthetic
which claims to render simultaneously the feelings expressed by the character and the inner thoughts which motivate him. . . In my opinion these are
two contradictory operations, from the operatic point of view, and bringing
them together can lead only to a mutual enfeeblement. Perhaps it is better

that music should by simple means – a chord? a curve? – try and render successive impulses and moods as they occur, rather than make laborious efforts to follow a symphonic development which is laid down in advance and *always arbitrary*, and to which one will inevitably be tempted to sacrifice the development of feelings. Maybe you'll produce a fine symphonic development. . .! But, as I say, that has no place in opera; what's more, it's a cheap way of getting round a difficulty. That's why there is no 'guiding thread' in *Pelléas* and why the characters are not subjected to the slavery of the 'leit-motif', as a blind man is the slave of his poodle or of his clarinet! – Notice that the motif which accompanies Mélisande is never altered; it comes back in the fifth act unchanged in every respect, because in fact Mélisande always remains the same and dies without anyone – only old Arkel, perhaps? – ever having understood her.

Emphasis must be laid on the simplicity in *Pelléas* – I spent twelve years removing anything *parasitic* that might have crept into it – At no time did I try and use it to revolutionise anything whatever. . . but the habit has grown up of dragging music into places of ill repute or of turning it into a game that no one can understand without a rigorous course of instruction.

I have tried to prove that when people sing they can remain human and natural, without having to look like idiots or conundrums! To begin with that upset the 'professionals' and also the man in the street who, accustomed as he was to being moved by means as false as they were bombastic, did not understand that he was not being asked for anything beyond a little goodwill – It is not in the least important for people to try and penetrate the secret of the technical means I have employed. Such curiosity is reprehensible, ridiculous and, to be frank, completely pointless.

. . . That is all, my dear Sir, that I can find to tell you. . . The rest belongs to anecdote on which I am not very well informed.

Please accept, along with my kind wishes, my thanks for your valuable help. With my best respects to Mrs Evans,

Yours sincerely,
Claude Debussy

Notes

For the sake of conciseness, the extensive quotations from Debussy's letters and articles have been referenced to the most accessible editions and their translations. Unless otherwise stated, for the original versions of letters, the reader is referred to *Claude Debussy: lettres, réunies et présentées par François Lesure* (Paris, 1980) (abbreviated to 'Lesure *Lettres*'). For an English translation, the reader is referred to Roger Nichols, *Debussy Letters* (London and Boston, 1988) (abbreviated to 'RN trans.'). Debussy's collected articles were first published as *Monsieur Croche et autres écrits*, edited by François Lesure (Paris, 1971). A revised edition appeared in 1988 and it is to this edition that references are given (abbreviated to *Croche*). A translation of the main articles of the 1971 edition, edited and translated by Richard Langham Smith, appeared in London and New York in 1977 as *Debussy on Music* (abbreviated to 'RLS trans.')

1 The play and its playwright

1 Letter in *Le Figaro*, 8 December 1962, from the Comtesse Renée Maurice Maeterlinck to the directors of the Opéra-Comique.

2 Octave Mirbeau, 'Maurice Maeterlinck', *Le Figaro*, 24 August 1890.

3 Letter from Maeterlinck to Octave Mirbeau of 1891. Entry 173 in Exhibition Catalogue 'Maurice Maeterlinck', Bibliothèque Nationale (Paris, 1962).

4 Maurice Maeterlinck, *Le Cahier bleu*, ed. J. Wieland Burston (Ghent, 1977).

5 Stéphane Mallarmé, "Théâtre", *National Observer*, 1 July 1893, reprinted in *Oeuvres complètes*, ed. H. Mondor and G. Jean-Aubry, p. 330.

6 Robert O. J. van Nuffel, 'Une conférence inédite d'Iwan Gilkin', *Annales de la Fondation Maeterlinck*, vol. 2 (1956), p. 18.

7 Charles van Lerberghe, '*Pelléas et Mélisande*: notes critiques' (Paris, 1962).

8 Martin Harvey, *The Book of Martin Harvey* (London, 1930), p. 133.

9 Undated Letter from Maeterlinck to Lugné-Poë, in N. D. Lugné-Poë, *Le Sot du tremplin* (Paris, 1930), p. 237.

10 Martin Harvey, *The Autobiography of J. Martin Harvey* (London, 1933), p. 198.

11 Maurice Maeterlinck, *Bulles bleues* (Monaco, 1948), p. 128.

12 Franz Hellens, 'Maurice Maeterlinck', in *Annales de la Fondation Maeterlinck*, vol. 3 (1957).

13 Maeterlinck, *Bulles bleues*, p. 25.
14 Charles van Lerberghe 'Journal', quoted by M. Postic, *Maeterlinck et le symbolisme* (Paris, 1970), p. 12.
15 Georges Rodenbach, *Le Rouet des brumes* (Paris, 1900), p. 210.
16 Van Nuffel, 'Une conférence', p. 25: 'C'est par eux [the essays]. . . que Maeterlinck a exercé une influence immense sur nombres d'âmes désemparées, qui se sont détachées de leur réligion, mais qui ont gardé le sentiment religieux.'
17 Charles Baudelaire, 'Le Paysage', *Salon de 1859. Oeuvres complètes*, ed. le Dantec, p. 1076: 'Si tel assemblage d'arbres, de montagnes, d'eaux et de maisons, que nous appelons un paysage, est beau, ce n'est pas par lui-même, mais par moi, par ma grâce propre, par l'idée ou le sentiment que j'y attache.'
18 F. Sarcey, 'Pelléas et Mélisande', *Le Temps*, 22 May 1893.
19 Arthur Symons, *'Plays, Acting and Music': Annotations by the Way* (London, 1903), p. 78.
20 Thomas Malory, *Le Morte d'Arthur* (fifteenth century), Book 4, XXI, XXII.
21 Alfred Lord Tennyson, 'Pelleas and Ettarre', based on Malory, and first published in 1869.
22 Walter Crane, *Valentine and Orson* (London, 1874).
23 See L.-F. Flutre, *Table des noms-propres des romans du moyen-age* (Poitiers, 1962).
24 The story was popular in the nineteenth century, several times translated from the Latin source of 1492 and published with illustrations. The quoted résumé of the tale comes from Matthias Emmich, *Geneviève de Brabant* (Paris, 1841).
25 Eugène Bossard, *Gilles de Rais dit Barbe-bleue* (Paris, 1886).
26 Jay S. Harrison, 'Maggie Teyte Recalls "Fiery" Debussy', *New York Herald Tribune*, 25 April 1954.
27 Christian Lutaud, 'La musique de *Pelléas*, de Maeterlinck à Debussy', in *Annales de la Fondation Maeterlinck*, vol. 23 (1977).
28 Hippolyte Taine, *Philosophie de l'art* (1872), p. 20.
29 Ibid., p. 161.
30 Maurice Maeterlinck, *Le Trésor des Humbles* (Paris, 1896); English trans. *The Treasure of the Humble*, by Alfred Sutro (London, 1897). Several of these articles had first appeared in *La Nouvelle Revue* (Paris) during 1895.
31 Rémy de Gourmont, *Le Livre des Masques*, vol. 1 (Paris, 1896), pp. 11–12.
32 In E. Dujardin, *Mallarmé* (Paris, 1936), p. 33.
33 Stéphane Mallarmé, 'Villiers de l'Isle Adam', 1889–90 (Conférence). Reprinted in *Oeuvres complètes*, p. 481.
34 J. Huret, *Enquête sur l'évolution littéraire* (Paris, 1913). Reprinted in Mallarmé, *Oeuvres complètes*, p. 869.
35 Debussy, letter to Ernest Chausson, 2 October 1893 (Lesure *Lettres* 55; RN trans., p. 54).
36 Preliminary versions of this essay were published twice in 1894: in *Le Figaro*, 2 April, and *L'écho de Paris*, 6 November.

37 Originally entitled 'Les jeunes morts', the essay was published in *L'In-dépendence belge* of 30 October 1892 before being included in *Le Trésor des Humbles*.)
38 Originally published in *La Nouvelle Revue*, 1 June 1895.
39 Maurice Maeterlinck, *The Treasure of the Humble* p. 83.
40 Maurice Maeterlinck, *Théâtre* (Brussels, 1901), Preface.
41 Robert O. J. van Nuffel 'Charles van Lerberghe and Maurice Maeterlinck', in *Annales de la Fondation Maeterlinck*, vol. 14 (1968).
42 Maurice Emmanuel, *Pelléas et Mélisande* (Paris, 1926), pp. 35–6.

2 The opera: genesis and sources

1 'A la veille de "Pelléas et Mélisande": Debussy interviewed by Louis Schneider,' *Croche*, p. 274.
2 Louis Laloy, *Claude Debussy* (Paris, 1909), p. 28.
3 Yvonne Tiénot and Oswald d'Estrade-Guerra, *Debussy: l'homme, son oeuvre, son milieu* (Paris, 1962), p. 83.
4 *Croche* pp. 62–4; RLS trans., pp. 74–5.
    Does this note really date from the beginning of April 1902, as was claimed by Georges Ricou, who solicited it from the composer? Debussy's reference to criticisms of the opera suggests that the note was written after, not before, the première. In fact, this note is extensively quoted and paraphrased in one sympathetic critic's defence of the opera – Louis Lastret's article in *Le Théâtre*, no. 84 (June 1902), pp. 17–22 – suggesting that it may have been written expressly for this purpose.
5 Louis Laloy, '*Pelléas et Mélisande*', in *Essays on Music: An Anthology from 'The Listener'*, ed. Felix Aprahamian (London, 1967), p. 75.
6 Paul Dukas, *Correspondance de Paul Dukas*, ed. Georges Favre (Paris, 1971), p. 21.
7 Gustave Charpentier, 'Hommage à Claude Debussy', *Chantecler*, no. 100, 24 March 1928, p. 1: 'C'est tellement contraire à tout ce que je désirerais exprimer. Le côté traditionaliste de ce sujet appelle des musiques qui ne sont pas les miennes. . .'
8 See Robert Orledge, *Debussy and the Theatre* (Cambridge, 1982), especially pp. 13–47, for information about Debussy's theatre projects prior to *Pelléas*.
9 This quotation comes from the transcribed notes Maurice Emmanuel claimed to have made during the conversation, rather than from the 'fleshed out' version which he published in his 1926 study of the opera. See Arthur Hoérée, 'Entretiens inédits d'Ernest Guiraud et de Claude Debussy, notés par Maurice Emmanuel (1889–1890)', in Hoérée, *Inédits sur Debussy*, (Paris, 1942). The translation is from Edward Lockspeiser, *Debussy, his Life and Mind* (London, 1962), vol. 1, p. 205.
10 Georgette Leblanc, *Souvenirs: My Life with Maeterlinck*, trans. by Janet Flanner (New York, 1932), p. 168.
11 André Boucourechliev *et al.*, *Debussy*, Collection Génies et Réalités (Paris, 1972), p. 111.

12 Robert Godet, 'En marge de la marge', *La Revue musicale*, 7:7 (1 May 1926), 174.
13 Claude Debussy, 'Correspondance de Claude Debussy et de Louis Laloy (1902–1914)', ed. François Lesure, *Revue de musicologie*, 48 (July–December 1962), 26.
14 Lesure *Lettres* p. 52; RN trans., p. 52.
15 Raymond Bonheur, 'Souvenirs et impressions d'un compagnon de jeunesse', *La Revue musicale*, 7:7 (1 May 1926), 103.
16 Carolyn Abbate, in '*Tristan* in the Composition of *Pelléas*', *Nineteenth-Century Music*, 5 (1981), 124, speculated that Debussy chose Act IV scene 4 as a 'trial' scene because of its structural parallels with Act II of *Tristan*.
17 Claude Debussy, 'Deux lettres de Debussy à Ernest Chausson', *La Revue musicale*, 7:7 (1 May 1926), 183–4; (RN trans., p. 62).
18 The terms 'preliminary' and 'developed drafts' were adopted from the Wagner literature in Abbate, 'Tristan', pp. 124–5.
19 See David A. Grayson, *The Genesis of Debussy's 'Pelléas et Mélisande'* (Ann Arbor, 1986), pp. 225–75, for further examples of motif substitutions as well as a broader discussion of Debussy's handling of leitmotifs, as revealed in the manuscripts.
20 See Marcel Dietschy, 'Une interview de Claude Debussy passée inaperçue', *Schweizerische Musikzeitung*, 121 (May–June 1981), 177.
21 James R. McKay, 'The Bréval Manuscript: New Interpretations', *Cahiers Debussy*, n.s. 1 (1977), 12.
22 Debussy's post-publication revisions of the vocal parts are discussed in Grayson, *The Genesis*, pp. 197–224.
23 Claude Debussy and Pierre Louÿs, *Correspondance de Claude Debussy et Pierre Louÿs (1893–1904)*, ed. Henri Borgeaud (Paris, 1945), p. 165.
24 Marcel Dietschy, *La Passion de Claude Debussy* (Neuchâtel, 1962), p. 139.
25 Henry Prunières, Robert Godet, and Léon Vallas, 'Autour de Debussy', *La Revue musicale*, 15:2 (June 1934), 24.
26 On several pages in Act II scene 1 the harp part was also entered by another hand, perhaps that of Raphaël Martenot, who played first harp in the *Pelléas* orchestra during the first season, and who advised the composer regarding harp notation, not only for *Pelléas*, but for *La Mer* (1905) and for the Sonata for Flute, Viola and Harp (1916).
27 For example, in Act I scene 1 the Golaud motif was added in the timpani for his entrance and in the horns beneath his first lines (see OS, pp. 5–6; these are not contained in VS). Similarly, this motif was added to the prelude and closing lines of Act IV scene 1, signifying Pelléas's fear that Golaud is eavesdropping on his conversation with Mélisande. (Again, these additions are not contained in VS; see OS, pp. 253–4 and 260–1.) Textually motivated additions of the Mélisande motif may be found, among other places, on OS, p. 66, bars 3–4 (violins); p. 157, bar 7 (horn); and p. 322, bars 4–5 (oboe and cor anglais).
28 Godet in Prunières, Godet, and Vallas, 'Autour de Debussy', p. 24. Albert Carré, *Souvenirs de théâtre*, ed. Robert Favart (Paris, 1950), p. 282.

29 According to the Opéra-Comique *livre de bord* (log-book), the décors for *Pelléas* were first tried out on the main stage on 17 March (décors by Jusseaume: the forest (Act I scene 1) and a room in the castle (Act II scene 2 and Act V)). Further trials occurred on 27 March (décors by Ronsin) and 29 March (the vaults (Act III scene 2) and the grotto (Act II scene 3)). The stage was reserved for the scene-shifters and stagehands on 2–3 April, and on the afternoon of the 3rd, there was a run-through of all of the décors, except the 'terrace' (Act I scene 3).

30 Carré, *Souvenirs de théâtre*, p. 229. Pierre Lalo, *La Musique, 1898–1899* (Paris, n.d.), pp. 66–7.

31 André Messager, 'Les premières représentations de *Pelléas*', *La Revue musicale*, 7:7 (1 May 1926), 207.

32 Messager described Debussy as 'ill-tempered and raving' while forced to write the interlude expansions, and claimed that he had to go daily to the composer to wrest the freshly written pages from him. Though it is virtually certain that the interludes were expanded in time for the première, they may have been revised after the first season of performances. Henri Busser, who served as *chef des chœurs* for the première and conducted many of the performances during the first season, wrote in his memoirs (*De Pelléas aux Indes Galantes* (Paris, 1955), p. 124) that there were 'new interludes' for the revival in October 1902. Indeed, the first interlude of Act II, as preserved in the manuscript full score, shows signs of substantial structural revision.

33 Debussy's use of particular themes to frame and organise scenes is discussed in Joseph Kerman, *Opera as Drama* (New York, 1956), pp. 183–4.

34 This is, incidentally, the only leitmotif which functions like the Wagnerian 'motif of reminiscence' defined in *Oper und Drama*, and is introduced in the voice (though the theme is actually more complete in the accompaniment, which it doubles).

35 It is possible, however, that these cuts were marked, not by Debussy, but by Pierre Monteux, who conducted from this score for a 1935 Amsterdam production.

36 The appearance of the manuscript full score suggests that the cut originally encompassed the two preceding bars as well.

37 The eight bars at the end of this cut, which feature the Golaud motif, appear to have been eliminated before the removal of Golaud's exit line.

38 These cuts removed the following in Act III scene 4: VS, p. 166, bar 5 – p. 167, bar 5 (10 bars); p. 174, bar 1 – p. 176, bar 12 (33 bars); and p. 178, bar 10 – p. 180, bar 6 (18 bars). In all, 89 of 348 bars were cut: more than a quarter of the scene. Two cuts were also made in Act III scene 1: VS, p. 137, bar 10 – p. 138, bar 8 (9 bars); and p. 139, bar 8. In addition, Mélisande's closing line in Act IV scene 2 was changed from 'je ne suis pas heureuse', which drew laughter from the dress rehearsal audience, to 'je suis si malheureuse'. Two of Golaud's lines, which the current Durand vocal score marks as traditional Opéra-Comique cuts – 'Evitez-la autant que possible; mais sans affectation, d'ailleurs, sans affectation. . .' (Act III scene 3: VS, pp. 156–7), and 'Simplement parce que c'est l'usage; simplement parce que c'est l'usage' (Act IV scene 2: VS, p. 218) – were never removed from the manuscript full score, but were crossed out in the

set of proofs from which André Messager conducted the performances at the Opéra-Comique during the 1903/4 season. This suggests that these cuts were not instituted until the third season of performances and may well have been introduced by Messager.

39 Maurice Emmanuel, 'Les ambitions de Claude Debussy', *La Revue Musicale*, 7:7 (1 May 1926), 144.

3 Synopsis

1 René Terrasson, *Pelléas et Mélisande, ou l'initiation* (Paris, 1982), p. 25.
2 Maurice Emmanuel, *Pelléas et Mélisande* (Paris, 1926), p. 135.
3 Terrasson, *Pelléas et Mélisande*, p. 26.
4 Joseph Kerman, *Opera as Drama* (New York, 1956), p. 186.
5 Quoted in Lucy Beckett, *Parsifal* (Cambridge, 1981), p. 25.
6 See, for example, Robert Orledge, *Debussy and the Theatre* (Cambridge, 1982), p. 55.
7 Pierre Boulez, 'Reflections on *Pelléas et Mélisande*', in *Orientations* (London, 1986), p. 308.
8 Bernard Williams, 'L'envers des destinées', *University Quarterly* (Autumn 1975), p. 392.
9 Emmanuel, *Pelléas et Mélisande*, p. 135.

4 Motives and symbols

1 Stéphane Mallarmé, 'Théâtre'. *National Observer*, 1 July 1893. Reprinted in *Oeuvres complètes*, ed. H. Mondor and G. Jean-Aubry (Paris, 1945), p. 330.
2 For a detailed study of this subject see A. G. Lehmann, *The Symbolist Aesthetic in France* (Oxford, 1968), ch. 4, and Léon Guichard, *La Musique et les lettres en France au temps de wagnérisme* (Paris, 1963).
3 *Lettres françaises de Richard Wagner*, ed. J. Tiersot (Paris, 1935), pp. 194–5.
4 Charles Baudelaire, 'Richard Wagner et *Tannhäuser* à Paris' (1861). Reprinted in *Oeuvres complètes*, vol. 2, ed. Pichois (Paris, 1976), p. 801.
5 Debussy, 'Critique des critiques: *Pelléas et Mélisande*, *Le Figaro*, 16 May 1902 (*Croche* p. 275; RLS trans., pp. 80–1).
6 Debussy, 'Opéras: *L'Ouragan*' (Alfred Bruneau), *La Revue blanche*, 15 May 1901' (*Croche* p. 41; RLS trans., p. 36).
7 Tristan: les thèmes de la symphonie sont les thèmes mêmes de l'action. La symphonie *ne violente* pas l'action.' Conversations between Debussy and Guiraud noted by Maurice Emmanuel. In *Inédits sur Debussy*, ed. Arthur Hoérée (Paris, 1942), p. 30. English trans. in Edward Lockspeiser, *Debussy, his Life and Mind* (London, 1962), vol. 1, pp. 204–8.
8 In one of his wittiest and most vitriolic jibes at the leitmotif Debussy writes: 'Ah! Mylord! que ces gens à casques et à peaux de bêtes deviennent insupportables à la quatrième soirée. . . Songez qu'ils n'apparaissent jamais sans être accompagnés de leur damné "leitmotiv"; il y en a même qui le chantent! Ce qui ressemble à la douce folie de quelqu'un qui, vous

remettant sa carte de visite, en déclamerait lyriquement le contenu!'
(My Lord! How intolerable these men in helmets and animal skins
become by the fourth evening. . . Remember they never appear unless
accompanied by their damnable leitmotif, and there are even those who
sing it! It's rather like those silly people who hand you their visiting cards
and then lyrically recite what is printed on them.)
(Debussy, 'Impressions de la Tétralogie à Londres', *Gil Blas*, 1 June
1903. *Croche*, p. 180; RLS trans., p. 203.)

9 'Quelles scies, ces leitmotif! Quelles sempiternelles catapultes!. . .Les
Niebelungen où il y a des pages qui me renversent, sont une machine à
trucs. Même ils déteignent sur mon cher *Tristan* et c'est un chagrin pour
moi de sentir que je m'en détache. . .' Debussy to Guiraud, September
1890. In Hoérée, *Inédits sur Debussy*, p. 33.

10 This letter is printed in full, with an English translation, in the Appendix
to this volume (pp. 184–6).

11 Adolphe Jullien, 'Pelléas et Mélisande', *Le Théâtre* (Paris), 84 (June,
1902), pp. 5–11.

12 Richard Wagner, Opera and Drama II, section 17, 'Harmony imparts
feeling tone to melody'. Reprinted in translation in *Wagner on Music and
Drama*, ed. A. Goldman and E. Sprinchorn (London, 1977), p. 214.

13 The term 'half-diminished' is used throughout in preference to the term
'Tristan-chord' used by some writers. It refers to a chord built on the
diminished triad, with a major third on top, forming one diminished and
one perfect fifth – thus *half* diminished as opposed to the *full* diminished
chord of the diminished seventh.

14 Maurice Emmanuel, *Pelléas et Mélisande* (Paris, 1926).

15 More fanciful is Terrasson's description of the motif as 'L'énigme du
monde', in his *Pelléas et Mélisande* (Paris, 1982).

16 See letter in Appendix.

17 Debussy, 'Opéras: *L'Ouragan*' (cited in n. 6 above).

18 Emmanuel, *Pelléas et Mélisande*.

19 'Une musique nouvelle deviendra nécessaire, écrite, non jouée, suggérant
l'émotion sans l'intermédiaire de sons entendus, la suggérant ainsi
meilleure et plus intime'. (A new form of music will thus become necessary, written but not played, evoking emotion without the intervention of
perceived sounds, thus rendering it more precisely and intimately.)
Téodore de Wyzewa: 'L'Art Wagnérien IV'. This article, which originally
appeared in *La Revue Wagnérienne* of 1886, is reprinted in I. Wyzewska,
La Revue Wagnérienne (Paris, 1934).

5 Tonalities of darkness and light

1 André Beaunier, *La poésie nouvelle* (Paris, 1920), p. 14.

2 Tzvetan Todorov, *Symbolism and Interpretation* (English trans., London,
1983), p. 89.

3 Untitled Maeterlinck manuscript *c.* 1892 (Heineman MS 279) in the Pierpont Morgan Library, kindly communicated to me by David Grayson.

4 Maurice Maeterlinck, *The Treasure of the Humble* (English trans.,
by Alfred Sutro (London, 1897)), pp. 61–2.

5 Ibid., p. 171.
6 Ibid., p. 174.
7 Ibid., p. 177.
8 Ibid., p. 187.
9 Ibid., p. 195.
10 Ibid., p. 180.
11 Octatonic here refers to the scale of alternate whole-tones and semitones.
12 Letter of Debussy to Henri Lerolle, 20 June 1895. In Maurice Denis, *Henri Lerolle et ses amis* (Paris, 1932), p. 31.
13 Carolyn Abbate, 'Tristan in the composition of *Pelléas*', *Nineteenth-Century Music*, 5 (1981), pp. 117–41.
14 Claude-Achille Debussy, *Esquisses de 'Pelléas et Mélisande'* (1893–95). Facsimile edition ed. by François Lesure (Geneva, 1977), p. 61.
15 Abbate, 'Tristan', p. 136.
16 Unpublished article kindly communicated by the author.

6 *Pelléas* in performance I – a history

1 Letters of Pierre Louÿs to Debussy of 31 May 1894 and 27 November 1895, in *Correspondance de C. Debussy et P. Louÿs, recueillie et annotée par Guy Tosi* (Paris, 1945), pp. 32, 65.
2 Letter of 13 October 1896 (Lesure *Lettres*, p. 83; RN trans., p. 87).
3 Letter of 5 May 1898, published in translation in Lockspeiser, *Debussy: His Life and Mind* (London, 1962), vol. 1, p. 166.
4 Dietschy lists three such occasions: 19 April 1897, 2 February 1899 and in 1900, when Ravel was one of the favoured few (*La Passion de Claude Debussy* (Neuchâtel, 1962), p. 129 n. 1).
5 Georgette Leblanc, *Souvenirs* (Paris, 1931), p. 169.
6 See David Grayson, 'Debussy in the opera house: an unpublished letter concerning Yniold and Mélisande', *Cahiers Debussy*, 9 (1985), pp. 17–28.
7 Mary Garden and Louis Biancolli, *Mary Garden's Story* (London, 1952), p. 64.
8 Grayson, 'Debussy in the opera house', pp. 17–28.
9 Letter of March 1902 (Lesure *Lettres*, p. 114; RN trans., pp. 123–24).
10 Printed in full in Dietschy, *La Passion*, pp. 141–2.
11 Garden and Biancolli, *Mary Garden's Story*, pp. 70–1.
12 Ibid., pp. 71–2.
13 Dietschy, *La Passion*, p. 148.
14 André Messager, 'Les premières représentations de *Pelléas*', *La Revue musicale* (May 1926), 113.
15 Unidentified source, quoted in *L'Echo musical* (November 1919), p. 52.
16 *Le Figaro*, 1 May 1902.
17 *Chronique des Arts et de la Curiosité*, 10 May 1902; reprinted in *Les Écrits de Paul Dukas sur la musique* (Paris, 1948), pp. 571–6.
18 Quoted by Pierre Lalo in *Le Temps*, 10 September 1941.
19 Cited in J.-M. Nectoux, 'Debussy et Fauré', *Cahiers Debussy*, 3 (1979), p. 23.
20 Ibid., p. 24.

21 Vincent d'Indy, 'A propos de Pelléas et Mélisande', *L'Occident* (Brussels), June 1902, pp. 374–81.
22 Quoted in Robert Jardillier, *Pelléas* (Paris, 1927), p. 26.
23 Letter to Messager of 9 May 1902 (Lesure *Lettres*, p. 117; RN trans., p. 126).
24 Letter of 13 June 1902 (Lesure *Lettres*, p. 118; RN trans., pp. 128–30).
25 Grayson, 'Debussy in the opera house', pp. 19, 27.
26 Letter of 26 October 1906 (Lesure *Lettres*, pp. 154–5; RN trans., p. 173).
27 Maggie Teyte, *Star on the Door* (London, 1958), p. 65.
28 Letter to Jacques Durand of 8 June 1908.
29 Letter to Godet of 18 January 1913 (RN trans., pp. 269–70).
30 Letter of 13 November 1908 in *Segalen et Debussy*, ed. Annie Joly-Segalen and André Schaeffner (Monaco, 1962), p. 105.
31 Letter to Jacques Durand of 18 June 1908 (Lesure *Lettres*, pp. 171–2; RN trans., pp. 191–2).
32 Letter to Godet of 18 January 1913.
33 Letter to Jacques Durand of 7 January 1907 (Lesure *Lettres*, p. 156; RN trans., pp. 174–5).
34 Letter to Louis Laloy of 23 January 1907, in *Claude Debussy: textes et documents inédits, Revue de Musicologie (numéro spécial)* 1962; pp. 23–4 RN trans., pp. 176–7.
35 Letter to Jacques Durand of 7 January 1907 (Lesure *Lettres*, p. 156; RN trans., pp. 174–5).
36 Lockspeiser, *Debussy: His Life and Mind* (London, 1962) vol. 2, p. 137 n. 2.
37 *Rivista musicale italiana*, June 1908, pp. 350–63.
38 Guglielmo Barblan, *Toscanini e la Scala* (Milan, 1972), p. 146 and plate facing p. 97.
39 Reprinted in translation in *The Musical Times*, June 1934.
40 Letter to Jacques Durand of 18 May 1909 (Lesure *Lettres*, p. 175; RN trans., p. 199).
41 Ibid.
42 Letter of 26 August 1911 (Lesure *Lettres*, p. 212; RN trans., pp. 246–7).
43 Letter of 29 May 1913. In *Lettres inédites à André Caplet*, recueillies et présentées par Edward Lockspeiser. Monaco 1957, p. 64; (RN trans., p. 270).
44 Quoted in Dietschy, *La Passion*, p. 153.
45 Stravinsky *Expositions and Developments* (London, 1962), p. 131 n. 1.
46 *L'Avant-scène*, 'Opéra 9: Pelléas et Mélisande', March–April 1977, p. 95.
47 Testimony of Henry Malherbe, as reported by Jean Gandrey-Rety, *Spectateur*, 24 June 1947.
48 *The Chesterian*, December 1919, p. 89.
49 *Le Courrier musical*, 1 January 1921.
50 'Projet de mise en scène pour *Pelléas*', *La Revue Musicale* December 1926, pp. 136–42.
51 Pierre Dominique in *Ecrits de Paris*, January 1963, pp. 54–8.
52 D.-E. Inghelbrecht, *Diabolus in Musica* (Paris, 1933), p. 58.
53 E. J. Dent, *Opera* (London, 1940), p. 136.

54 Gandrey-Rety in *Spectateur* (see n. 47 above).
55 In *Le Figaro littéraire*, 1962, exact date unknown.
56 In conversation with Roger Nichols.
57 *The Musical Times*, July 1949, signed 'R.C.'
58 Gandrey-Rety; see n. 47 above.
59 Dominique, *Ecrits*.
60 Quoted by Jacques Longchampt, *Le Monde*, 25 September 1962.
61 Jean Mistler, *La Revue de Paris*, January 1963.
62 In *Combat*, 25 September 1962.
63 'Reflections on Pelléas et Mélisande' in *Orientations* (London, 1986), pp. 306–17.
64 See Robin Holloway, *Debussy and Wagner* (London, 1979), especially pp. 76–113.
65 'Pour échapper à la loi du château', in *L'Avant-scène*, March–April 1977, p. 104.
66 Interview with John Higgins, *The Times*, 1 December 1981.
67 Andrew Porter in *Opera*, February 1982, p. 198.
68 *The Times Literary Supplement*, 4 December 1981.
69 *The Sunday Times*, 29 November 1981.
70 This translation is printed in the *English National Opera Guide no. 9* (London, 1982).
71 'The "Authentic" *Pelléas*', paper given at the Debussy conference in Milan, June 1986, p. 10.

7 *Pelléas* in performance II – ideals and enigmas

1 Exposition de l'Opéra-Comique, Paris, 1942, cat. no. 249.
2 Letter to André Messager of 29 June 1903. Lesure *Letters*, p. 124; RN trans., p. 135.
3 Letter to Pierre Louÿs of 6 February 1900 (Lesure *Lettres* pp. 102–3; RN trans., pp. 110–11).
4 Letter of 9 May 1902 (Lesure *Lettres* p. 117; RN trans., p. 126).
5 Letter of May 1902, kindly communicated by Edward Blakeman.
6 Garry O'Connor, *The Pursuit of Perfection* (London, 1979), p. 70.
7 BBC interview with John Amis, 27 September 1966.
8 In the Bibliothèque de l'Association des Régisseurs de Théâtre in Paris (P.4.1), dated 27 April 1902.
9 Andrew Porter in *Opera*, February 1982, p. 198.
10 *Le Figaro*, 18 May 1893.
11 Gabriel Astruc, *Le Pavillon des fantômes* (Paris, 1929), p. 47.
12 Joseph Kerman, *Opera as Drama* (New York, 1956), p. 179.
13 Pierre Boulez, *Orientations* (London, 1986), p. 311.
14 Ibid., p. 308.
15 D.-E. Inghelbrecht, *Comment on ne doit pas interpréter Carmen, Faust, Pelléas* (Paris, 1933), p. 58.
16 Maggie Teyte, *Star on the Door* (London, 1958), p. 73.
17 *Times Literary Supplement*, 4 December 1981.

18 O'Connor, *The Pursuit*, p. 80n.

19 Review of 30 January 1944, printed in *The Musical Scene* (New York, 1945), p. 165.

20 See Appendix to this volume.

21 Kerman, *Opera*, p. 176.

22 See note 2, letter 140 of 20 October 1906.

23 Boulez, *Orientations*, p. 310.

24 Bernard Williams, 'L'envers des destinées', *University Quarterly* (Autumn 1975), p. 392.

25 See note 1; cat. nos. 275, 276, 277.

26 Inghelbrecht, *Comment*, p. 61.

27 'Pelléas et Mélisande', *L'Avant-scène*, March–April 1977, no. 9, p. 92.

28 Kerman, *Opera*, p. 177.

29 Robin Holloway, *Debussy and Wagner*, (London, 1979), p. 62.

30 Ibid., p. 134.

31 *Le Côté de Guermantes*, ed. de la Pléiade (Paris, 1954), vol. 2, p. 66.

32 *Le Théâtre*, May 1907.

33 Georgette Leblanc, *Souvenirs* (Paris, 1931), pp. 50, 51.

34 Unpublished critique, kindly communicated by Robert Orledge.

35 Andrew Porter in *Opera*, February 1982, p. 199.

36 *Le Ménestrel*, 29 December 1901, p. 415.

37 Mary Garden and Louis Biancolli, *Mary Garden's Story* (London, 1952), p. 69.

38 Ibid., p. 111.

39 *The New York Sun*, 28 January 1920.

Select bibliography

Literature on Debussy is most comprehensively listed in Claude Abravanel, *Claude Debussy: A Bibliography* (Detroit Studies in Music Bibliography no. 29), Information Coordinators Inc., Detroit, 1974. This listing has been updated by the author in subsequent issues of the *Cahiers Debussy*, the bulletin of the Centre de documentation Claude Debussy (Minkoff). See also David Grayson, *The Genesis of Debussy's* 'Pelléas et Mélisande' (Studies in Musicology no. 88), UMI Research Press, Ann Arbor, 1986.

Editions and manuscripts

Principal editions of the play

Maurice Maeterlinck, *Pélléas et Mélisande*, Paul Lacomblez, Brussels, 1892 (Debussy's copy was this edition, with Pélléas spelt with 2 accents).
Théâtre, Paris, 1901–2.
Pelléas et Mélisande, Préface by Henri Ronse, *lecture* by Christian Lutaud, Brussels–Paris, 1983.

Principal translations

Maurice Maeterlinck, *Pélléas and Mélisande*, trans. Erving Winslow, New York, 1894.
Pelleas et Melisanda [sic] and *The Sightless*, two plays trans. from the French by Laurence Alma Tadema, London, 1895.
Pelléas et Mélisande trans. by Richard Hovey, Chicago, 1896.
Pelléas et Mélisande trans. by J. W. Mackail (unpublished MSS in existence). This was the translation used for the English première in June 1898, in which the incidental music by Fauré was used. Mrs Patrick Campbell's prompt script is in the Enthoven collection in the Theatre Museum, Covent Garden, London.
Claude Debussy, *Pelléas et Mélisande*, English National Opera, Opera Guide 9, London, 1982. Contains dual language libretto including the scenes Debussy cut or omitted. English trans. by Hugh Macdonald.

The sources of the opera

Preliminary draft (sketches)

*1 Paris, Bibliothèque Nationale, MS 20631 ('Meyer' MS, former collection André Meyer): Act I scenes 1–2 (fragments); Act II; Act IV scene 4 (incomplete); Act V; [September 1893], June–July 1895.

2 Paris, Bibliothèque Nationale, MS 20703: Act IV scene 3, [August 1894].

3 Austin, Humanities Research Center, University of Texas: sketch of an interlude?

Developed draft (*particelle*)

1 New York, Pierpont Morgan Library, Robert Owen Lehman Collection, on deposit ('Legouix' MS, former collection Robert Legouix): Act IV scene 4 (incomplete, lacking 6 ff., which were incorporated into Bréval MS), September–October 1893.

*2 Paris, Bibliothèque Nationale, MS 1206 ('Bréval' MS, former collection Lucienne Bréval): Act IV scene 1 (incomplete); Act IV scene 4, September–October 1893, May 1895.

3 New York, Pierpont Morgan Library, Frederick R. Koch Foundation Collection, on deposit, Koch 15 ('NEC' MS, former collection New England Conservatory of Music, Boston): Act I (December 1893, January–February 1894); Act II (June–17 August 1895); Act III (undated); Act IV (September–October 1893, May 1895, January 1900, September 1901); Act V (undated).

Piano–vocal score

A Manuscripts
1 Basel, private collection: Act IV scenes 1–2 (incomplete, preliminary version).
2 Paris, Bibliothèque Nationale, MS 17686: Act IV scenes 1–2; Act V (*Stichvorlage*).
3 Paris, Bibliothèque Nationale, Françoise Prudhomme Collection, on deposit, MS 17683: Act IV scenes 3–4 (*Stichvorlage*).

B Corrected proofs
1 Paris, Bibliothèque Nationale, Françoise Prudhomme Collection, on deposit, Rés. Vma. 237: 2 sets (Acts I–III, Acts II–IV, with annotations by Jean Périer).

C Editions
1 French language, Fromont, 1902 (E. 1416. F.). Later printings with corrections.
2 Interludes, arr. for piano by Gustave Samazeuilh, Durand, 1905 (D. & F. 6590).
3 French language, Durand, [1906] (D. & F. 6576). Reprinted in 1907 with extensive revisions.
4 German language, Durand, 1906 (D. & F. 6774).
5 French–English language, Durand, 1907 (D. & F. 6953). Later printings with extensive revisions.

6 Italian language, Durand, 1908 (D. & F. 6576).

Full score

A Manuscripts

1 Paris, Bibliothèque Nationale, MSS 961–5: Acts I–V (*Stichvorlage*).
2 Austin, Humanities Research Center, University of Texas: 3 ff. rejected from MS 961.
3 Location unknown (former collection Georges Van Parys, sold at auction, 7–8 March 1979, Paris): 1 p. with revisions to pp. 385 and 391 of published score (facsimile in auction catalogue).

B. Collected proofs

1 Paris, Bibliothèque Nationale, MS 1029: Act I (first proofs), Act III (second proofs).
2 New York, Pierpont Morgan Library, Robert Owen Lehman Collection, on deposit: Act I (second proofs), Act II (second proofs), Act III (first proofs), Act IV (first proofs?), Act V (first proofs).
3 Location unknown: Act I (third proofs?), pp. 65–68. Listed in Coulet & Faure sale catalogue, *Spectacles* (1972), p. 175, no. 1045.
4 Asnières, Durand archives: Acts I–V. Used by André Messager to conduct performances at Opéra-Comique, 1903–4.
5 Paris, Bibliothèque Nationale, Rés. Vma. 281: Acts I–V (final proofs), 29 June 1904.

C Editions

1 Conductor's score, Fromont, 1904 (E. 1418. F.).
2 Conductor's score, Durand, [1905] (D. & F. 6577 on p. 1; E. 1418. F. on pp. 3–409).
3 Conductor's score, revised edition, Durand, 1966 (D. & F. 6577).
4 Study score, Durand, [1908] (D. & F. 7018).
5 Study score, revised edition, Durand, 1950 (D. & F. 6577).

D Annotated scores

1 Asnières-sur-Oise, Bibliothèque Musicale François Lang, Fondation Royaumont: conductor's score (Fromont, 1904) which belonged to Debussy, with autograph corrections and revisions.
2 Paris, Bibliothèque Nationale, Rés. Vma. 339: conductor's score (Fromont, 1904), used at the Opéra-Comique, with annotations in many hands.
3 Paris, Durand archives: conductor's score (Durand, 1905), with autograph and non-autograph corrections and revisions, 25 August 1905.
4 Paris, Bibliothèque Nationale, Rés. 2729: study score (Durand, 1908), with autograph corrections and revisions on pp. 1–2, 4–5, 10–18, and 391.

Orchestra parts

1 Durand, 1905 (D. & F. 6578). Parts reprinted with revisions.
2 Paris, Bibliothèque Nationale, Rés. Vma. 338. Incomplete set of printed parts used at the Opéra-Comique, including one MS viola part (with autograph corrections and annotations) and one MS part for the bell in Act V.

Chorus parts
1 Durand, [1905] (men: D. & F. 6579, women: 6579bis).
2 Paris, Bibliothèque de l'Opéra, Mat. F. 230. Printed parts used at the Opéra-Comique, including one MS part for contraltos and a MS choral score.

* *Esquisses de 'Pelléas et Mélisande' (1893–1895)*, ed. François Lesure, Publications du Centre de Documentation Claude Debussy, vol. 2 (Geneva: Minkoff, 1977), contains facsimiles of the 'Meyer' and 'Bréval' MSS.

Debussy on *Pelléas*

The principal published primary sources of Debussy's commentary on *Pelléas* are in letters and articles written by the composer. The former are in various published editions (see Abravanel, *Claude Debussy: A Bibliography* (Detroit, 1974), with important selected letters in *Claude Debussy: lettres*, réunies et présentées par François Lesure (Paris, 1980). These letters, plus additional published and unpublished letters, have been translated by Roger Nichols in *Debussy Letters* (London and Boston, 1987). Articles can be found in Claude Debussy, *Monsieur Croche et autres écrits*, ed. François Lesure (Paris, 1971, revised edition 1987). The majority of these articles and interviews, plus additional articles, are included in *Debussy on Music*, translated and edited by Richard Langham Smith (London and New York, 1977). Where no notes or references to letters or articles are given in the text of this volume, the source may be found in the above collections.

Other source material may be found in Mary Garden, *Souvenirs de Mélisande* (Foreword by Debussy) (Liège, 1962); and 'Pelléas et Mélisande', by Adolphe Jullien; 'Autour de la pièce' by Louis Lastret, *Le Théâtre* (Paris); no. 84, June 1902, pp. 5–22 (contains facsimiles of manuscript musical examples by Debussy).

Commentaries on *Pelléas*

Abbate, Carolyn, '*Tristan* in the composition of *Pelléas*', *Nineteenth-Century Music*, 5 (1981), pp. 117–41.
Ackere, Jules van, *Pelléas et Mélisande* (Brussels, 1952).
L'Avant-scène no. 9, 'Pelléas et Mélisande', Mars–Avril 1977.
Boulez, Pierre, 'Reflections on *Pelléas et Mélisande*', *Orientations* (London, 1986) (previously issued separately with his recording of the work on Columbia M3 30119 in 1970).
Chailley, Jacques, 'Le symbolisme des thèmes dans *Pelléas et Mélisande*', *L'information musicale*, 3 (April 1942), pp. 889–90.
Dietschy, Marcel, *La passion de Claude Debussy* (Neuchâtel, 1962).
Dukas, Paul, 'Pelléas et Mélisande', *La Chronique des arts et de la curiosité*, 10 May 1902. Reprinted in *Les Écrits de Paul Dukas sur la musique* (Paris, 1948), pp. 571–6.

Emmanuel, Maurice, *Pelléas et Mélisande* (Paris, 1926).

English National Opera, Opera Guide 9, ed. Nicholas John (London, 1982). Contains articles by Hugh Macdonald, Roger Nichols, Alan Raitt and Nicholas John.

Garden, Mary, and Biancolli, Louis, *Mary Garden's Story* (London, 1952).

Gilman, Lawrence, *Debussy's 'Pelléas et Mélisande': A guide to the opera* (New York, 1907).

Golea, Antoine, *Pelléas et Mélisande* (Paris, 1962).

Grayson, David, *The Genesis of Debussy's 'Pelléas et Mélisande'* (Ann Arbor, 1986).

'The Libretto of Debussy's *Pelléas et Mélisande*', *Music and Letters* (January 1985), pp. 34–50.

Hoérée, Arthur, ed. *Inédits sur Debussy* (Paris, 1942).

Holloway, Robin, *Debussy and Wagner* (London, 1979).

Howat, Roy, 'Dramatic shape in *Jeux de vagues* and its relationship to *Pelléas, Jeux* and other scores' *Cahiers Debussy*, n.s. 7 (1983).

Debussy in Proportion (Cambridge, 1983).

D'Indy, Vincent, 'A propos de *Pelléas et Mélisande*', *L'Occident*, June 1902.

Inghelbrecht, D.E. *Comment on ne doit pas interpréter 'Carmen', 'Faust', 'Pelléas'* (Paris, 1933).

Jankelevitch, Vladimir, *De la musique au silence 2: Debussy et le mystère de l'instant* (Paris, 1976).

Jardillier, Robert, *Pelléas* (Paris, 1927).

Kerman, Joseph, *Opera as Drama* (New York, 1956).

Laloy, Louis, *Claude Debussy* (Paris, 1909).

'Pelléas et Mélisande'. In *Essays on Music: An Anthology from 'The Listener'*, ed. Felix Aprahamian. (London, 1967), pp. 74–7.

Leblanc, Georgette, *Souvenirs* (Paris, 1931).

Lockspeiser, Edward, *Debussy his Life and Mind* (London, 1962).

Mellers, Wilfrid, *Caliban Reborn* (London, 1968).

Messager, André, 'Les premières représentations de Pelléas', *La Revue musicale*, 7 (May 1926), pp. 206–10.

Nattiez, J.-J. and Hirbour-Paquette, L., 'Analyse musicale et sémiologie à propos du Prélude de *Pelléas*', *Musique en jeu* 10 (March 1973), pp. 42–69.

O'Connor. Garry, *The Pursuit of Perfection: A Life of Maggie Teyte* (London and New York, 1979).

Orledge, Robert, *Debussy and the Theatre* (Cambridge, 1982).

Rolf, Marie, 'Structural coherence in Act IV scene 4, of Debussy's *Pelléas et Mélisande*', paper given at the Society for Music Theory, Vancouver, Nov. 1985.

Smith, Richard Langham, 'Debussy and the Pre-Raphaelites', *Nineteenth-Century Music*, 5 (1981), pp. 95–109.

Stewart, Madeau, 'The first Mélisande: Mary Garden on Debussy, Debussy on Mary Garden', *Opera* (May 1962).

Terrasson, René, *'Pelléas et Mélisande' ou l'initiation* (Paris, 1982).

Teyte, Maggie, *Star on the Door* (London, 1958).

Vallas, Léon, *Claude Debussy, his Life and Works*, trans. Maire and Grace O'Brien (1929; reprinted New York, 1973).

Williams, Bernard, 'L'envers des destinées', *University Quarterly* (Cambridge Autumn 1975).

Books on Maeterlinck

The *Annales de la Fondation Maurice Maeterlinck* (Ghent) contain many articles, a few of them in English. Of special interest are the following:

Halls, W.D. 'Maeterlinck and Anglo-American literature', vol. 1, 1955.

Hermans, George, 'Les cinq chansons de Mélisande', vols. 20–1, 1974–5.

Lutaud, Christian, 'La musique de *Pelléas*', vol. 23, 1977.

Nuffel, R. van, 'Une conférence inédite d'Iwan Gilkin sur Maeterlinck', vol. 2, 1956.

Slomkowska, Anièle, 'Le paysage dans le Théâtre de Maeterlinck', vol. 9, 1963.

Van Lerberghe, Charles, 'Sur le IVe Acte de *Pelléas et Mélisande*', vol. 6, 1960.

Other works

Halls, W.D. *Maurice Maeterlinck* (London, 1960).

Knapp, Bettina, *Maurice Maeterlinck* (Boston, 1975).

Lecat, Maurice, *Bibliographie de Maurice Maeterlinck* (Brussels, 1939).

Maeterlinck, Maurice, *Le Trésor des Humbles* (Paris, 1896), trans. by Alfred Sutro as *The Treasure of the Humble* (London, 1897).

Preface to Théâtre, vol. 1 (Brussels, 1901). Reprinted Geneva, 1979.

Le Cahier bleu, critical edition by Joanne Wieland-Burston (Ghent, 1977). (1977 volume of the *Annales de la Fondation Maeterlinck*).

Bulles bleues (Monaco, 1948).

Schillings, Anne, 'La genèse de *Pelléas et Mélisande*', in *Souvenir du symbolisme* (Brussels, 1970), pp. 120–31.

Symons, Arthur, *Plays, Acting and Music* (London, 1903).

Van Lerberghe, Charles, '*Pelléas et Mélisande*: notes critiques' (Paris, 1962).

Discography

BY MALCOLM WALKER

All recordings are in stereo unless otherwise stated.

Symbols used

(m) mono recording   (4) cassette version   (CD) Compact Disc version
* 78 rpm

Mélisande *M*; Pelléas *P*; Golaud *G*; Arkël *A*; Geneviève *Gen*; Yniold *Y*;
Doctor *D*

Complete recordings

1941 Joachim *M*; Jansen *P*; Etcheverry *G*; Cabanel *A*; Cernay *Gen*; ben
    Sedira *Y*; Narçon *D*; Gouverné Chorus; SO / Desormière
                EMI (m) 112513-3
                CD: CHS 7 61038 2

1952 Danco *M*; Mollet *P*; Rehfuss *G*; Vessières *A*; Bouvier *Gen*; Wend *Y*;
    Olsen *D*; chorus; Suisse Romande Orch / Ansermet
                Decca (m) 414 510-1DM3
                Richmond (m) R63013

1953 Micheau *M*; Maurane *P*; Roux *G*; Dépraz *A*; Gorr *Gen*; Simon *Y*;
    Vigneron *D*; Elisabeth Brasseur Chorale; Lamoureux Orch / Fournet
                Philips (m) ABL3076/8
                Epic (m) SC6003

1954 (public broadcast performance) Schwarzkopf *M*; Haefliger *P*; Roux
    G; Petri *A*; Gayraud *Gen*; Sciutti *Y*; Calabrese *D*; RAI Rome Chorus
    and Orch / Karajan
                Rudolphe (m) RP12393/5

1957 De los Angeles *M*; Jansen *P*; Souzay *G*; Froumentary *A*; Collard
    Gen; Ogéas *Y*; Vieuille *D*; Raymond St Paul Chorus; French National
    Radio Orch / Cluytens
                World Records (m) OC210/2

1963 Grandcher *M*; Maurane *P*; Mars *G*; Vessières *A*; Bellary *Gen*; Ogéas
    Y; Vigneron *D*; Chorus; ORTF / Inghelbrecht
                Barclay 995 014/6
                CD: TCE8710

1964 Spoorenberg *M*; Maurane *P*; London *G*; Hoekmann *A*; Veasey *Gen*; Brédy *Y*; Olsen *D*; Geneva Grand Theatre Chorus; Suisse Romande Orch / Ansermet
>Decca SET277/9
>London OSA1379

1970 Söderström *M*; Shirley *P*; McIntyre *G*; Ward *A*; Minton *Gen*; Britten *Y*; Wicks *D*; Royal Opera Chorus; Royal Opera House Orch, Covent Garden / Boulez
>CBS (UK) 77324
>CBS M3-30119

1978 Command *M*; Dormoy *P*; Bacquier *G*; Soyer *A*; Taillon *Gen*; Pouradier-Duteil *Y*; Tamalet *D*; Bourgogne Vocal Ensemble; Orchestre de Lyon / Baudo
>Eurodisc 25.396

1978 Von Stade *M*; Stilwell *P*; van Dam *G*; Raimondi *A*; Denize *Gen*; Barbaux *Y*; P. Thomas *D*; Berlin German Opera Chorus; Berlin PO / Karajan
>EMI SLS5172 (4) TC-SLS5172
>*CD*: CDS7 49350-2

1979 Yakar *M*; Tappy *P*; Huttenlocher *G*; Loup *A*; Taillon *Gen*; Alliot-Lugaz *Y*; Brodard *D*; Monte Carlo National Opera Chorus and Orch / Jordan
>Erato STU71296

Extended excerpts

1924 Brothier *M*; Panzéra *P*; Vanni-Marcoux *G*; Tubiana *A*; orch / Coppola
>EMI P520/2; DA677; W614/7*

1927 Brothier *M*; Panzéra *P*; Vanni-Marcoux *G*; Tubiana *A*; orch / Coppola
>EMI D2083/6; E603/5*

1928 Nespoulos *M*; Maguenat *P*; Dufranne *G*; Narçon *A*; Croiza *Gen*; orch / Truc
>CBS (m) RL3092
>Pearl (m) GEMM145

1948 (public performance) Teyte *M*; *P*; *A*; *Gen*; *Y*; *D*; Ranck (pno)
>Desmar (m) GHP4003

Historic excerpt

1904 Mary Garden *M*; Debussy (pno) (Act II: *Mes longs cheveux*)
>MCA (m) MCK502
>*CD*: EMI CDH 7 61041 2

Index